Communications
in Computer and Information Science   984

Commenced Publication in 2007
Founding and Former Series Editors:
Phoebe Chen, Alfredo Cuzzocrea, Xiaoyong Du, Orhun Kara, Ting Liu,
Krishna M. Sivalingam, Dominik Ślęzak, and Xiaokang Yang

More information about this series at http://www.springer.com/series/7899

Shikai Shen · Kaiguo Qian
Shaojun Yu · Wu Wang (Eds.)

Wireless Sensor Networks

12th China Conference, CWSN 2018
Kunming, China, September 21–23, 2018
Revised Selected Papers

 Springer

Editors
Shikai Shen
Kunming University
Kunming, China

Shaojun Yu
Kunming University
Kunming, China

Kaiguo Qian
Kunming University
Kunming, China

Wu Wang
Yunnan Nationalities University
Kunming, China

ISSN 1865-0929   ISSN 1865-0937   (electronic)
Communications in Computer and Information Science
ISBN 978-981-13-6833-2   ISBN 978-981-13-6834-9   (eBook)
https://doi.org/10.1007/978-981-13-6834-9

Library of Congress Control Number: 2019932166

This Springer imprint is published by the registered company Springer Nature Singapore Pte Ltd.
The registered company address is: 152 Beach Road, #21-01/04 Gateway East, Singapore 189721,
Singapore

Preface

The China Wireless Sensor Network Conference (CWSN) is an annual conference sponsored by the China Computer Federation (CCF). The 12th China Wireless Sensor Network Conference (CWSN2018) was cosponsored by the China Computer Federation Technical Committee on Internet of Things and took place at Kunming University, China. CWSN is a premier event that aims to provide a high-level forum to bring together academic researchers, engineering professionals, and industry experts to exchange information, share achievements, and discuss key challenges and research hotspots related to research and applications in the Internet of Things wireless sensor networks.

The papers contained in these proceedings address challenging issues in energy-efficient network infrastructure, network architecture, wireless communication systems and protocols, power control and management, positioning and location-based services, new models of sensor usage, security and privacy, performance modeling and analysis, as well as the Internet of Things.

This book constitutes the refereed proceedings of the 12th China Wireless Sensor Network Conference (CWSN 2018), held in Kunming, China, during September 21–23, 2018. The 16 revised full papers underwent careful two-way anonymous reviewing and were selected from 177 submissions. Each submission received around three reviews, and for those recommended for CCIS, we further improved the technical quality and the language with one more careful review round. In these proceedings, papers are organized in topical sections on algorithms for wireless sensor networks, energy efficiency and harvesting, privacy and security, neural network, positioning and location, and image processing.

November 2018

Jianzhong Li
Huadong Ma
Yinhai Ma
Li Cui
Limin Sun
Shikai Shen
Yuyan Liu

Organization

CWSN 2018 (the 12th China Wireless Sensor Network Conference) was sponsored by CCF and cosponsored by the China Computer Federation Technical Committee on Internet of Things. The Tridium Company, Lianyi Technology, Inspur Group, Ruijie Technology, and H3C Group were corporate sponsors. The conference was organized by Kunming University, China.

Conference Chairs

Jianzhong Li	Harbin Institute of Technology, China
Yinhai Ma	Kunming University, China

Honorary Chair

Hao Dai	Chinese Academy of Engineering, China

Technical Program Committee Chairs

Huadong Ma	Beijing University of Posts and Telecommunications, China
Yuyan Liu	Kunming University, China
Li Cui	Chinese Academy of Sciences, China

Technical Program Committee Co-chairs

Limin Sun	Chinese Academy of Sciences, China
Jun He	Kunming University, China
Kaijia Li	Kunming University, China

Best Paper Award Chair

Xue Wang	Tsinghua University, China

Outstanding Young Research Workshop Chairs

Huadong Ma	Beijing University of Posts and Telecommunications, China
Zheng Yang	Tsinghua University, China

Enterprise Workshop Chair

Ming Bao	Chinese Academy of Sciences, China

Local Organization Chairs

Shikai Shen	Kunming University, China
Jun Tao	Kunming University, China
Zhihong Zhang	Kunming University, China

Technical Program Committee

Hongbang Han	Kunming University, China
Kaiguo Qian	Kunming University, China
Yujian Wang	Kunming University, China
Shaojun Yu	Kunming University, China
Wu Wang	Yunnan Minzu University, China
Sunyan Hong	Kunming University, China
Zhenbi Liang	Kunming University, China
Song Tan	Kunming University, China
Hui Fu	Kunming University, China
Yunchun Yang	Kunming University, China
Wei Chen	Kunming University, China
Yanqing Lang	Kunming University, China
Yong Yang	Kunming University, China
Zhilin Zhang	Kunming University, China
Donghong Shi	Kunming University, China
Xiaoru Qian	Yunnan Normal University, China

Program Committee

Guangwei Bai	Nanjing Technology University, China
Ming Bao	Chinese Academy of Sciences, China
Qingsong Cai	Beijing Technology and Business University, China
Shaobin Cai	Huaqiao University, China
Bin Cao	Harbin Institute of Technology, China
Fanzi Zeng	Hunan University, China
Guihai Chen	Nanjing University, China
Hong Chen	Renmin University of China, China
Jiaxing Chen	Hebei Normal University, China
Xi Chen	State Grid Information and Telecommunication Company Ltd., China
Xiaojiang Chen	Northwest University, China
Yongle Chen	Taiyuan University of Technology, China
Zhikui Chen	Dalian University of Technology, China
Li Cui	Institute of Computing Technology, Chinese Academy of Sciences, China
Xunxue Cui	Chinese People's Liberation Army Academy, China
Zhidong Deng	Tsinghua University, China
Wei Dong	Zhejiang University, China

Hongwei Du	Harbin Institute of Technology Shenzhen Graduate School, China
Dingyi Fang	Northwest University, China
Xiufang Feng	Taiyuan University of Technology, China
Deyun Gao	Beijing Jiao Tong University, China
Hong Gao	Harbin Institute of Technology, China
Jibing Gong	Yanshan University, China
Songtao Guo	Southwest University, China
Zhongwen Guo	Ocean University of China, China
Guangjie Han	Hohai University, China
Yanbo Han	North China University of Technology, China
Daojing He	East China Normal University, China
Shibo He	Zhejiang University, China
Chengquan Hu	Jilin University, China
Yanjun Hu	Anhui University, China
Qiangsheng Hua	Huazhong University of Science and Technology, China
He Huang	Soochow University, China
Liusheng Huang	University of Science and Technology of China, China
Hongbo Jiang	Huazhong University of Science and Technology, China
Qi Jing	School of Software and Microelectronics, Peking University, China
Bo Jing	Air Force Engineering University, China
Deying Li	Renmin University of China, China
Fan Li	Beijing Institute of Technology, China
Fangmin Li	Wuhan University of Technology, China
Guanghui Li	Jiangnan University, China
Guorui Li	Northeastern University at Qinhuangdao, China
Hongwei Li	University of Electronic Science and Technology of China, China
Jianbo Li	Qingdao University, China
Jianzhong Li	Harbin Institute of Technology, China
Jinbao Li	Heilongjiang University, China
Minglu Li	Shanghai Jiao Tong University, China
Renfa Li	Hunan University, China
Shining Li	Northwestern Polytechnical University, China
Xiangyang Li	University of Science and Technology of China, China
Zhetao Li	Xiangtan University, China
Hongbin Liang	Southwest Jiaotong University, China
Jiuzhen Liang	Changzhou University, China
Wei Liang	Shenyang Institute of Automation, Chinese Academy of Sciences, China
Yaping Lin	Hunan University, China
Jiajia Liu	Xidian University, China
Liang Liu	Beijing University of Posts and Telecommunications, China
Min Liu	Chinese Academy of Sciences, China
Xingcheng Liu	Sun Yat-sen University, China

Geng Yang	Nanjing University of Posts and Telecommunications, China
Weidong Yang	Henan University of Technology, China
Weidong Yi	University of Chinese Academy of Sciences, China
Ruiyun Yu	Northeastern University, China
Jiguo Yu	Qufu Normal University, China
Shigeng Zhang	Central South University, China
ShuQin Zhang	Zhongyuan University of Technology, China
Yunzhou Zhang	Northeastern University, China
Junhui Zhao	East China Jiaotong University, China
Zenghua Zhao	Tianjin University, China
Jiping Zheng	Nanjing University of Aeronautics and Astronautics,
Hongzi Zhu	Shanghai Jiao Tong University, China
Hongsong Zhu	Institute of Information Engineering, Chinese Academy of Sciences, China
Yihua Zhu	Zhejiang University of Technology, China
Liehuang Zhu	Beijing Institute of Technology, China
Shihong Zou	Beijing University of Posts and Telecommunications, China
Wei Chen	Beijing Jiaotong University, China
Haiming Chen	Ningbo University, China
Honglong Chen	China University of Petroleum, China
Xu Chen	Sun Yat-sen University, China
Siyao Cheng	Harbin Institute of Technology, China
Kaikai Chi	Zhejiang University of Technology, China
Xiaochao Dang	Northwest Normal University, China
Guangsheng Feng	Harbin Engineering University, China
Zhitao Guan	North China Electric Power University, China
Zhanjun Hao	Northwest Normal University, China
Jie Jia	Northeastern University, China
Feng Li	Shandong University, China
Jie Li	Northeastern University, China
Yanjun Li	Zhejiang University of Technology, China
Zhuo Li	Beijing Information Science and Technology University, China
Tie Qiu	Dalian University of Technology, China
Yiran Shen	Harbin Engineering University, China
Xiaoxia Song	Shanxi Datong University, China
Xiaohua Tian	Shanghai Jiao Tong University, China
Qingshan Wang	Hefei University of Technology, China
Tian Wang	Huaqiao University, China
Hejun Wu	Sun Yat-sen University, China
Ling Xiao	Hunan University, China
Lei Xie	Nanjing University, China
Yuan Yan	CIT-CHINA, China
Guisong Yang	University of Shanghai for Science and Technology, China
Zuwei Yin	Information Engineering University, China
Ju Zhang	PLA 61785 Troops, China

Lei Zhang	Tianjin University, China
Lichen Zhang	Shaanxi Normal University, China
Lianming Zhang	Hunan Normal University, China
Jumin Zhao	Taiyuan University of Technology, China
Anfu Zhou	Beijing University of Posts and Telecommunications, China
Changbing Zhou	China University of Geosciences, China
Hui Wen	Chinese Academy of Sciences, China

Organizers

Organized by

China Computer Federation, China

Hosted by

Kunming University

Corporate Sponsors

Tridium Company

Lianyi Technology

Inspur Group

Ruijie Technology

New H3C Group

Contents

Neural Network

Energy Efficiency and Harvesting

Privacy and Security

Image Processing

Algorithm for Wireless Sensor Network

Cost-Aware Cooperative Theory Based Routing in Mobile Opportunistic Networks

Sui Yu[1,2,3], Lichen Zhang[1,2,3(✉)], Lixia Li[1,2,3],
and Xiaoming Wang[1,2,3]

[1] Key Laboratory of Modern Teaching Technology,
Ministry of Education, Xi'an 710062, China
zhanglichen@snnu.edu.cn
[2] Engineering Laboratory of Teaching Information
Technology of Shaanxi Province, Xi'an 710119, China
[3] School of Computer Science, Shaanxi Normal University,
Xi'an 710119, China

Abstract. Mobile Opportunistic Networks (MONs) are a class of wireless Delay Tolerant Networks that have been widely utilized in the areas of sporadic network connectivity. Many routing protocols in MONs assume that nodes are willing to forward messages to others. However, in real world scenarios, nodes behave selfishly and do not choose to be cooperative throughout due to a variety of reasons, ranging from lower energy levels to buffer shortages. Thus, it is imperative to develop incentive mechanisms to reward nodes for cooperation. In this paper, we propose a cost-aware cooperative theory-based routing protocol called CACR that is able to improve the delivery ratio and reduce the cost of nodes as well as incentivize them to participate in message routing. CACR is based on cooperative theory and adopts Shapley value to distribute the extra payoff for all participants to achieve the payment fairness according to the contribution of each participant. Subsequent simulations based on real-life traces show that CACR provides higher delivery rate and less transmission overheads than the existing routing protocols in MONs with selfish nodes.

Keywords: Opportunistic mobile networks · Cooperative theory · Shapley value · Routing

1 Introduction

Mobile Opportunistic Networks (MONs) can be formed by wireless portable devices such as iPad, PDA, smart phone, etc., which are usually carried by human beings. Due to the random mobility of nodes, there are no persistent connections between any two nodes. For data transmission, each node stores data to be sent, then forwards to the encounter nodes. Such data delivery process refers to "storage-carry-and-forward" mechanism, which is the basic principle for data transmission and routing in MONs. Since the path from a source to a destination is intermittently connected, the conventional routing protocols are generally not applicable, and routing becomes a challenging issue in MONs [1].

© Springer Nature Singapore Pte Ltd. 2019
S. Shen et al. (Eds.): CWSN 2018, CCIS 984, pp. 3–11, 2019.
https://doi.org/10.1007/978-981-13-6834-9_1

Generally speaking, some classical routing algorithms [2] (e.g., Epidemic, Prophet and Spray-Wait) work with a premise that each node were a volunteer for assisting others to forward messages in opportunistic networks. Based on basic routing, some researchers focus on some critical factors, such as social feature [5, 9], contact history [3], multi-replica [4], energy [6, 8] and mobility [7], to improve routing performance. Unfortunately, some assumption in above models is not applicable in the actual wireless network environment. Specifically, few nodes are selfless to connect with others unconditionally when the devices with the confined processing power, buffer, and battery capacity are controlled by people or other rational entities. Thus the active cooperation between the nodes can not be taken for granted. Therefore, several incentive schemes have been proposed to stimulate selfish nodes for cooperation. Li et al. [10] proposed the IAR-GT scheme which considers the individual selfishness and social selfishness simultaneously and use Rubinstein-Stahl bargaining game model to map the message transmission. Shevade *et al.* [11] proposed an incentive aware routing, which exploits pair-wise tit for tat (TFT) mechanism for DTNs. Wu *et al.* [12] proposed a game-theoretic approach based on bargaining to incentive selfish nodes for cooperation in probabilistic routing over OPPNETS. Zhu *et al.* [13] proposed a secure multilayer credit-based incentive (SMART) scheme for DTNs with selfish nodes. In 2016, Cai *et al.* [14] presented an efficient incentive compatible routing protocol (ICRP) with multiple copies for two hop DTNs based on game theory and optimal sequential stopping rule. However, these proposed approaches have not considered the timeliness of message. If the message could not arrive at destination in a limited time, some specific messages, such as weather forecast, real-time news and disaster warning, will lose its timeliness. For example, the value of real-time news will decrease greatly with time being. In addition to the selfish issue, delay constraint issue would be a challenging in MONs. Lo *et al.* [15] considers the time-sensitive scheme to improve the efficiency. Huang *et al.* [16] proposed TTL sensitive social-aware routing to calculate the community and centrality metric of nodes. The most previous works simply consider the social characteristic of the node and mainly applied to community-based map to solve the delay constraint problem. Lu *et al.* [17] proposed an IPAD scheme based on incentive and privacy-ware to incent nodes to forward messages, in which value of the message is changed with the change of TTL, but it assumes that the cost of each node is the same and do not consider the differences between people. Therefore, how to simultaneously address selfish and delay constraint becomes particularly challenging in MONs.

Motivated by these observations, in this paper, we present a Cost-Aware Cooperative Theory based Routing (CACR) in Mobile Opportunistic Networks, which jointly considers selfishness of nodes and delay constraint of message to improve network performance. Firstly, we define a new cost function, which considers the consumption of both energy and buffer resource in storing and transmitting messages. Base on the above cost function, we then propose a cooperative forwarding scheme to improve the total utility by considering whether including the encountered node into the current coalition, and adopt Shapley value to distribute the extra payoff among participants in coalition. Finally, we evaluate the performance of our CACR scheme with reality trace. Through the evaluation, we validate the effectiveness of the proposed incentive routing scheme in MONs.

2 Models and Assumptions

In MONs, we assume that participants are characteristically selfish, which means mobile nodes will refuse to consume their energy, buffer and bandwidth resources to help forwarding other mobile users' message. This will lead to poor network performance. However, mobile nodes are rational and can be made to participate in message relaying by giving them a reward. In other words, they perform cooperative data forwarding only if they gain payoff. So an incentive mechanism is necessary. Nodes' contact in the network can be described as a graph $G(V, E)$, where the random contact process between a node pair n_i, $n_j \in V$ can be modeled as an edge $e_{ij} \in E$. The characteristics of an edge $e_{ij} \in E$ are mainly determined by the properties of inter-contact time among mobile nodes. Recently, some studies [18, 19] in MONs found that the pair-wise inter-contact time in realistic traces follows an exponential distribution. Specifically, authors in [18] conduct the χ^2 hypothesis test on each contacted node pair in the Infocom06 [19] traces, to test whether "the pair-wise inter-contact time of nodes follows an exponential distribution." Their results show that when a large enough number of test intervals (≥ 10) is used, over 85% Hence, the contact between nodes n_i and n_j becomes a homogeneous Poisson process with a contact frequency of λ_{ij} and the inter-contact time among nodes follows an exponential distribution. We assume that each node n_i hold a contact probability list called CP list (i.e., Φ_i) that record meeting history, and the encounter time interval of each pair (i.e., node n_i and node n_j) nodes is defined as T_{ij}.

Without loss of generality, we assume that buffer space of nodes in the network are all equal. Furthermore, messages generated in the network have the same volume capacity; thus when nodes exchange messages with each other, they will exchange their encounter information. Finally, during each contact, we assume that the contact duration between pair-wise nodes is long enough to complete the message exchange.

3 The CACR Scheme

In this section, we first introduce the architecture of our proposed scheme, CACR to stimulate the cooperation among mobile nodes and to find the best strategy for each selfish node. To facilitate our exposition, we first introduce several basic definitions that serve as the basis for proposed incentive schemes.

Based on above definitions, our proposed incentive scheme is outlined below. To facilitate our discussions, we assume that each data message m at node n_i, is associated with a descriptive metadata, which includes its basic value (i.e., V_m), Time-to-Live (i.e., TTL), appraisal (i.e., $V(m, t)$) and destination (i.e., n_d). Let N denotes the set of participated nodes of transmitting message m, Φ_i the list of CPs of node n_i, and Li the set of metadata of the messages at node n_i.

3.1 Design Basic

3.1.1 Message Appraisal

Each message is associated with a descriptive meta data, which includes its base value V_m. Time-to-Live TTL, current value $V(m, t)$ and destination n_d. Let $V(m, t)$ denote the appraisal of message m at t time. For example, if node n_i receives message m at time t, the value $V(m, t)$ to n_i is defined as

$$V(m,t) = \begin{cases} V_m \cdot e^{-k_m \cdot (t-t_0)}, & 0 < t - t_0 \leq TTL \\ 0, & t - t_0 > TTL \end{cases} \qquad (1)$$

where V_m is the initial value of message m, t_0 is the message generation time, and k_m is the decrease rate.

3.1.2 Cost Function

Because the nodes are rational, they will be selfish due to limited resources. During carrying and forwarding message m, a node will consume some energy and buffer resource. The resource consumed is divided into two types (i.e., transmitting consumption C_t and forwarding/receiving consumption C_r). We define $C(n_i, m)$ as the cost that node n_i carries and transmits message m.

$$C(n_i, m) = C_t \cdot T_i^m + C_r \cdot f \qquad (2)$$

where T_i^m is the time that node n_i carries the message m, and f is the number of forwarding and receiving message m for node n_i.

3.1.3 Expected Utility Gain

In this paper, we focus on cooperative game among nodes in transmitting message. The larger the overall payoff is, the more an individual earns. Assuming that set N is all the participated nodes in transmitting with message m, we adopt $U(m, S)$ as the payoff for coalition $S \subseteq N$ with the message m.

$$U(m, S) = V(m, t) - \sum_{h=1}^{|S|} C(n_h, m) \qquad (3)$$

3.1.4 Calculation of Shapely Value

The Shapley value is one way to distribute the total gains to the nodes, assuming that they all collaborate. It is a "fair" distribution in the sense that it is the only distribution with certain desirable properties listed below. According to the Shapley value [14], the amount that node n_k gets given in a coalitional game is

$$\phi_k(U_s) = \sum_{S \subseteq N \setminus \{k\}} \frac{|S|! \cdot (|N| - |S| - 1)!}{|N|!} \cdot (U(S \cup \{k\}) - U(S)) \qquad (4)$$

where $|N|$ is the total number of nodes in transmitting message m and the sum extends over all subsets S of N not containing node n_k.

3.2 The Proposed Incentive Scheme

Based on the above definitions, our proposed incentive scheme is outlined in process of encounter of a pair of nodes. To facilitate our discussions, we assume that message m has been forwarded by nodes in set S and the current value of message m is $V(m, t)$, and the total payoff of coalition S is $U(m, S)$. Moreover, if node n_j is invited to join the coalition, S' (i.e., $S' = S + \{n_j\}$) is the new coalition and $U(m, S')$ is the total payoff of the coalition S'. In addition, Φ_i and L_m are the list of CPs of node n_i and the set of metadata of the message m respectively.

When node n_i with the message m encounters another node, e.g., node n_j at time t, it follows four steps to acquire necessary information and makes decisions. First, node n_i sends node n_j a control message, which includes Φ_i and L_m. Meanwhile, node n_i receives a similar control message from node n_j too. Both nodes update their CPs. Second, node n_i decides whether the node n_j is the destination of the message m, if not, it adds node n_j into coalition S and creates new coalition S', and node n_i computes the $U(m, S')$ by formula (3), otherwise node n_i transmits the message m to node n_j. Third, if the $U(m, S') > U(m, S)$, node n_i further computes the shapely value $\phi_i(U_{S'})$ and $\phi_j(U_{S'})$ using formula (4). Finally, nodes n_i transmits the message m to node n_j. Furthermore, if the time that node n_i carries the message m is beyond the expected time $T_{i,d}^m$ and the extra cost $C'(n_i, m)$ is larger than its payoff ϕ_i, node n_i will drop the message m to stop loss (Fig. 1).

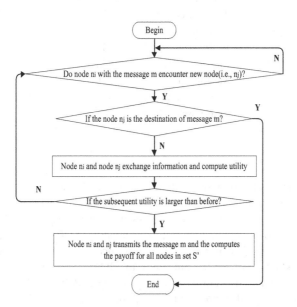

Fig. 1. The process of message exchange

4 Performance Evaluation

4.1 Simulation Setup

We evaluate the performance of proposed incentive routing scheme in Opportunistic Network Environment simulator (ONE). We use Infocom 2006 (INF06) [19] reality data traces to evaluate the performance of incentive-aware routing, which consists of Bluetooth sightings 78 iMotes carried by humans for 4 days in a conference environment. We compare CACR with Epidemic, GAER and SSAR, GAER [20] describes an energy efficient routing protocol that is based on the genetic evolutionary algorithm used. [21] proposes a social selfishness aware routing (SSAR) algorithm to allow user selfishness by considering both users' willingness to forward and their contact opportunity (Table 1).

Table 1. Simulation parameters.

Parameter	Values
Device	iMote
Number of nodes	78
Duration	24 h
Network type	Bluetooth
Initial energy	500 U
Transmit energy	0.2 U
Base energy	0.1 U
Buffer size	3 MB
Message TTL	10 min
Message size	25 KB
Transmission range	10 m
Transmission speed	250 Kbps

4.2 Results

Figure 2 shows the delivery ratio with different selfish ratio. As we can see, the delivery ratio of four different schemes will decline with increasing of percentage of selfish nodes. Non-cooperative routing schemes (GAER and Epidemic) achieve lower delivery ratio than that of cooperative routing schemes (CACR and SSAR). CACR has the highest delivery ratio because it considers the incentive scheme and cost of nodes simultaneously, which improve the efficiency in MONs with selfish nodes. SSAR is also a cooperative-compatible routing and it has a smaller delivery ratio, this is because it does not consider the cost of node in messages transmission. On the contrary, GEAR simply considers the cost of node and leads to a lower delivery ratio.

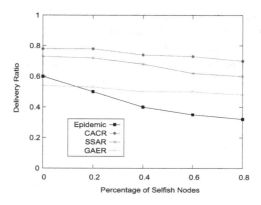

Fig. 2. Delivery ratio with different selfish ratio

Figure 3 shows the average delay with different selfish ratio. From Fig. 3, all routings schemes will increase the average delay with the increasing selfish ratio, but Epidemic and CACR increases smoothly. This is because that Epidemic adopts flooding scheme and messages can be transmitted to destinations quickly. In CACR scheme, nodes will likely to help other nodes with the payoff gained, if the node encounters destinations more frequently, it will help the neighbor to transmit the message to get more total payoff and individual payoff. GEAR does not consider the cooperative scheme and increase the message delay correspondingly. However, SSAR considers the cooperative scheme, but nodes will be more selfish with the cost increasing, which increases the average delay lastly.

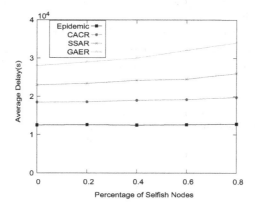

Fig. 3. Average delay with different selfish ratio

Figure 4 shows the overhead with different selfish ratio. Epidemic is a flooding-based routing and the packet loss is extremely serious when nodes are selfish with limited resources, which causes that its overhead is far larger than others. In order to clearly display the overhead of other 3 protocols, we adopt the subfigure to display the comparison results. From the subfigure, we find that the overhead of and GAER is similar with the selfish ratio increasing and overhead of CACR is slightly lower than that of SSAR. This is because that CACR scheme incents more selfish nodes into participating forwarding and relays more selfish nodes to improve the delivery ratio and reduce the average delay. Similarly, SSAR relays more messages and causes a larger overhead.

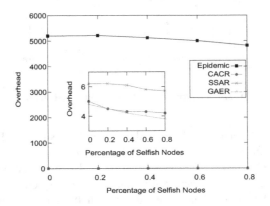

Fig. 4. Overhead with different selfish ratio

5   Conclusion

In this paper, we proposed a cost-aware cooperative theory based routing, CACR, in MONs, which mainly exploits how to accelerate the cooperation among nodes in a limited delay constraint and provide a fair incentive distribution for all participated nodes in the coalition. The simulation results show that the proposed CACR routing scheme can achieve better performance. In the future work, we will consider the multi-copies into model and continue to focus on the efficiency of incentive aware routing scheme.

Acknowledgments. This work is partly supported by the National Key R&D Program of China (No. 2017YFB1402102), the Natural Science Basis Research Plan in Shaanxi Province of China (Nos. 2017JM6060, 2017JM6103), and the Fundamental Research Funds for the Central Universities of China (No. GK201801004).

References

1. Fall, K.: Delay-tolerant network architecture for challenged internets. In: Annual Conference on the Special Interest Group on Data Communication, pp. 27–34. ACM, Karisruhe (2003)
2. Zhang, Z.: Routing in intermittently connected mobile ad hoc networks and delay tolerant networks: overview and challenges. IEEE Commun. Surv. Tutor. **8**(1), 24–37 (2006)
3. Zhang, L., Wang, X., Lu, J., Ren, M., Duan, Z., Cai, Z.: A novel contact prediction-based routing scheme for DTNs. Trans. Emerg. Telecommun. Technol. **28**(1), 1–12 (2017)

4. Zhao, R., Wang, X., Lin, Y., Yang, Y., Hui, T., Zhang, L.: A controllable multi-replica routing approach for opportunistic networks. IEEJ Trans. Electr. Electron. Eng. **12**(4), 589–600 (2017)
5. Zhao, R., Wang, X., Zhang, L., Lin, Y.: A social-aware probabilistic routing approach for mobile opportunistic social networks. Trans. Emerg. Telecommun. Technol. **28**(12), 1–19 (2017)
6. Zhang, F., Wang, X., Jiang, L., Zhang, L.: Energy efficient forwarding algorithm in opportunistic networks. Chin. J. Electron. **25**(5), 957–964 (2016)
7. Zhang, L., Cai, Z., Lu, J., Wang, X.: Mobility-aware routing in delay tolerant networks. Pers. Ubiquit. Comput. **19**(7), 1111–1123 (2015)
8. Chen, Q., Cheng, S., Gao, H.: Energy-efficient algorithm for multicasting in duty-cycled sensor networks. Sensors **15**(12), 31224–31243 (2015)
9. Lin, Y., Wang, X., Hao, F., Wang, L., Zhang, L., Zhao, R.: An on-demand coverage based self-deployment algorithm for big data perception in mobile sensing networks. Future Gener. Comput. Syst. **82**, 220–234 (2018)
10. Li, L., Qin, Y., Zhong, X.: An incentive aware routing for selfish opportunistic networks: a game theoretic approach. In: IEEE 8th International Conference on Wireless Communications and Signal Processing, pp. 1–5. IEEE, Yang Zhou (2016)
11. Shevade, U., Song, H., Qiu, L.: Incentive-aware routing in DTNs. In: IEEE 16th International Conference on Network Protocols, pp. 238–247. IEEE, Orlando (2008)
12. Wu, F., Chen, T., Zhong, S., Qiao, C., Chen, G.: A game-theoretic approach to stimulate cooperation for probabilistic routing in opportunistic networks. IEEE Trans. Wirel. Commun. **12**(4), 1573–1583 (2012)
13. Zhu, H., Lin, X., Lu, R., Fan, Y., Shen, X.: SMART: a secure multilayer credit-based incentive scheme for delay-tolerant networks. IEEE Trans. Veh. Technol. **58**(8), 4628–4639 (2009)
14. Cai, Y., Fan, Y., Wen, D.: An incentive-compatible routing protocol for two-hop delay-tolerant networks. IEEE Trans. Veh. Technol. **65**(1), 266–277 (2016)
15. Lo, C., Kuo, Y., Jiang, J.: Data dissemination strategy based on time validity for opportunistic networks. In: 8th International Conference on Ubiquitous and Future Networks, pp. 1040–1045. IEEE, Vienna (2016)
16. Huang, Y., Dong, Y., Zhang, S.: TTL sensitive social-aware routing in mobile opportunistic networks. In: 15th Consumer Communications and Networking Conference, pp. 810–814. IEEE, Las Vegas (2014)
17. Lu, R., Lin, X., Shi, Z.: IPAD: an incentive and privacy-aware data dissemination scheme in opportunistic networks. In: 32nd International Conference on Computer and Communications, pp. 445–449. IEEE, Turin (2013)
18. Gao, W., Li, Q., Zhao, B., Cao, G.: Multicasting in delay tolerant networks: a social network perspective. In: 10th ACM International Symposium on Mobile Ad Hoc Network and Computing, pp. 299–308. ACM, New Orleans (2009)
19. Scott, J., Gass, R., Crowcroft, J., Hui, P., Diot, C., Chaintreau. A.: Crawdad data set Cambridge/Haggle (2009). http://crawdad.cs.dartmouth.edu/cambridge/haggle/imote/infocom2006. Accessed 29 May 2009
20. Dhurandher, S., Sharma, D., Woungang, I.: GAER: genetic algorithm-based energy-efficient routing protocol for infrastructure-less opportunistic networks. J. Supercomput. **69**(3), 1183–1214 (2014)
21. Li, Q., Zhu, S., Cao G.: Routing in socially selfish delay tolerant networks. In: 29nd International Conference on Computer and Communications, pp. 445–449. IEEE, San Diego (2010)

An Efficient Task Allocation Scheme with Capability Diversity in Crowdsensing

Lixia Li[1,2,3], Lichen Zhang[1,2,3]([✉]), Xiaoming Wang[1,2,3], Sui Yu[1,2,3],
and Ana Wang[1,2,3]

[1] Key Laboratory of Modern Teaching Technology, Ministry of Education,
Xi'an 710062, China
[2] Engineering Laboratory of Teaching Information Technology
of Shaanxi Province, Xi'an 710119, China
[3] School of Computer Science, Shaanxi Normal University,
Xi'an 710119, China
zhanglichen@snnu.edu.cn

Abstract. Crowdsensing offers an effective data collection platform where data requesters can create tasks dynamically and workers are assigned to tasks. Task assignment is a vital part in crowdsensing. Most existing researches consider single capability and basic cost of workers, while ignoring the diverse capabilities and both the basic and additional cost of performing a task. In this paper, we introduce the capability diversity of tasks and workers' additional cost of workers and formulate the task assignment as a one-to-many matching problem, in which multiple workers with different capabilities are assigned to execute one task, and a task can be successfully completed only if all the required capabilities are fully covered by the capabilities of its assigned workers within its limited budget. Based on relationship between capability and profit, we propose three heuristic algorithms that try to increase the total profits of assigned workers within budget constraint. Through extensive simulations, we show that the proposed algorithms greatly improve the total profits and the coverage ratio of task accomplishment.

Keywords: Crowdsensing · Task allocation · Capability diversity ·
Additional cost

1 Introduction

Crowdsensing is a new mechanism for efficient data collection, in which a sensing task is assigned to and performed by a crowd of individuals equipped with mobile devices capable of sensing and computing [1]. Task assignment is one of the most essential problems in crowdsensing [2–7]. In general, research efforts on task assignment have focused on different aspects, such as task's budget [8, 9], traveling cost [10], capability [11] and quality [12–14] of workers. In [10], authors present the one-to-one assignment problem and aim to maximize the utility as well as minimize the traveling costs of tasks. In [11], authors explore the problem of assigning workers, with certain quality to

S. Shen et al. (Eds.): CWSN 2018, CCIS 984, pp. 12–20, 2019.
https://doi.org/10.1007/978-981-13-6834-9_2

tasks with different quality requirements and budget constraints. In [12], researchers consider an online task assignment scenario, where each worker has a set of experienced capabilities, whereas specific task is budget-constrained and requires a certain capability. To *et al.* [15] study many-to-one allocation problem with maximizing the number of assigned tasks under the budget constraint, in which multiple simple tasks are assigned to a worker. Another research topic of task assignment in crowdsensing is over the opportunistic networks [16, 17], in which workers encounter with each other and could reassign their tasks to the neighbors.

Existing works mostly focused on single capability requirement of a task. Currently, complex tasks with multiple capabilities requirement arise and should be executed by the cooperation of multiple workers. Thus, the capability diversity is essential in crowdsensing. Moreover, we consider two kinds of costs, basic and additional cost. For instance, an employee takes time and resources to complete a project, that is time and resources is regular wage; in addition, the employer may pay the employee certain additional reward due to the employee completing the project. Therefore, the regular wage is the basic cost of a worker for completing a task and the reward is as the additional cost. The main contributions of this paper are as follows:

(1) We formally define the task assignment problem with diverse capabilities in Sect. 2, under the constraints of diverse capabilities covering, time, budget for tasks and basic and additional cost for workers in the Crowdsensing system.
(2) For the task assignment problem, we present three heuristic algorithms, respectively named by Basic Greedy Algorithm (BG), Profit-Based Greedy Algorithm (P-BG), and Profit and Budget-Based Greedy Algorithm (PB-BG) in Sect. 3.
(3) We conduct extensive experiments, and the results show that the Profit and Budget-Based Greedy Algorithm achieves both higher profit value and assignment ratio than the other two algorithms in Sect. 4.

2 Problem Formulation

In our model, we define a task t_i as (A_i, b_i, d_i), where A_i, b_i and d_i denote the set of required capabilities, the budget, and the deadline of task t_i, respectively. A task expires if it has not been assigned before its deadline. Each worker w_j is defined as (A_j, c_j), where A_j denotes w_j's capabilities, c_j is the basic cost of performing a task.

Supposing there are m tasks, n workers and τ kinds of capabilities, the platform should choose some tasks and then assign them to some workers with the objective of maximizing the total profit. Each worker w_j must support the capabilities required by task t_i if w_j is assigned to t_i. The capability of a worker has great impact on his/her profit of performing a task. Generally, if a worker possesses more required capabilities of a task, he/she will make greater contribution to this task and obtain more profit. Consider a scenario of developing an application, it is not an easy task, which requires many challenging works (capabilities), such as designing software front-end, developing the backend of application, and testing developed application. If worker A has capabilities of designing software front-end and developing the backend of application and worker

B owns capability of testing developed application, worker A will get more profit than B after they work together to develop the software application.

Besides the basic cost of performing a task, the request of a task will pay additional costs for workers who complete the task. And the larger number of capability that a task required of a worker possessing is, the more profit the worker will obtain. Thus, we use p_{ij} and ac_{ij} respectively denote the profit and additional cost of worker w_j performing a task. The task allocation problem is formulated as a following linear programming problem.

$$\max \sum_{i=1}^{m} \sum_{j=1}^{n} p_{ij} \cdot y_{ij}$$

$$\text{s.t.} 1. \sum_{i=1}^{m} \sum_{j=1}^{n} ac_{ij} \cdot y_{ij} + \sum_{j=1}^{n} c_j \cdot x_j \leq \sum_{i=1}^{m} b_i, \forall i \in \{1,\ldots,m\}, \forall j \in \{1,\ldots,n\}$$

$$2. \sum_{i=1}^{m} y_{ij} \leq 1, \quad \forall j \in \{1,\ldots,n\}$$

$$3. \sum_{j=1}^{n} y_{ij} \geq 1, \quad \forall i \in \{1,\ldots,m\}$$ \hfill (1)

$$4. \sum_{j=1}^{n} b_{ik} \cdot y_{ij} \geq a_{ik}, \quad \forall i \in \{1,\ldots,m\}, \quad \forall k \in \{1,\ldots,\tau\}$$

$$5. y_{ij} \in \{0,1\}, \quad \forall j \in \{1,\ldots,m\}, \quad \forall j \in \{1,\ldots,n\}$$

$$6. x_j \in \{0,1\}, \quad \forall j \in \{1,\ldots,n\}$$

where $a_{ik} \in \{0,1\}$, and if $a_{ik} = 1$, the k-th capability is required by task t_i, otherwise, $a_{ik} = 0$; $b_{jk} \in \{0,1\}$, and if $b_{jk} = 1$, worker w_j has the k-th capability, otherwise, $b_{jk} = 0$. The objective is restricted by Constraints 1–6. Constraint 1 implies the total cost of all the assigned workers should not exceed total budget of all the assigned tasks. Constraints 2 and 3 mean that each worker can only focus on one task and each task can involve multiple workers. Constraint 4 indicates that for any task that has been assigned, all the required capabilities by the task should be satisfied. In Constraints 5 and 6, x_j and y_{ij} are indicators. If worker w_j is assigned to a task, $x_j = 1$; otherwise, $x_j = 0$. If worker w_j is assigned to task t_i, $y_{ij} = 1$; otherwise, $y_{ij} = 0$.

3   The Proposed Task Assignment Scheme

Apparently, the above-mentioned optimization problem (1), which could be reduced from the maximum coverage problem (MCP) [18], is NP-hard. In order to solve it efficiently, we present 3 greedy algorithms, namely by Basic Greedy (BG), Profit-Based Greedy (P-BG) and Profit and Budget-Based Greedy (PB-BG).

3.1   Basic Greedy Algorithm

As shown in Table 1, the temporal urgency of a task is considered in BG. Near-deadline tasks should have higher priorities to be assigned than others (Line 5). At the beginning of each time period, Line 4 removes the expired tasks from the previous time period. Basically, each task firstly sorts the workers according to the profits paid to the workers by the task t_i and then selects the worker with the maximal profit, depicted in Line 7 and 8 of Algorithm 1. Only the total cost of a worker being less than the budget of the task t_i can he/she may be selected, depicted in Line 9. If the capability requirement of task t_i is satisfied by w_j, $y_{ij} = 1$. The algorithm goes to the next cycle when either running out of budget (Line 9) or the capabilities are unsatisfied (Line 10). At the end of the algorithm, the result of task assignment $\{y_{ij} \mid t_i \in T, w_j \in W\}$ is returned in line 18.

BG can achieve fast task assignment by simply selecting the worker with maximum profit. However, it treats all tasks equally without considering the relationship between capability and profit of worker and between budget and deadline of task. Below we introduce two assignment algorithms that explicitly model the task priority given worker priority given profits and its deadline.

Table 1. Basic Greedy Algorithm.

Algorithm 1 BASIC GREEDY ALGORITHM
1:    **Input**: worker set W, task set T, capability set A
2:    **Output**: the task assignment result $\{y_{ij} \mid t_i \in T, w_j \in W\}$
3:    **for** each time period q **do**
4:        Remove expired tasks and update task set
5:        Sort tasks based on their deadline
6:        **for** each $t_i \in T$ **do**
7:            Sort workers based on the benefits paid to the workers by the task t_i
8:            **for** each $w_j \in W$ **do**
9:                **while** budget of $t_i >$ cost of w_j **do**
10:                   **if** sectional capabilities requirement can be satisfied **then**
11:                       $y_{ij}=1$
12:                       Update the budget of the task t_i
13:                   **end if**
14:               **end while**
15:           **end for**
16:       **end for**
17:   **end for**
18:   Return $\{y_{ij} \mid t_i \in T, w_j \in W\}$

3.2   Profit-Based Greedy Algorithm

To maximize total profit in the long term, we consider the relation between capability and profit of worker. The intuition is that a worker who has more capabilities will get more profit which is paid by a task, and vice versa. Because the task t_i selects workers based on the profits paid to the workers by the task t_i, where is a positive relationship between the amount of capabilities and the amount of profit, more required capabilities of t_i are satisfied. The P-BG Algorithm adapts BG by selecting the worker with more capabilities at each stage. To implement P-BG, we preprocess before Algorithm 1 by updating values of profits that are paid for workers by tasks based on the capabilities of these workers.

3.3   Profit and Budget-Based Algorithm

One approach to set budgets of tasks is by considering their temporal urgency. The intuition is that a task which is further away from its deadline has larger budget, and vice versa. As a result, near-deadline tasks should have higher budget than others. We model the budget of a task based on the remaining time of each task. To implement PB-BG Algorithm, we preprocess before PBG by updating values of budgets of tasks based on the deadlines of these tasks.

With m tasks and n workers, in the worst case, since each worker can only be assigned to one task, there are an exponential number of possible task-worker assignments, which leads to time complexity of $O(m^n)$. While in our greedy algorithms, the number of iterations of the two-layer loop is at most m or n. Therefore, the total time complexity of our greedy algorithms is $O(m \cdot n)$.

4   Simulation Evaluation

In this section, we evaluate the performance of the proposed algorithms. The parameter details are shown in Table 2. We base our simulations on two inter-related metrics: (i) *total profit* and (ii) *coverage ratio*.

Table 2. Simulation parameters.

Parameter	Value
Number of tasks	{10, 15, 20, 25, 30, 35}
Number of workers	{100, 110, 120, 130, 140, 150}
Number of capabilities	{5, 6, 7, 8, 9, 10}
Budget of task	[2.5, 4]
Basic cost of worker	[1, 1.5]
Additional cost of worker	[0.1, 1]
Deadline of task	[1, 50]

4.1   Total Profit

Figure 1(a) shows that the total profits of all algorithms increase with the number of workers for a fixed value of the number of tasks. Compared with the P-BG, PB-BG achieves 10% of profit with the same value of worker numbers. While the number of workers is fixed, the total profit increases substantially with the increase of tasks' number, as shown in Fig. 1(b). Clearly, the gap among three algorithms is narrow, but compared with others, PB-BG can achieve higher profit. In Fig. 1(c), the total profit of assigned workers increases when the number of capability increases from 5 to 9, while it declines as the number of capability increases from 9 to 10. The number of capabilities that tasks require will increase as the increase of capability kinds, and accordingly the number of required workers by tasks also will increase.

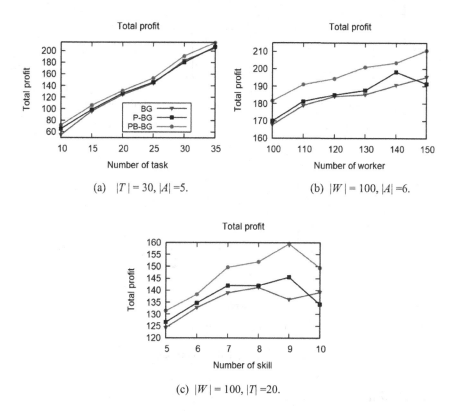

(a) $|T| = 30, |A| = 5$.

(b) $|W| = 100, |A| = 6$.

(c) $|W| = 100, |T| = 20$.

Fig. 1. Total profit comparison.

4.2   Coverage Ratio

Coverage ratio is defined as the ratio of successfully completed tasks over all tasks. Naturally, the coverage ratio increases with the number of workers, as shown in Fig. 2 (a). Compared with the BG, PB-BG can achieve up to 16% improvement when the number of workers is relatively small. As expected, the coverage ratio will reach 95% when the number of workers is large enough for all tasks to fill up their capability requirement. In Fig. 2(b), when the number of tasks increases, the coverage ratio decreases. The reason is that, when the number of workers is fixed, uncompleted of task increase with the increase of number of tasks. The coverage ratio also decreases with the increase of capability kinds in Fig. 2(c). Because of the increase of capability number, a task needs more workers to satisfy its capability requirement. Uncompleted tasks will increase as the total number of worker is decreased.

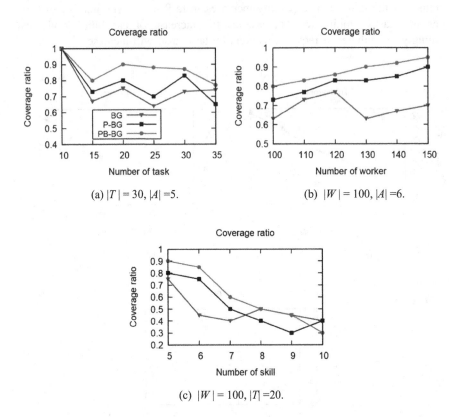

(a) $|T| = 30$, $|A| = 5$.

(b) $|W| = 100$, $|A| = 6$.

(c) $|W| = 100$, $|T| = 20$.

Fig. 2. Coverage ratio comparison.

5   Conclusions

In this paper, we propose a one-to-many matching problem of task assignment, which assigns budget-constrained and capability-diversity tasks with workers, such that the required capabilities of tasks can be satisfied by the capabilities of workers and the total profit of all assigned workers can be maximized. We consider the capability diversity, the relationship between capability and profit of worker, and the relationship between budget and deadline of task. We propose efficient task assignment algorithms to maximize the total profit with budget constraint. Through extensive simulations, the results show that the proposed PB-BG algorithm is superior to other task allocation algorithms when there are more tasks, fewer users for maximizing overall profit. As for future work, we will consider complex task assignment where task requester may require multiple workers who have diverse capabilities with different degrees.

Acknowledgments. This work is partly supported by the National Key R&D Program of China (No. 2017YFB1402102), the Natural Science Basis Research Plan in Shaanxi Province of China (Nos. 2017JM6060, 2017JM6103), and the Fundamental Research Funds for the Central Universities of China (No. GK201801004).

References

1. Arkian, H., Diyanat, A., Pourkhalili, A.: MIST: fog-based data analytics scheme with cost-efficient resource provisioning for IoT crowdsensing applications. J. Netw. Comput. Appl. **82**, 152–165 (2017)
2. Ganti, K., Ye, F., Lei, H.: Mobile crowdsensing: current state and future challenges. IEEE Commun. Mag. **49**(11), 32–39 (2011)
3. Ho, J., Vaughan, J.: Online task assignment in crowdsourcing markets. In: Hoffmann, J., Selman, B. (eds.) Proceedings of the Twenty-Sixth AAAI Conference on Artificial Intelligence, pp. 45–51. AAAI, Toronto (2012)
4. Boutsis, I., Kalogeraki, V.: On task assignment for real-time reliable crowdsourcing. In: 2014 IEEE 34th International Conference on Distributed Computing Systems, ICDCS, pp. 1–10. IEEE, Madrid (2014)
5. Feng, Z., Zhu, Y., Zhang, Q.: Towards truthful mechanisms for mobile crowdsourcing with dynamic smart-phones. In: 2014 IEEE 34th International Conference on Distributed Computing Systems, ICDCS, pp. 11–20. IEEE, Madrid (2014)
6. He, Z., Cao, J., Liu, X.: High quality participant recruitment in vehicle-based crowdsourcing using predictable mobility. In: 2015 IEEE Conference on Computer Communications, INFOCOM, pp. 2542–2550. IEEE, Kowloon (2015)
7. Xiao, M., Wu, J., Huang, L.: Multi-task assignment for crowdsensing in mobile social networks. In: 2015 IEEE Conference on Computer Communications, INFOCOM, pp. 2227–2235. IEEE, Kowloon (2015)
8. Shi, Z., Huang, H., Sun, Y.-E., Wu, X., Li, F., Tian, M.: An efficient task assignment mechanism for crowdsensing systems. In: Sun, X., Liu, A., Chao, H.-C., Bertino, E. (eds.) ICCCS 2016. LNCS, vol. 10040, pp. 14–24. Springer, Cham (2016). https://doi.org/10.1007/978-3-319-48674-1_2
9. Zhang, X., Yang, Z., Liu, Y., Tang, S.: On reliable task assignment for spatial crowdsourcing. IEEE Trans. Emerg. Top. Comput. **PP**(99), 1 (2016)
10. Wang, X., Wang, S.: An optimal assignment for mobile sensing tasks in spatial crowdsourcing. In: 2016 5th International Conference on Computer Science and Network Technology, ICCSNT, pp. 681–687. IEEE, Changchun (2016)
11. Yin, X., Chen, Y., Li, B.: Task assignment with guaranteed quality for crowdsourcing platforms. In: 2017 IEEE 25th International Symposium on Quality of Service, IWQoS, pp. 1–10. IEEE, Vilanova i la Geltru (2017)
12. Qin, H., Zhang, Y., Li, B.: Truthful mechanism for crowdsourcing task assignment. In: Fox, G. (ed.) 2017 IEEE 10th International Conference on Cloud Computing, CLOUD, pp. 520–527. IEEE Computer Society, Honolulu (2017)
13. Kang, Y., Miao, X., Liu, K., Chen, L., Liu, Y.: Quality-aware online task assignment in mobile crowdsourcing. In: 12th IEEE International Conference on Mobile Ad Hoc and Sensor Systems, MASS, pp. 127–135. IEEE Computer Society, Dallas (2015)
14. Lee, S., Park, S., Park, S.: A quality enhancement of crowdsourcing based on quality evaluation and user-level task assignment framework. In: 2014 International Conference on Big Data and Smart Computing, BIGCOMP, pp. 60–65. IEEE, Bangkok (2014)

15. To, H., Fan, L., Tran, L., Shahabi, C.: Real-time task assignment in hyperlocal spatial crowdsourcing under budget constraints. In: 2016 IEEE International Conference on Pervasive Computing and Communications, PerCom, pp. 1–8. IEEE, Sydney (2016)
16. Zhang, L., Cai, Z., Lu, J., Wang, X.: Mobility-aware routing in delay tolerant networks. Pers. Ubiquit. Comput. **19**(7), 1111–1123 (2015)
17. Lin, Y., Wang, X., Hao, F., Wang, L., Zhang, L., Zhao, R.: An on-demand coverage based self-deployment algorithm for big data perception in mobile sensing networks. Future Gener. Comput. Syst. **82**, 220–234 (2018)
18. Feige, U.: A threshold of ln n for approximating set cover. J. ACM (JACM) **45**(4), 634–652 (1998)

VDTS: A Voronoi Diagram Based Tracking Schemes in Wireless Sensor Networks

Qianqian Ren[1,2(✉)], Jinbao Li[1,2(✉)], and Yong Liu[1,2(✉)]

[1] Key Laboratory of Database and Parallel Computing of Heilongjiang Province,
Harbin, China
[2] School of Computer Science and Technology, Heilongjiang University,
Harbin, China
{renqianqian, jbli}@hlju.edu.cn, acliuyong@sina.com

Abstract. Sleeping scheduling has been widely employed in target tracking due to its energy conservation. However, the randomness of target's trajectory makes it difficult to implement with accuracy and real time guarantee. We propose VDTS, a novel, simple and efficient tracking technique. VDTS first constructs a Voronoi based network model, then makes nodes in the Voronoi polygon that the target is in work and others sleep. The target is hence detected by nodes closest to it. VDTS further presents a weighted centroid based algorithm to locate the target with the chosen nodes and reduce the influence of data noise on localization accuracy. We have implemented VDTS, and our extensive simulation show the excellent performs of our schemes.

Keywords: Wireless sensor network · Target tracking · Voronoi

1 Introduction

In wireless sensor networks (WSNs), tracking is an essential function for many networking application in which nodes return the location of interested targets periodically [1, 2]. However, the characteristics of wireless sensor networks make the energy of networks is very limited. To reduce the energy consumption, some energy efficient mechanisms and duty-cycled schemes are usually used. In theses mechanisms, sensor nodes are assigned two states, that's the active state and sleep state. Nodes that do not participate in tracking are turned to sleep state to save energy. In this paper, our aim is to detect and track a target with an unknown trajectory, i.e., a vehicle on a road or a wild animal in its habit environment. Since sensor nodes can be deployed in difficult or inaccessible areas, we can not control them during the tracking procedure. However, we can design a scheduling for sensor nodes so that they can turn to work and sleep as the schedule. To minimize the energy cost of the networks, active nodes that monitor the target should be minimum, which is decided by specific applications. Moreover, the target is subject to move in an unexpected trajectory, that requires waking up nodes surrounding the target in advance to sample the target. Therefore, our main purpose is to construct a working schedule of sensor nodes, which can detect and sample the target in time and accurately.

© Springer Nature Singapore Pte Ltd. 2019
S. Shen et al. (Eds.): CWSN 2018, CCIS 984, pp. 21–32, 2019.
https://doi.org/10.1007/978-981-13-6834-9_3

Presently, the received signal strength indicator (RSSI) based localization is nearly ubiquitous as its simplicity. However, the received signal is often influenced by many factors such as noise and hardware characteristic of the device [3–5] As RSSI-localization uses the signals decay with distance to estimate the distance between the target and nodes. The signal information from the nodes near to the target is more accurate. However, in order to improve the accuracy of RSSI based localization, we have to find and update the neighbor nodes of the target as the target moving.

In this paper, we study the problem of tracking a single target in wireless sensor networks. The nodes can be active or sleeping at a period, and only parts of nodes are active at each time step. The key problem we need to solve is to balance the amount of sensed data and the energy consumption, meanwhile make guarantee of response time to the target moving. The paper contains three contributions to the target tracking problem in WSNs.

1. Developing a nodes scheduling policy: In the paper, we construct a nodes schedule policy considering the distance between the target and sensor nodes. A Voronoi graph based network model is first constructed, then node schedule algorithm is given to make nodes closest to the target be in active state and others in sleep state.
2. Designing a weighted centroid based localization algorithm to locate the target with distance information from nodes closest to the target to reduce the influence of noise on localization accuracy.
3. Analyzing the performance of the algorithms: A set of simulations are implemented to evaluate the performance of the proposed algorithms.

The rest of the paper is organized as follows. The related work is reviewed in Sect. 2, Sect. 3 presents the Voronoi based network model and 4 presents the scheduling based algorithms. Section 5 illustrates the performance of our algorithms. Section 6 gives the conclusion of the paper.

2 Related Work

Many existing mechanisms and algorithms are proposed to solve the problem of target tracking in WSNs. Usually they make assumptions about extra expensive equipments requirement, device capabilities (static nodes or mobile nodes), network makeup (homogeneous vs. heterogeneous), network size, node deployment and predicted target trajectory model. In this section, we review existing works in target tracking from two aspects.

2.1 Target Tracking Solutions

The authors in [6] presents an area location prediction based tracking algorithm making guarantee of QoT and energy efficiency. Vasuhi et al. [7] construct moving models to track targets, which makes multiple sensor nodes discover and identify the targets. Yu proposes a distributed target tracking mechanism with uncertainty considering [8]. The algorithm focuses on the data uncertainty in the network. The author in [9] gives a weighted centroid target locating method, which is implemented in a distributed way.

The authors in [10] propose two low computational RSSI based algorithms that's the weighted centroid localization algorithm and the relative-span exponential weighted localization algorithm. The authors in [1] design an energy efficient Localization and Tracking system, which use a serial a set of low cost and portable device with guarantee of tracking accuracy.

The above works consider the problem of energy efficiency when design the tracking algorithms.

2.2   Node Schedule Solutions

The authors in [11] propose a mobile sensors scheduling and a fixed sensors scheduling mechanisms for target tracking. Atia et al. [12] design a serial of strategies to schedule sensors to optimize the balance between tracking performance and energy cost. Moreover, they solve the scheduling problem via a partially observable Markov decision process. Lersteau et al. build a sensing activities scheduling for target tracking with tracking quality guarantee [13], which is based on the assumption that the trace of the target is known. In real applications, getting the trace of the target in advance is not feasible.

For above reviews, we can see that the existing work on tracking and nodes schedule only consider the energy efficient problem, or only address the problem under uncertain data or tracking policies based on a determined trajectory model. The aim of this paper is to solve the combination problem of tracking under energy efficiency and data uncertainty, moreover we do not make any assumption on the target trajectory.

3   Preliminary

In this section, a Voronoi model is constructed first to search the nearest nodes of the target participate in tracking.

3.1   Voronoi Diagram Based Network Model

Assumed that the number of sensor nodes in the network is m, the set of nodes is denoted as $N = \{n_1, n_2, ..., n_m\}$. All nodes know their own position [14, 15]. These sensor nodes are deployed with certain uniformity and density guarantee. Thus, the target can be discovered by more than one node at any time step. The Voronoi diagram of a collection of sensor nodes divide the space into a lot of polygons. The feature of Voronoi diagram confirms that the target in a given polygon is closer to the sensor nodes in this polygon than to any other sensor nodes. Figure 1 is an example of Voronoi diagram of the network.

The Voronoi polygon of each node n_i can be denoted as $G_i = <P\ N_i,\ V_i,\ E_i>$, where $P\ N_i$ is the subset of sensor nodes in G_i, V_i is the subset of Voronoi vertices of G_i, and E_i is the subset of Voronoi edges. As shown in Fig. 2, $PN_i = \{pn_{i1}, pn_{i2}, pn_{i3}, pn_{i4}\}$, $V_i = \{v_1, v_2, v_3, v_4, v_5\}$, $E_i = \{v_1v_2, v_2v_3, v_3v_4, v_4v_5, v_5v_1\}$. We construct the Voronoi polygons as the method in [16], that's each node first calculates the bisector of its neighbors and itself. All bisectors can form several polygons. Among these

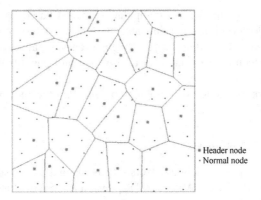

Fig. 1. An example of Voronoi model

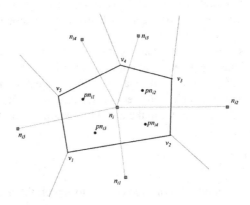

Fig. 2. Voronoi polygon Gi of n_i.

polygons, the smallest one enclosing the sensor node is its Voronoi polygon. In each polygon, one header node is chosen and the others are normal nodes. The nodes in the same polygon can communicate directly. In order to balance the energy consumption of nodes, the partition of polygons is updated periodically according to the application requirement. However it is at the price of extra energy cost. For simplicity, we use header to denote header node and node to denote normal node for short.

3.2 Choosing Header Node

For arbitrary sensor node n_i, it first generates a number $s_i(s_i \in \{0, 1\})$ randomly, then n_i creates a threshold ts_i according to the probability of being chosen as header and the fact that if it has been a header before. ts_i is defined as:

$$ts_i = \frac{p}{1 - p \times (r \bmod \frac{1}{p})} \tag{1}$$

where p is the probability that n_i is chosen as a header, r is the round number of choosing header. Initially, $r = 1$, NH is the nodes set has not been chosen as header in the latest $\frac{1}{p}$ rounds. If $s_i \leq ts_i$, then n_i becomes a header.

After deciding the headers, a Voronoi diagram is constructed. $H = \{h_1, h_2 \cdots\}$ is the headers set. tt_i is the polygon that enclose header h_i. When the target moves into the polygon of n_i, the characteristics of Voronoi guarantee that the distance from the target to each node in polygon G_i is less than the distance from the target to any node outside this polygon, that's nodes in the polygon of G_i are the closest nodes set to the target.

3.3 Adjusting Normal Nodes

The random distribution of headers makes the size of each polygon different, moreover the number of normal nodes in each polygon different. However, there are usually minimum nodes number constraint in target localization. To ensure that the number of nodes in each polygon is no less than a given threshold T_v, we give a normal nodes adjusting scheme. The idea of the scheme is to make nodes in the polygons with more members move to the polygons of which nodes number is less than T_v. We divide the algorithm into two steps, that's searching for the destination polygons and nodes moving.

Searching for Destination Polygons. Initially, header h_k broadcasts a Member Request packet (MREQ) to confirm its member nodes. MREQ is consisted of a binary tuple $<h_k, V_k>$. When node n_i receives MREQ, it decides whether it should stay within polygon G_k which is those vertexes in V_k have constructed. If it does, n_i sends a reply packet MREP to h_k, otherwise it ignores the message. After these information exchange, each node determines the polygon it belongs to.

Nodes Moving. Header h_k collects MREPs and counts the number of nodes in its G_k, denoted as c_k. Then h_k broadcasts c_k. If $c_k < T_v$, h_k sends Node Request (NREQ) packet to request new members. NREQ is a tuple consisted of $<h_k, qc, x_k, y_k>$. Where qc is the required nodes number, (x_k, y_k) is the coordinate of h_k. The scheme works in three steps:

a. Collect the number of nodes information from neighbor polygons, and sort neighbor polygons (of which nodes number is greater than T_v) in descending order of nodes number, the sorted neighbor polygons list is denoted as SP.
b. From the first element G_f in SP, sends NREQ to its header h_f and request for M in $(qc, c_f - T)$ normal nodes.
c. If M in $(qc, c_f - T)$ equals to qc, the procedure ends. Otherwise, $qc = qc - M$ in (qc, c_fGT), repeat step b and send NREQ to the next element in SP until all elements in SP have been processed.

4   A Voronoi Diagram Based Tracking Scheme

In the section, a Voronoi diagram based tracking scheme is presented, which is named VDTS. VDTS first divides the monitoring area into multiple Voronoi polygons, then it designs a Voronoi diagram based method to implement tracking. Nodes in the polygon that the target resides must be the closest nodes to the target, which provide more accurate sensed data, moreover better results.

4.1   Main Algorithm

At the initial phase, the Voronoi diagram is determined based on the location information of sensor nodes. The nodes location information is obtained through certain localization mechanism. Initially, the target must enter the monitoring environment from the network boundary, we assume that when the target has not entered into the monitor area, only boundary nodes of the network stay in active and others keep in sleep state. As shown in Fig. 3, when the target appears in a Voronoi polygon, the header in the Voronoi polygon can detect it. The header sends awakening message to wake up normal nodes in the polygon to sample the target. When these normal nodes are wakened up, they estimate the distance to the target via RSSI method or other distance estimation mechanisms, then transmit distance information to header node for performing location estimating.

As the moving of the target, we should predict the target appearing Voronoi polygons and activate headers in these polygons in advance. Considering the target's moving trajectory is undetermined or unknown, how to predict the target's appearing Voronoi polygons is a problem. We will describe the solutions in the next sections.

4.2   Target Appearing Polygon Prediction

At a certain time t, the target is in Voronoi polygon G_i, its estimated position is L_t. The neighbor polygons of G_i is denoted as G_{i1}, G_{i2}, G_{i3} and G_{i4}, respectively.

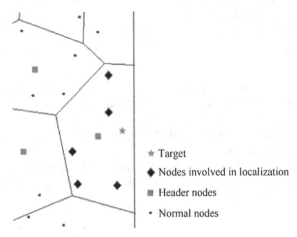

Fig. 3. An example of target in boundary cells

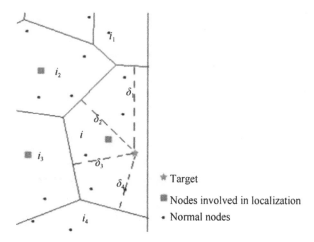

Fig. 4. An example of Case 1

The corresponding edges set is denoted as $V_t = \{v_0v_1,\ v_1v_2,\ v_2v_3,\ v_3v_4\}$. Header h_i calculates the distance between L_t and each edge, the distances set is denoted as $\Delta_i = \{\delta_1, \delta_2, \delta_3, \delta_4\}$, as shown in Fig. 4.

Case 1. Given threshold δ and $j = 1, 2, 3, 4$, if $\delta_j < \delta$, then G_j is the target's appearing polygon for the next time step $t + 1$. The value of δ is decided by sample frequency f and target's maximum velocity v_{max} [17], we formulate it as:

$$\delta = \frac{1}{f} \times \frac{v_{max}}{2} \tag{2}$$

From the formula, we know that δ is the half distance of the target in time $\frac{1}{f}$. The setting of δ makes sure that the target can be detected wherever it leaves the current Voronoi polygon.

Case 2. Given δ_j and δ_k, $(j, k = 1, 2, 3, 4 \wedge j f = i)$, if $\delta_j < \delta \wedge \delta_k < \delta$, then both polygon G_j and G_k are target's possible appearing polygons for the next time step $t + 1$, as shown in Fig. 5.

4.3   Awaking up Sleeping Nodes

When the target's appearing polygons G_j and G_k (or only G_j) are determined for the next time is determined, header h_i starts to broadcast awaking packet (ANP) to wake up normal nodes in the destination polygons. ANP is a tuple consisted of $<h_i, n_G, G_{des}[]>$. Where n_G is the number of destination polygons, $G_{des}[]$ is the destination polygons ID.

When the headers h_j (and h_k) in the destination polygons receives ANP, they wake up normal nodes in their polygons to perform tracking task. Meanwhile, h_i send a sleeping message to inform normal nodes in ins polygon turn to sleep.

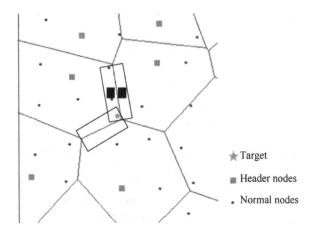

Fig. 5. An example of Case 2

4.4 Estimating Target's Coordinates

When normal nodes in the Voronoi polygon that the target resides, the information from these nodes are obtained to locate the target. Many excellent localization algorithms are proposed [18, 19]. In our simulations, we take weighted centroid based localization algorithm as an example for its simplicity and robustness.

Supposed the target is in polygon G_i, the normal nodes that participate in localization is defined as $P\ N_i = \{pn_1, ..., pn_{|pNi|}\}$. Instead of treating the weights of nodes equally, the weighted average of all involved nodes is considered.

4.5 An Example Illustration

In this section, an example on how the involved polygons are predicted and normal nodes are wakened is illustrated, as shown in Fig. 6. At time step t, the target is in G_i, the five neighbors of G_i is G_{i1}, G_{i2}, G_{i3}, G_{i4} and G_{i5}. The distance from the target to G_{i1}, G_{i2}, G_{i3}, G_{i4} and G_{i5} are $\delta_1 = 3$, $\delta_2 = 1.5$, $\delta_3 = 2$, $\delta_4 = 3$ and $\delta_5 = 2.5$, respectively.

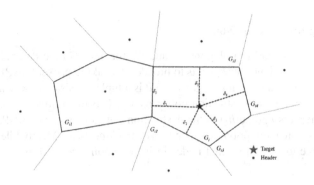

Fig. 6. An example of the tracking scheme

Given $\delta = 2$, then the appearing polygons of the moving target at the next time step $t + 1$ is G_{i2} and G_{i3}.

5   Simulation Results

To validate the proposed algorithms, we use HP X230 computer, windows 7 OS and Java eclipse to construct a simulation environment. The Voronoi diagram based network partition is constructed using node by node insertion method. We evaluated the influence of parameters p and δ on the algorithms. In the simulations, sensor nodes are distributed uniformly in the environment with size of 600 580 units. Sensor nodes number varies from 100 to 150, the default value is 122. The number of headers is random, which is decided by probability p. p varies between 0.10–0.40, the default value is 0.25. δ varies between 10 to 40 and the default value is 30. When one parameter is evaluated, the others are default value.

5.1   The Influence of p

In these simulations, the impact of p on sensor nodes number being in active state and transmission times are evaluated. Figure 7 illustrates the results when the nodes number is 100, 121 and 144, respectively. From these figures, we can see that as the increasing of p, active nodes number reduces. That's because raising p increases the ratio of headers and the number of Voronoi polygons, while the number of normal nodes reduces which leads to the decreasing of nodes being active. When the working nodes number reaches to a fixed value, the change trend is not obvious, that's because we have set the minimum normal nodes number limit, which is 2.

Figure 8 shows the influence of p on transmission times. When the nodes number is fixed, the transmission times reduces as the raising of p. The reason is that the increasing of p leads to the decreasing of active nodes, which makes the transmission times for each localization reduce. Moreover, the transmission amounts for activating nodes in new Voronoi polygons is reduced too. Although increasing p contributes to energy conservation of the network, while it is at the price of tracking quality.

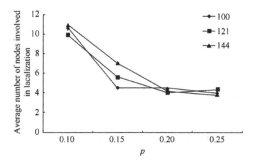

Fig. 7. The influence of p on active nodes

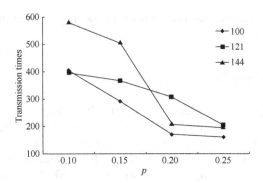

Fig. 8. The influence of p on transmission times

5.2 The Influence of δ

Figure 9 shows the influence of δ on transmission times. As the main energy consumption of the network is from transmission, we use transmission times to reflects the energy consumption. The figure also describes the influence of δ on energy consumption. With the increasing of δ, transmission times increases. When the distance between the target and any edge of the polygon is less than δ, the nodes from the neighbor polygons will be awakened up, which leads to unnecessary nodes be active, thus brings extra transmission cost.

Figure 10 shows the relationship between δ and active nodes number. As the raising of δ, the number of nodes being awakened up increases. As raising δ means the distance threshold between the target and edges of polygons increases, that's nodes satisfies the given threshold will be awakened up. The raising δ increases the probability of nodes being active.

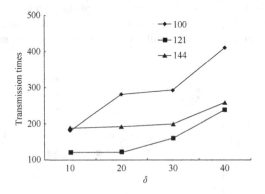

Fig. 9. The influence of δ on transmission times

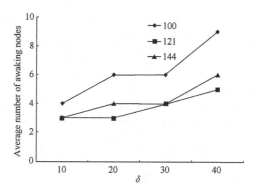

Fig. 10. The influence of δ on Average number of awaking nodes.

6 Conclusions

This paper presents a Voronoi diagram based scheduling and tracking scheme in wireless sensor networks, which constructs a network model based on the property of Voronoi diagram, and selects sensor nodes closest to the target that participate in tracking to reduce the influence of data noise on tracking accuracy. The proposed algorithm minimizes the number of awaking nodes with tracking quality guarantee. Finally, a set of simulation experiments are made to evaluate the influence of various parameters on the performance of the proposed schemes. Experimental results show the excellent performance of the proposed algorithm in terms of energy saving.

References

1. Zheng, K., et al.: Energy efficient localization and tracking of mobile devices in wireless sensor networks. IEEE Trans. Veh. Technol. **66**(3), 2714–2726 (2017)
2. Ahmadi, H., Viani, F., Bouallegue, R.: An accurate prediction method for moving target localization and tracking in wireless sensor networks. Ad Hoc Netw. **70**, 14–22 (2018)
3. Martin, E., Vinyals, O., Friedland, G., Bajcsy, R.: Precise indoor localization using smart phones. In: Proceedings of the 18th ACM International Conference on Multimedia (MM 2010), NewYork, NY, October 2010, pp. 787–790 (2010)
4. Yiu, S., et al.: Wireless RSSI fingerprinting localization. Signal Process. **131**, 235–244 (2017)
5. Xing, G., Tan, R., Liu, B., Wang, J., Jia, X., Yi, C.-W.: Data fusion improves the coverage of wireless sensor networks. In: Proceedings of the 15th Annual International Conference on Mobile Computing and Networking, MobiCom 2009. ACM, New York, pp. 157–168 (2009)
6. Bhuiyan, M.Z.A., Wang, G., Vasilakos, A.V.: Local area prediction-based mobile target tracking in wireless sensor networks. IEEE Trans. Comput. **64**(7), 1968–1982 (2015)
7. Vasuhi, S., Vaidehi, V.: Target tracking using interactive multiple model for wireless sensor network. Inf. Fusion **27**, 41–53 (2016)
8. Yu, Y.: Distributed target tracking in wireless sensor networks with data association uncertainty. IEEE Commun. Lett. **21**(6), 1281–1284 (2017)

9. Wang, J., et al.: Weighted centroid localization algorithm: theoretical analysis and distributed implementation. IEEE Trans. Wirel. Commun. **10**(10), 3403–3413 (2011)
10. Pivato, P., Palopoli, L., Petri, D.: Accuracy of RSS-based centroid localization algorithms in an indoor environment. IEEE Trans. Instrum. Meas. **60**(10), 3451–3460 (2011)
11. Wang, T., et al.: Following targets for mobile tracking in wireless sensor networks. ACM Trans. Sens. Netw. (TOSN) **12**(4), 31 (2016)
12. Atia, G.K., Veeravalli, V.V., Fuemmeler, J.A.: Sensor scheduling for energy-efficient target tracking in sensor networks. IEEE Trans. Signal Process. **59**(10), 4923–4937 (2011)
13. Lersteau, C., Rossi, A., Sevaux, M.: Robust scheduling of wireless sensor networks for target tracking under uncertainty. Eur. J. Oper. Res. **252**(2), 407–417 (2016)
14. Han, G., et al.: A survey on mobile anchor node assisted localization in wireless sensor networks. IEEE Commun. Surv. Tutor. **18**(3), 2220–2243 (2016)
15. Rezazadeh, J., et al.: Superior path planning mechanism for mobile beacon-assisted localization in wireless sensor networks. IEEE Sens. J. **14**(9), 3052–3064 (2014)
16. Wang, G., Cao, G., La Porta, T.F.: Movement assisted sensor deployment. IEEE Trans. Mob. Comput. **5**(6), 640–652 (2006)
17. Ren, Q., Li, J., Liu, H.: Energy efficient tracking in uncertain sensor networks. Ad Hoc Netw. **81**, 45–55 (2018)
18. Mizmizi, M., Reggiani, L.: Binary fingerprinting-based indoor positioning systems. 2017 International Conference on Indoor Positioning and Indoor Navigation (IPIN). IEEE (2017)
19. Lasla, N., et al.: An effective area-based localization algorithm for wireless networks. IEEE Trans. Comput. **64**(8), 2103–2118 (2015)

Improved Lightweight RFID Bidirectional Authentication Protocol LMAP++

Xiaohui Cheng, Shuai Shen, and Qiong Gui[✉]

Guangxi Key Laboratory of Embedded Technology and Intelligent System,
College of Information Science and Engineering,
Guilin University of Technology, Jiangan road No. 12, Guilin 541000, China
cxiaohui@glut.edu.cn, 1403229316@qq.com,
guilucky@163.com

Abstract. The security of the lightweight LMAP++ bidirectional authentication protocol commonly used in low-cost RFID systems is studied. The vulnerability of LMAP++ authentication protocol is analyzed, and the reason of LMAP++ authentication protocol vulnerabilities is studied. An improved lightweight LMAP++ bidirectional authentication protocol is proposed and a concrete formula is given to prove the protocol security. After comparison, the improved lightweight LMAP++ bidirectional authentication protocol can meet the security requirements such as confidentiality and traceability faced in RFID systems. Attacks such as tracking, counterfeit tags, replay, and positioning can be resisted, making it more adaptable to the security needs of low-cost RFID systems.

Keywords: RFID · Lightweight · Security of protocol · LMAP++

1 Introduction

Radio frequency identification (RFID) system is an important part of the perception layer of the Internet of Things. As a mature automatic identification technology, it saves costs and improves efficiency. It is widely used in various fields, but it also brings with a series of security and privacy issues [1]. Most of the existing RFID authentication protocols are based on Hash function or cryptographic technology [2, 3]. Although the security of tag information is largely guaranteed, there is a certain requirement on the computing power and storage space of the tags, not lightweight, not universal [4–7]. Therefore, an improved lightweight RFID bidirectional authentication protocol LMAP is proposed. The protocol has relatively low computing power and storage space requirements for tags, and has relatively high security performance.

2 LMAP++ Protocol Overview

LMAP++ is a lightweight bidirectional authentication protocol. It is an improved version of the LMAP protocol. It guarantees the security of tag information through the mutual authentication of tags and readers. The operation of the protocol is simple, just use OR, AND, XOR. Multiplication and Hash function are not used [9]. The LMAP++

© Springer Nature Singapore Pte Ltd. 2019
S. Shen et al. (Eds.): CWSN 2018, CCIS 984, pp. 33–40, 2019.
https://doi.org/10.1007/978-981-13-6834-9_4

authentication protocol's power consumption is slightly more than the super light-weight authentication protocol SASI, but the LMAP^{++} protocol is more secure than the SASI protocol, and has the ability to prevent the following hazards, such as tracking attacks and location attacks [8, 10]. The LMAP^{++} authentication protocol makes up for the shortcomings of the SASI protocol and prevents tracking and positioning.

As shown in Fig. 1, the LMAP^{++} original authentication system consists of three parts: tags, readers and back-end databases. The channel is assumed to be safe between the reader and the back-end database, therefore, The simplified model only considers the communications security between the reader and tag [6]. The data in the back-end database is stored in the reader. The identifier ID is stored in the ROM of the tag, and the pseudo-identifier PID of the tag is stored in the EEPROM.

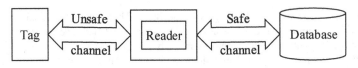

Fig. 1. LMAP^{++} protocol main body

The three goals of LMAP^{++} protocol are: ① To ensure privacy, that is, the tag unique ID will not appear in Plaintext during authentication, and the pseudo identifier PID will update automatically after each protocol is executed; ② To ensure security, that is, the protocol can resist a series of attack methods such as man-in-the-middle attacks, replay attacks, and tracking attacks; ③ To ensure lightweight, that is, only lightweight functions are used in the authentication process, and the hardware system can only be at the level of several hundred gate circuits.

2.1 Symbol Definition in LMAP^{++}

LMAP^{++} protocol is lightweight because it only uses bit operations such as modulo 2n plus (+), XOR ($\oplus$), and does not use complex operations such as Hash. Random number is generated only in the reader. As shown in Table 1.

Table 1. Symbol meaning of LMAP^{++} protocol

Symbol	Meaning
ID	Tag unique identifier
$PID^{(n)}$	The pseudo-ID of the tag at the nth execution of the protocol
$K_1^{(n)}$, $K_2^{(n)}$	The key to execute the nth protocol
+	Modulo 2n plus operation
$\parallel$	Digital connector
$\oplus$	XOR operation
r	Random

Each tag has two identifiers, one is a unique identifier ID with a constant tag, and the other is a pseudo-identifier PID that changes after each round of protocol execution. Each tag has two keys, K_1 and K_2. Both the pseudo-identifier and the key are represented in 96-bit long binary. Since the PID, K_1, and K_2 are all updated, the tag requires a 96*3-bit EEPROM to store the data, and a 96-bit ROM to store ID.

2.2 LMAP^{++} Protocol Execution Procedure

The execution of the LMAP^{++} protocol is shown in Fig. 2. R is used to represent Reader and T is used to represent Tag.

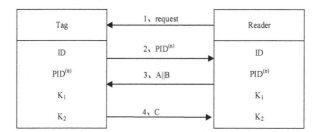

Fig. 2. LMAP^{++} protocol execution process

(1) R $\rightarrow$ T: request。
(2) T $\rightarrow$ R: The tag responds to the request and returns PID$^{(n)}$. The reader queried the PID$^{(n)}$. If there is no match, the authentication fails and the process ends. If there is a match, the reader calculates A and B according to formulas (1) and (2):

$$A = PID^{(n)} \oplus K_1^{(n)} + r \tag{1}$$

$$B = PID^{(n)} + K_2^{(n)} \oplus r \tag{2}$$

(3) R $\rightarrow$ T: The reader sends A$\|$B to the tag. The tag separates random numbers r from A and B:

$$r_1 = A - PID^{(n)} \oplus K_1^{(n)}$$

$$r_2 = (B - PID^{(n)}) \oplus K_2^{(n)}$$

If $r_1 = r_2$, the tag completes the authentication of the reader and tag. Otherwise, the protocol execution process is terminated.

(4) T → R: The tag calculates C according to the formula (3):

$$C = \left(PID^{(n)} + ID \oplus r \right) \oplus \left(K_1^{(n)} + K_2^{(n)} + r \right) \tag{3}$$

And send C to the reader. Then, the tag updates $PID^{(n)}, K_1^{(n)}, K_2^{(n)}$ according to the formula (4), (5), (6):

$$PID^{(n+1)} = \left(PID^{(n)} + K_1^{(n)} \right) \oplus r + \left(ID + K_2^{(n)} \right) \oplus r \tag{4}$$

$$K_1^{(n+1)} = K_1^{(n)} \oplus r + \left(PID^{(n+1)} + K_2^{(n)} + ID \right) \tag{5}$$

$$K_2^{(n+1)} = K_2^{(n)} \oplus r + \left(PID^{(n+1)} + K_1^{(n)} + ID \right) \tag{6}$$

(5) The reader calculates the value of C as follows:

$$C' = \left(PID^{(n)} + ID \oplus r \right) \oplus \left(K_1^{(n)} + K_2^{(n)} + r \right)$$

If $C = C'$, the reader completes the authentication of the tag. Finally, the reader updates $PID^{(n)}, K_1^{(n)}, K_2^{(n)}$ according to the formula (4), (5), (6).

3 LMAP⁺⁺ Protocol Vulnerabilities

The LMAP⁺⁺ protocol has a loophole in the minimum bit tracking defense.

According to the execution process of LMAP⁺⁺ protocol, as long as A, B, and C are monitored, the unique identifier ID of the tag can be calculated. This leads to a tracking attack, which is equal to expose the location of the protocol's tag. The tag information will bring users the threat of location threats and motion trajectory analysis. The process of attack is as follows:

Attack process: The attacker listens successfully to the authentication process. That is, get $PID^{(n)}$, A, B, and C.

Analysis process: Assume that the IDs of the two tags are ID_0 and ID_1, the lowest bits are 0 and 1, that's $(ID_0)_0 = 0$, $(ID_1)_0 = 1$, only consider the lowest bit, then there are:

$$(A)_0 = \left(PID^{(n)} \right)_0 \oplus \left(K_1^{(n)} \right)_0 \oplus (r)_0 \tag{7}$$

$$(B)_0 = \left(PID^{(n)} \right)_0 \oplus \left(K_2^{(n)} \right)_0 \oplus (r)_0 \tag{8}$$

$$(C)_0 = \left(PID^{(n)}\right)_0 \oplus (ID)_0 \oplus (r)_0 \oplus \left(\left(K_1^{(n)}\right)_0 \oplus \left(K_2^{(n)}\right)_0 \oplus (r)_0\right) \qquad (9)$$

Available from (7), (8):

$$\left(K_1^{(n)}\right)_0 = \left(PID^{(n)}\right)_0 \oplus (A)_0 \oplus (r)_0 \qquad (10)$$

$$\left(K_2^{(n)}\right)_0 = \left(PID^{(n)}\right)_0 \oplus (B)_0 \oplus (r)_0 \qquad (11)$$

Substituting (10) and (11) into (9) can be obtained by

$$(C)_0 = \left(PID^{(n)}\right)_0 \oplus (ID)_0 \oplus (A)_0 \oplus (B)_0$$

After the transfer:

$$(ID)_0 = \left(PID^{(n)}\right)_0 \oplus (A)_0 \oplus (B)_0 (C)_0$$

From this it can be seen that $(ID)_0$ can be calculated, that means the attacker can distinguish which tag is in use from the two tags, so as to achieve the purpose of tracking.

4   Improved Lightweight Bidirectional Authentication Protocol LMAP^{++}

4.1   Improved Lightweight Bidirectional Authentication Protocol LMAP^{++} Execution Procedure

Since the LMAP^{++} protocol cannot solve the least-bit tracking problem based on the operation of modulo 2 plus and the like, the value of C can be modified when the tag transfers C to the reader. Therefore, when attacking a RFID system with a trace attack method, the attacker cannot calculate the ID value, thereby ensuring the system has the ability to resist the threat of tracking attacks. The specific method is as follows:

(1) R → T: Request。
(2) T → R: The tag responds to the request and returns PID$^{(n)}$. The reader queries the PID$^{(n)}$. If there is no match, the authentication fails and the process ends. If there is a match, the reader calculates A and B according to formulas (12) and (13):

$$A = PID^{(n)} \oplus K_1^{(n)} + r \qquad (12)$$

$$B = PID^{(n)} + K_2^{(n)} \oplus r \qquad (13)$$

(3) R → T: The reader sends A∥B to the tag. The tag separates random numbers r from A and B:

$$r_1 = A - PID^{(n)} \oplus K_1^{(n)}$$

$$r_2 = \left(B - PID^{(n)}\right) \oplus K_2^{(n)}$$

If $r_1 = r_2$, the tag completes the authentication of the reader. Otherwise, the protocol is terminated.

(4) T → R: The tag calculates C according to the formula (3):

$$C = \left(PID^{(n)} + ID \oplus r\right) \oplus \left(K_1^{(n)} + K_2^{(n)} + r\right) + r \tag{14}$$

And send C to the reader. Then, the tag updates $PID^{(n)}, K_1^{(n)}, K_2^{(n)}$ according to the formula (15), (16), (17):

$$PID^{(n+1)} = \left(PID^{(n)} + K_1^{(n)}\right) \oplus r + \left(ID + K_2^{(n)}\right) \oplus r \tag{15}$$

$$K_1^{(n+1)} = K_1^{(n)} \oplus r + \left(PID^{(n+1)} + K_2^{(n)} + ID\right) \tag{16}$$

$$K_2^{(n+1)} = K_2^{(n)} \oplus r + \left(PID^{(n+1)} + K_1^{(n)} + ID\right) \tag{17}$$

(5) The reader calculates the value of C as follows:

$$C' = \left(PID^{(n)} + ID \oplus r\right) \oplus \left(K_1^{(n)} + K_2^{(n)} + r\right) + r$$

If $C = C'$, the reader completes the authentication of the tag. Finally, the reader updates $PID^{(n)}, K_1^{(n)}, K_2^{(n)}$ according to the formula (15), (16), (17).

4.2 Improved LMAP^{++} Protocol Analysis Result

Assume that the attack is as follows:

The attack process is shown below: The attacker successfully listens to the authentication process. That means that the attacker gets $PID^{(n)}$, A, B, and C.

Analysis process: Assume that the IDs of the two tags are ID_0 and ID_1, the lowest bits are 0 and 1, that means $(ID_0)_0 = 0$, and $(ID_1)_0 = 1$, only considering the lowest bit, then there are:

$$(A)_0 = \left(PID^{(n)}\right)_0 \oplus \left(K_1^{(n)}\right)_0 \oplus (r)_0 \tag{18}$$

$$(B)_0 = \left(PID^{(n)}\right)_0 \oplus \left(K_2^{(n)}\right)_0 \oplus (r)_0 \tag{19}$$

$$(C)_0 = \left(PID^{(n)}\right)_0 \oplus (ID)_0 \oplus (r)_0 \oplus \left(\left(K_1^{(n)}\right)_0 \oplus \left(K_2^{(n)}\right)_0 \oplus (r)_0\right) \oplus (r)_0 \tag{20}$$

Available from (18), (19):

$$\left(K_1^{(n)}\right)_0 = \left(PID^{(n)}\right)_0 \oplus (A)_0 \oplus (r)_0 \tag{21}$$

$$\left(K_2^{(n)}\right)_0 = \left(PID^{(n)}\right)_0 \oplus (B)_0 \oplus (r)_0 \tag{22}$$

Substituting (21) and (22) into (20) can be obtained by,

$$(C)_0 = \left(PID^{(n)}\right)_0 \oplus (ID)_0 \oplus (A)_0 \oplus (B)_0 \oplus (r)_0$$

After the transfer:

$$(ID)_0 = \left(PID^{(n)}\right)_0 \oplus (A)_0 \oplus (B)_0 (C)_0 \oplus (r)_0$$

Since there is a random number r in the $(ID)_0$ calculation formula, even if A, B and C are all heard, the attacker still cannot crack the tag unique identifier ID.

5 Conclusion

Based on the analysis of the RFID system security authentication LMAP protocol, this paper presents a more secure and improved lightweight LMAP^{++} bidirectional authentication protocol. The security of the improved LMAP^{++} protocol is described from both the theoretical proof and the security analysis. The analysis results show that the improved LMAP^{++} protocol compensates for the original protocol's lowest bit traceable threat. At the same time, the protocol can resist attacks such as tag replay and positioning. The lightweight advantages of LMAP^{++} protocol make the protocol more suitable for the application security requirements of low-cost RFID systems.

Acknowledgements. As the research of the thesis is sponsored by National Natural Science Foundation of China (No: 61662017, No: 61262075), Key R & D projects of Guangxi Science and Technology Program (AB17195042), Guangxi Natural Science Foundation (No: 2017GXNSFAA198223), Guilin Science and Technology Project Fund (No: 2016010408) and Guangxi Key Laboratory Fund of Embedded Technology and Intelligent System, we would like to extend our sincere gratitude to them.

References

1. Zhou, S.J., Zhang, W.Q., Luo, J.Q.: Overview of radio frequency identification (RFID) privacy protection technology. J. Softw. **26**(4), 960–976 (2015)
2. Zhang, B., Ma, X.X., Qin, Z.G.: Design and analysis of lightweight RFID bidirectional authentication protocol. J. Univ. Electron. Sci. Technol. China **42**(3), 425–430 (2013)
3. Gao, S.J., Zhang, R.Q.: Lightweight RFID privacy protocol based on universal hash function. In: International Symposium on Knowledge Acquisition and Modeling (2015)
4. Sicari, S., Rizzardi, A., Miorandi, D., et al.: A secure and quality-aware prototypical architecture for the Internet of Things. Inf. Syst. **58**, 43–55 (2016)
5. Namin, M.E., Hosseinzadeh, M., Bagheri, N., et al.: A secure search protocol for lightweight and low-cost RFID systems. Telecommun. Syst. **3**, 1–14 (2017)
6. Wang, K.H., Chen, C.M., Fang, W., et al.: On the security of a new ultra-lightweight authentication protocol in IoT environment for RFID tags. J. Supercomput. **15**, 1–6 (2017)
7. Zhuang, X., Zhu, Y., Chang, C.C., et al.: Security issues in ultra-lightweight RFID authentication protocols. Wirel. Pers. Commun. **4**, 1–36 (2017)
8. Ma, Q.M., Wang, S.P.: An ultra-lightweight RFID authentication protocol. Comput. Eng. **38**(2), 151–152 (2012)
9. Zeng, F.: Research on Lightweight RFID Security Authentication Protocol for Internet of Things. Beijing Jiaotong University (2014)
10. Ma, Q., Guo, Y.J., Zeng, Q.J., et al.: A new ultra-lightweight RFID bidirectional authentication protocol. Inf. Netw. Secur. **5**, 44–50 (2016)

Matching Model of Flow Table
for Software-Defined Internet of Things

Yiheng Su, Ting Peng, Xiaoxun Zhong, and Lianming Zhang[✉]

Key Laboratory of Internet of Things Technology and Application,
College of Information Science and Engineering, Hunan Normal University,
Changsha 410081, China
yhsu@smail.hunnu.edu.cn, zlm@hunnu.edu.cn

Abstract. The heterogeneity of the IoT devices increases the difficulty of management. Software-defined Internet of Things (SD-IoT) provides a workable and practical paradigm for designing more efficient and flexible IoT. Matching strategy in the flow table of SD-IoT switches is most crucial. In this paper, we use a classification approach to analyze the structure of packets based on the tuple-space lookup mechanism, and propose a matching model of the flow table in SD-IoT switches by classifying packets based on a set of fields, which is called an F-OpenFlow. The experimental results show that the proposed F-OpenFlow effectively improves the utilization rate and matching efficiency of the flow table in SD-IoT switches.

Keywords: Software-Defined IoT (SD-IoT) · Matching model · F-OpenFlow · Tuple-space search

1 Introduction

Internet of Things (IoT) contains a larger number of interconnected devices. According to Gartner, there will be 24 billion devices connected to IoT by 2020. Heterogeneity of the IoT devices increases the difficulty of management. Software-defined networking (SDN) [1, 2] is a new networking innovation paradigm that separates the control plane from the data plane, offering a well-defined programmable interface for the management of IoT devices. In the recent years. Lin et al. presented a forward-looking view of the convergence of IoT, big data, cloud and SDN technologies along with the arrival of 5G mobile broadband networks [3]. Yin et al. presented a general framework for software-defined Internet of Things (SD-IoT) based on the software-defined anything paradigm [4].

The two main components of SD-IoT are SD-IoT controllers and SD-IoT switches. SD-IoT controllers are mainly responsible for the centralized management and remote control of network devices. The SD-IoT switches relying on flow tables are only in charge of forwarding data. However, global deployment of SD-IoT encounters some issues. With the increasing number of flow tables and the complicated structure of flow entries, the size of flow tables in SD-IoT switches explosively grows, which poses difficulties for practicing flow tables.

© Springer Nature Singapore Pte Ltd. 2019
S. Shen et al. (Eds.): CWSN 2018, CCIS 984, pp. 41–54, 2019.
https://doi.org/10.1007/978-981-13-6834-9_5

To solve the scalability problem of flow table items, the present study can be divided into the following categories. (1) Optimizing the flow table, designing flow table structure combining software and hardware to expand capacity [5–7]. (2) Compressing the size and number of flow table items so that the original flow table can hold more flow table items [8–10].

The Open vSwitch kernel has been adopted Microflow Cache method [11], where the Hash's exact lookup table and wildcard lookup table they use it to reduce the number of lookups in a multilayer flow table. Since Open vSwitch utilizes a tuple-space lookup method, the average number for searching the original lookup table is half of what adopts the tuple-space table based on the kernel. The core of this idea is to minimize the number of messages in the lookup of multilayer flow tables, and to increase the number of access to the lookup table in the cache of switches.

In this paper, we present a matching model of the flow table in SD-IoT switches by classifying packets based on matching a set of fields, which are short for F-OpenFlow, to search flow tables of OpenFlow switches. The main contributions of this paper are as follows:

- Proposing the method that the matching field can improve the matching probability of the table entries by classifying packets.
- Using tuple-space search to analyze the structure of the flow table in existing networks, and finding the matching rules of the same type for SD-IoT.
- Integrating the analysis model with the dictionary tree using a tuple-space approach, and obtaining a rule matching strategy.

The rest of the paper is organized as follows. In Sect. 2, we introduce challenges for flow tables of OpenFlow switches. We describe the problem of flow tables of SDN switches and present a system model for flow tables in Sect. 3. In Sect. 4, we realize the flow tables and design the structure of packets and flow tables. Section 5 presents the experimental results and evaluates the performance of the proposed matching model. Finally, conclusions are given in Sect. 6.

2 Challenges for the Flow Table of OpenFlow Switches

In traditional network devices, the data forwarding of switches and routers depends on the MAC forwarding table on Layer 2 or the IP address routing table on Layer 3. The flow table of OpenFlow switches is the entry of network devices integrating other levels of OpenFlow networks. Each flow table of OpenFlow switches consists of three parts: header fields for matching packets (Header Fields), counters for counting the number of packets (Counters) and actions on how to process a matching packet (Actions). The OpenFlow header field is used to match the header of the packets received by switches. In OpenFlow v1.0, the header of the flow table contains twelve tuples. However, there are still following challenges for flow tables of OpenFlow switches.

(1) The number of matching fields of flow entries is increasing rapidly. OpenFlow v1.0 defines a 12-tuple matching field. OpenFlow v1.3 defines forty matching fields, including thirteen matching fields that the switches must support. It is an inevitable trend for networked big data to extend matching field types and increase the number of flow tables.

(2) The scale of flow tables grows exponentially. Along with the expansion of the network, the number of flow entries and the number of matching entries will continue to grow. OpenFlow v1.1 points out the scalability of flow tables by introducing a multilayer structure. However, flexibility of multilayer flow tables is far beyond the capacity of data forwarding processing of traditional switching chip. It will add the complexity of designing hardware and software of OpenFlow switches.

(3) According to the application scenario of switches and the types of flow actions supported by switches, OpenFlow switches are classified into OpenFlow-only and OpenFlow-enabled, and the latter is also called OpenFlow-hybrid after OpenFlow v1.1. The former only supports OpenFlow protocol, while the latter considers the incompatibility between the OpenFlow switches and traditional switches when they are mixed. It can run the OpenFlow protocol and traditional Layer 2 or Layer 3 protocol stacks simultaneously. As a result, the latter is able to support NORMAL action in the optional forward action in OpenFlow.

(4) After a switch receives network packets, the processing of 802.1d protocol in the flow will become an optional step in the process. When the OpenFlow switch receives a packet, it will match entries with its local flow table according to the priority. As the result of matching, it takes the matching entry with the highest priority as the matching result based on the corresponding action to operate the packet. At the same time, once the matching is successful. The corresponding counter will update. If the packet cannot find a matching entry, it will forward to the controller.

3   Structure of F-OpenFlow

3.1   Problem Description

In recent years, the SDN has been widely used in the current experimental environments for network innovation, and it has broad application prospects as well as data centers. However, many critical technologies of the SDN have no mature solutions [12]. One of them is the update and design scheme of flow tables in switches.

The flow table of SDN switches contains a large number of matching rules. When a packet enters the flow table, it is matched in accordance with a specified search algorithm. Consequently, some matching algorithms, including linear and sequential search algorithms, will have a great effect on the pros and cons of SDN switches in the matching performance of data packets. The order of matching rules is limited by the search speed of the design level. Some linear and sequential rules in flow tables are analyzed, and a new pre-match method is formed by the hierarchical structure of data packets. Each packet, passing through flow tables in SDN switches, needs to be compared with the pre-model.

With the extension of OpenFlow applications, the scale of flow tables in OpenFlow switches is escalating, and the number of matching fields becomes larger and larger. The OpenFlow v1.1 [13] is proposed to compress the storage space and improve the lookup speed by a multilayer flow table and pipeline structure. The flow table of OpenFlow switches is divided into several work tables based on the protocol level of the header in the matching field. When the flow table is used for matching rules, the packet header is divided into multiple fields. We make a search operation in each field independently, use the method of sorting and grouping to find and integrate returned data, and return them to the flow table in OpenFlow switches for finding the rules of the Action.

3.2 Structure of F-OpenFlow

A flow entry is composed of six parts, including the matching field, table item priority, counter, table item instruction, timeout period, and cookie. The matching field and the table item priority in the flow table of OpenFlow switches define a unique flow table entry. The matching field contains many matches, which cover most of the character set in the link layer, network layer, and transport layer. The table item priority indicates the execution order of the flow entry. The table item instruction shows that the packet executes next instruction to match the table entry. The counter collects the statistics of the data flow, including the number and the length of matching the data flow. Devices in the OpenFlow network will no longer distinguish between routers and switches. In order to improve the efficiency of the flow table lookup, the current lookup uses the multilayer flow table and pipeline mode to obtain the corresponding operation. The OpenFlow pipeline of each switch contains multiple levels of flow tables that contain multiple flow entries. In this section, we present the structure of a matching model of the flow table in SD-IoT switches, F-OpenFlow for short, as showed in Fig. 1.

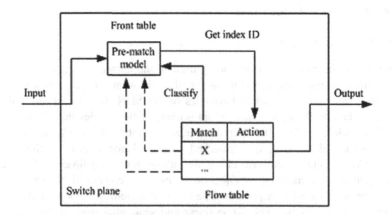

Fig. 1. Structure of F-OpenFlow

Firstly, the data packets enter into the OpenFlow switch via a port of network devices. Secondly, by applying a specific analytical model, we gain a pre-match model for the corresponding packet inside the matching field. Thirdly, according to adopt the layered protocol, the packet data are able to be classified by the tuple-space lookup. Fourthly, we can obtain the corresponding front table model by adopting the results that are obtained in the third step. Finally, we get the index ID of the flow table to fetch an instruction from the action field in the table, and perform the instruction of action.

4   Design Approach of F-OpenFlow

4.1   Implementation of Flow Tables

The matching features of packets are as follows: Layer 1 is the ingress port (Ingress-Port) in switches. Layer 2 is made up of five parts which are the source MAC address (Ethersource), destination MAC address (Etherdst), Ethernet type (EtherType), VLAN tag (VLANid), and VLAN priority (VLANpriority). Layer 3 includes the source IP (IPsrc), destination IP (IPdst), IP protocol field (IP proto), and IP service type (IP ToS bits). Layer 4 contains TCP/UDP source port number (TCP/UDP src port), and TCP/UDP destination port number (TCP/UDP dst port).

Based on the concept of TCP/IP layers, we classify the matching fields of data packets. At the same time, we can gather the counts for the fields under the classification phase. Figure 2 shows the implementation process of the flow table in the F-OpenFlow. The information of data packets is resolved, classified and counted. This categorization only considers the pre-match model of the field and ignores the specific value of the latter entry.

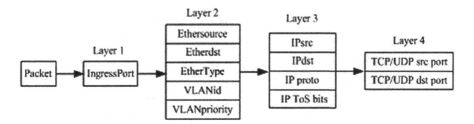

Fig. 2. Implementation process of the flow table in the F-OpenFlow

4.2   Feature Structure of Data Packets

Here are five data packets for analyzing the samples whose statistics are stored in a database table for comparison and classification, as shown in Table 1. It shows the relationship between the ID of packets and the number of matching fields in the corresponding layer.

From Table 1, we can see that Packet 1 contains one first-level matching field, two second level matching fields, third third-level matching fields, and one fourth-level

Table 1. Flow characteristic structure

Packet	Layer 1	Layer 2	Layer 3	Layer 4
Packet 1	1	2	3	1
Packet 2	0	3	2	1
Packet 3	1	1	1	1
Packet 4	1	3	2	1
Packet 5	1	2	3	1

matching field. The structure of Packet 5 is similar to that of Packet 1. Obviously, we can classify the data according to the number of hierarchical statistics. For example, the structural model of Packet 1 and Packet 5 can be classified the two as a homogeneous structure. When the pre-matching model matches the corresponding structure, the number of matches in the corresponding type of flow tables can be found quickly.

4.3   Feature Structure of Flow Table Rule

Figure 3 shows rules for classifying flow tables. For each table, we count the matching fields based on the previous entries, and ignore other parameters. Assume that there are sixty tables, using the above classification method, we can find that there are seven tables in the first layer, twenty-one tables in the second layer, nineteen tables in the third layer, and thirteen tables in the fourth layer for meeting the requirement.

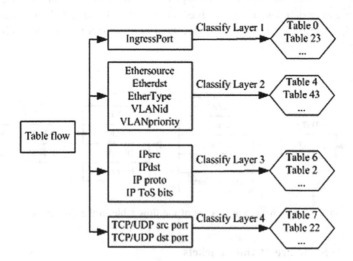

Fig. 3. F-OpenFlow rules for classifying flow tables

At the same time, we gain the index ID of each table in order to find the root, as shown in Table 2. In this way, it is helpful to locate the approximate position of all matching fields in the flow table quickly and precisely.

Table 2. Statistics on all tables

Table	Layer 1	Layer 2	Layer 3	Layer 4
Table number	7	21	19	13
Table ID	0, 1, 3, 5,...	4, 9, 11, 13,...	6, 12, 14,...	7, 22, 24,...

4.4   Classification Algorithm

We categorize data packets on the concept of TCP/IP layer and obtain layered packets, and it shortens the matching range of packets in switches. The specific methods to achieve the following: (1) getting all matching fields in the data packet; (2) omitting specific parameters after the field and only matching the first item; (3) classifying statistics and getting fuzzy results; (4) converting a corresponding numeric string into resulting statistics. We implement this method with the code shown in Algorithm 1.

Algorithm 1. Packet classification.

Input: Data packets.

Output: Layered packets.

1: **for** *Packge* in *TCP=IP* **do**

2:      **if** *Packget:String = TCP=IP:String* **then**

3:          *Packget:layer = TCP=IP:layer*

4:          *Packget:Number = Packget:Number* + 1

5:      **end if**

6: **end for**

The core idea of OpenFlow flow tables passing through F-OpenFlow transformation is: (1) obtaining the results of both sides of the classification algorithm; (2) comparing and confirming a rough rule model of flow tables; (3) finding the specific model ID in the front table, and getting its corresponding rules ID in original tables; (4) according to the ID of the original flow table, matching all the operation of Action. The code is shown in Algorithm 2.

Algorithm 2. Flow table term hierarchy.

Input: OpenFlow flow table.

Output: F-OpenFlow fuzzy hierarchical model.

   1: **for** *Flow* in *TCP=IP* **do**

   2:    **if** *Flow:T able = TCP=IP:String* **then**

   3:       *Flow:layer = TCP=IP:layer*

   4:       *Flow:Number = Packget:Number + 1*

   5:       *Flow:Tableid:add(Flow:id)*

   6:    **end if**

   7: **end for**

The matching becomes the principle of fuzzy matching after getting the packet feature code and the fuzzy classification structure of the flow table. There are two reference elements during the period: the hit rate and the tuple length. Where A represents the data package and B represents the flow.

The fuzzy matching code between the data packet and the two features of the flow table entries is given in Algorithm 3.

Algorithm 3. F-OpenFlow.

Input: Data packets and stream tables correspond to the F-OpenFlow model.

Output: Hit rate and length of tuple.

   1: **for** *A;B* in *F-OpenF low* **do**

   2:    **if** *A:layer = Flow:layer:number* **then**

   3:       **for** *A:layer:MatchinF low:layer:Match* **do**

   4:          **if** *A:layer:Mathch == Flow:layer:Match* **then**

   5:             *A:Hit:number + +*

   6:          **end if**

   7:       **end for**

   8:    **end if**

   9:    *A:Hit = A:Hit:number=A:layer:Length*

  10: **end for**

---

5   Experimental Results and Analysis

In order to ensure the efficiency and practicability of the proposed architecture, we have built a data model which is similar to the flow table in the database. By using Java language, we design the flow table architecture for optimizing OpenFlow.

By using OpenFlow 1.0, we first find and match twelve elements, and then we carry on the data consolidation according to the data warehouse theory. The basic database is constructed to be used in real-time data, and it is the basis for establishing analysis platform.

5.1   Hit Rate

We use the proposed F-OpenFlow and the original flow table structure to carry on the related data in our test experiments. We compare the two groups of data packets through two different designs.

Figure 4 shows the impact of the time (in ms) to enter the flow table from a single data flow to the Action instruction on the hit rate of the data flow to the field in the forward model of flow tables.

From Fig. 4, the overall trend of the curve is similar for different values of tuple lengths. When the hit rate is 10% and the tuple lengths are 10, the time based on F-OpenFlow and OpenFlow is 550 and 641, respectively. When the hit rate is 90% and the tuple lengths are 10, the time based on F-OpenFlow and OpenFlow is 579 and 512, respectively. Obviously, the efficiency of the proposed F-OpenFlow exceeds that of the OpenFlow. Compared with the original structure, the F-OpenFlow has more steps, so there is a higher time. When the hit rate is 20%, 30%, and 40%, respectively, the time has declined while the effect is not obvious. But the gap between the two structures is constantly narrowing. When the hit rate is equal to 50%, and there is a critical point that indicates that the original structure and the proposed F-OpenFlow are mutually balanced. When the hit rate is more than 50%, the superiority is quite obvious.

From Fig. 4, it can be seen that when the contrast value of the matching rate between the data flow and the field in the pre-model flow table is very low, the flow table structure of the proposed F-OpenFlow does not have the original structure quickly. However, with the improvement of the hit rate, it can be seen that there are obvious changes in the structural design of the proposed F-OpenFlow. When the hit rate is close to 50%, the time required for both structures is very close. When the hit rate is equal to 70%, the F-OpenFlow is significantly better than the original design.

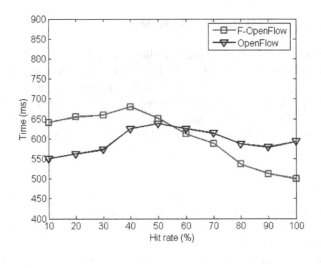

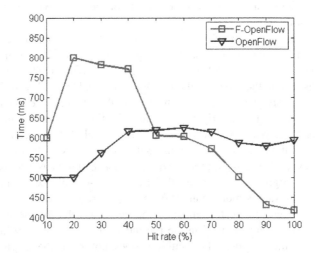

Fig. 4. Hit rate vs. Time (top: 10 tuples; bottom: 12 tuples).

5.2 Tuple Lengths

Figure 5 shows the impact of the time to enter the flow table from a single data flow to the Action instruction on the tuple length of the matching field. The single data flow gets into the flow table for getting the time to get the Action command (in ms), and the matching field is the one that is in the flow table of the proposed OpenFlow.

From Fig. 5, the overall trend of the curve is similar for average hit rate and the rate of 100%. When the tuple length is 2 and the hit rate is 100%, the time based on F-OpenFlow and OpenFlow is 398 and 400, respectively. When the hit rate is 100% and the tuple length are 10, the time based on F-OpenFlow and OpenFlow is 501 and 513, respectively. The efficiency of the proposed F-OpenFlow is better than that of the

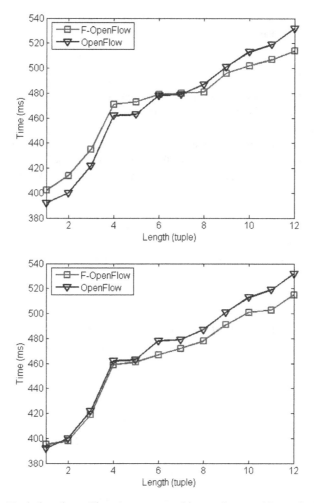

Fig. 5. Tuple length vs. Time (top: average hit rate; bottom: hit rate is 100%).

OpenFlow. It can be seen that for a tuple length, the original structure is shorter than the structure of the F-OpenFlow, because of the very short length. This phenomenon is not static. The time for the two structures increases on 2, 3, 4, 5, and 6 tuple lengths. The growth rate of the optimized structure of the F-OpenFlow is lower than that of the original structure. When the length of the tuple exceeds seven, the time of the optimizing structure of the F-OpenFlow is less than that of the original structure.

We have simulated twelve test cases of tuple length. We found that when the length is relatively short and the inner tuple capacity is small. The proposed F-OpenFlow does not match the OpenFlow fast. But with the increase of the tuple length, we can see that the F-OpenFlow matching structure design has a relatively good development trend in the experimental results. When the tuple length increases to eight, the advantages and disadvantages of F-OpenFlow and OpenFlow have obvious difference. Accordingly, it can directly verify that the structural design of the F-OpenFlow has the advantage of shortening the time of the long data flow.

5.3   Frequency

Figure 6 shows the impact of the time (in ms) that a single data flow enters the flow table until it gets the Action instruction on the number of repeated tests for the same data flow table.

From the above two tests, the overall trend of the curve is similar for the hit rate of 100% and the tuple length of 12. When the frequency is 3, the time based on F-OpenFlow and OpenFlow is 395 and 419, respectively. When the frequency is 18, the time based on

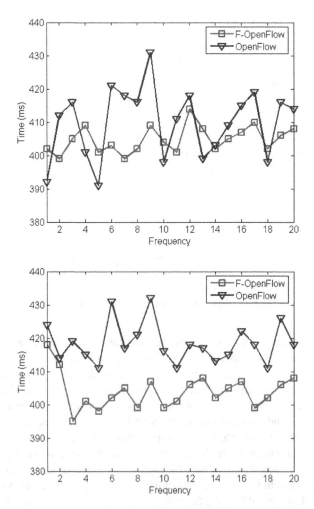

Fig. 6. Frequency vs. Time (top: hit rate is 50% and 8 tuples; bottom: hit rate is 100% and 12 tuples).

F-OpenFlow and OpenFlow is 402 and 411, respectively. The efficiency of the proposed F-OpenFlow is better than that of the OpenFlow. We have chosen the middle segment of a group of data packets, and the data packets with two dimensions of hit rate and tuple length are the 50% of the length and the eight elements. The difference between the two can be seen in terms of the data. The stability of the new proposed structure of the F-OpenFlow is better than that of the original design.

6 Conclusion

SD-IoT is an efficient solution to simplify the management of heterogeneous IoT, the performance of SD-IoT switches directly affects the speed of information exchange and the management process. The proposed F-OpenFlow structure is different from the OpenFlow. It is optimized on the basis of the original one. The purpose is to solve the problem of packet matching speed. The core idea of the F-OpenFlow is to give priority to the analysis of the content structure of flow table rules, and to establish a simple model of the front table. In the proposed F-OpenFlow structure, the packet matching can quickly locate the specific Action instruction of the flow table. In case of the packet length is longer. F-OpenFlow matching is better than OpenFlow matching. The future work will also take advantage of the previous historical data of matching. It will be more accurate to analyze the relationship between the location of the message and the flow table. In this way, we can improve the hit rate and matching speed of the flow table.

Acknowledgment. This research is supported in part by the grant from the National Natural Science Foundation of China (61572191 and 61672447), the Natural Science Foundation of Hunan Province (2018JJ4058).

Conflict of Interests. The authors declare that there is no conflict of interests regarding the publication of this paper.

References

1. Dave, T.: OpenFlow: enabling innovation in campus networks. Acm Sigcomm Comput. Commun. Rev. **38**(2), 69–74 (2008)
2. Jarraya, Y., Madi, T., Debbabi, M.: A Survey and a layered taxonomy of software-defined networking. IEEE Commun. Surv. Tutor. **16**(4), 1955–1980 (1955)
3. Lin, B.S.P., Lin, F.J., Tung, L.P.: The roles of 5G mobile broadband in the development of IoT, big data. Cloud SDN. Commun. Netw. **8**(1), 9–21 (2016)
4. Yin, D., Zhang, L., Yang, K.: A DDoS attack detection and mitigation with software-defined Internet of Things framework. IEEE Access **6**(1), 24694–24705 (2018)
5. Curtis, A.R., Mogul, J.C., Tourrilhes, J., et al.: DevoFlow: scaling flow management for high-performance networks. Acm Sigcomm Comput. Commun. Rev. **41**(4), 254–265 (2014)
6. Katta, N., Alipourfard, O., Rexford, J., et al.: CacheFlow: dependency-aware rule-caching for software-defined networks. In: Symposium on Sdn Research, pp. 1–12. ACM (2016)

7. Li, X., Xie, W.: CRAFT: a cache reduction architecture for flow tables in software-defined networks. In: IEEE Computers and Communications, pp. 967–972 (2017)
8. Casado, M., Koponen, T., Shenker, S., et al.: Fabric: a retrospective on evolving SDN. In: The Workshop on Hot Topics in Software Defined Networks, pp. 838–839. ACM (2012)
9. Iyer, A.S., Mann, V., Samineni, N.R.: SwitchReduce: reducing switch state and controller involvement in OpenFlow networks. In: IFIP NETWORKING Conference, pp. 1–9. IEEE (2013)
10. Schwabe, A., Karl, H.: Using MAC addresses as efficient routing labels in data centers. In: The Workshop on Hot Topics in Software Defined NETWORKING, pp.115–120. ACM (2014)
11. Pfaff, B., Pettit, J., Koponen, T., et al.: The design and implementation of open vSwitch. In: Proceedings of the 12th USENIX Conference on Networked Systems Design and Implementation, pp. 117–130 (2015)
12. Wang, S., Li, D., Xia, S.: The problems and solutions of network update in SDN: a survey. In: Computer Communications Workshops, pp. 474–479. IEEE (2015)
13. Sun, X., Ng, T.S.E., Wang, G.: Software-defined flow table pipeline. In: IEEE International Conference on Cloud Engineering, pp. 335–340. IEEE (2015)

A Collision-Free Path Planning Approach for Multiple Robots Under Warehouse Scenarios

Xiaoxiao Zhuang[1], Guangsheng Feng[1(✉)], Haibin Lv[1], Hongwu Lv[1],
Huiqiang Wang[1], Liqiang Zhang[1], Junyu Lin[2], and Mao Tang[3]

[1] College of Computer Science and Technology,
Harbin Engineering University, Harbin 150001, China
fengguangsheng@hrbeu.edu.cn
[2] Institute of Information Engineering,
Chinese Academy of Sciences, Beijing 100093, China
[3] Science and Technology Resource Sharing Service Center of Heilongjiang,
Harbin 150001, China

Abstract. Coordinating the motion of multi-robot is one of the fundamental problems in robotics, and how to find collision-free paths efficiently is an open issue. The high time complexity in existing methods severely hinders the applications of multi-robot in practice, especially in an overloaded warehouse scenario. To overcome this difficulty, we propose a collision-free search algorithm based on Jump point search (JPS) to improve the searching efficiency, where a reverse search path is employed to estimate the distance from the current position of one robot to the target position during traversing the root node. The experimental results show that the proposed method can achieve a higher efficiency compared with the traditional methods.

1 Introduction

Multi-robot systems have been effectively employed in various application domains, including search and rescue [1], mine exploration [2], land mine removal [3], logistics [4], and a wide variety of other intriguing tasks. For example, Kiva warehouse management system [5] is a typical multi-robot application, where multiple robots are coordinated to bypass possible obstacles and no collisions among these robots are allowable. Planning collision-free optimal paths for multiple robots (or named agents) is a multi-agent path finding (MAPF) problem, in which agent collision caused by resource competition is unavoidable, e.g., space competition [6–9].

In this work, we mainly consider time-slotted MAPF systems used in automatic warehouses, where one agent independently makes a decision whether it move to an adjacent vertex or stay still in the beginning of each time slot [10]. During the movement of multiple agents, two or more agents are prohibited to appear at the same position simultaneously. Otherwise, the vertex collision event

© Springer Nature Singapore Pte Ltd. 2019
S. Shen et al. (Eds.): CWSN 2018, CCIS 984, pp. 55–63, 2019.
https://doi.org/10.1007/978-981-13-6834-9_6

occurs. Besides, multiple agents are not allowed to move along the same edge to avoid edge collision. Unfortunately, MAPF is proven to be an NP-hard problem, and there is no efficient method to obtain optimal solutions [11].

Conventional approaches, e.g., Hierarchical Cooperative A* (HCA*), greedily arrange the traverse locations of agents according to their appearing orders, i.e., later agents may not traverse locations in collision with previous agents [6]. However, the greedy nature of this kind of approaches results in suboptimal solutions, in which some agents might never reach their destinations. Guni et al. [12] propose a cooperative path finding approach to avoid collision using multi-tree processing. However, it causes an unbearable time complexity. Felner et al. [10] propose an improved collision-based Search (CBS) algorithm using differentiated admissible heuristics, which aggregates cardinal collision among agents to improve CBS.

From the above literatures, the solution to the MAPF problem in an automatic warehouse has been transformed to an optimal method from a suboptimal one, but there are still some open issues. On the one hand, the obstacles in the real environment are usually overlooked when estimating the two-point distance. As a result, the resulting paths often deviating from the real ones. On the other hand, to achieve an efficient path-searching, it is necessary to develop an admissible heuristic approach to meet the requirements in practice. To this end, we propose an improved MAPF algorithm based on Jump point search (JPS), which improves the accuracy and reduces the time complexity by storing the estimated distance.

2   System Model

We mainly consider the multi-robot path planning problem under the scenario of warehouse management system, where multiple "urban site" shelves are used to store goods from different cities. Generally, the warehouse system contains a "manager" and multiple robots, the manager uniformly plans the paths of all robots, and each robot responsible for a urban site is required to reach the corresponding target according to the manager's instruction. Due to the huge number of goods and the high-efficiency requirement of goods transportation, it is necessary for multiple robots to transport the goods to their respective target locations efficiently. Assume that there are n robots with different start and target positions, and they cannot collide with the "urban site" and other obstacles including other agents during the movement. The scenario is illustrated in Fig. 1.

To ease the path planning design, we use grid method to model the storage scene, in which all the "urban site" shelves and other infeasible regions are considered as obstacle regions. The grid size is determined by the robot's step size. Furthermore, the entire area of the warehouse is rasterized and abstracted as a data map to assist path planning.

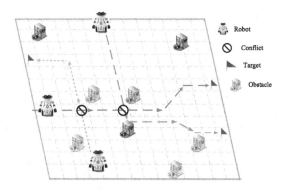

Fig. 1. Multi-robot path planning under warehouse scenario.

The location of the agent a_i is a pair $v(a_i, t)$, which is composed by agent a_i and time t. The edge of the agent from vertex v_p to vertex v_q is denoted by E, which is a set $E(a_i, v_p, v_q, t)$ that composed by agent a_i, vertex v_p, v_q, time t. The number of vertices is P, and the set of vertices is $V = 1, 2, ..., P$. Obstacles can be represented by set V_o, and then the set of vertices that the agents can pass is $V_c = V - V_o$. When agent a_i moves, it cannot collide with the "urban site" shelves and other obstacles, so we have

$$v(a_i, t) \in V_c. \tag{1}$$

Besides, the following constraints (2) and (3) can guarantee no collision events between two agents, which are given by

– **Different agents can not appear in the same place at the same time, which can be denoted by**

$$v(a_i, t) \neq v(a_j, t), \tag{2}$$

– **Two agents cannot move along the same edge of the grid at the same time, which can be denoted by**

$$E(a_i, v_p, v_q, t) \neq E(a_j, v_q, v_p, t). \tag{3}$$

The objective of the system is to minimize the overall arrival time of all agents, i.e., $\min \sum_{i=1}^{n} t_i$, where t_i denotes the system runtime of the agent a_i. Therefore, we can formulate the problem as follows:

$$\min \sum_{i=1}^{n} t_i$$

$$s.t. (1), (2) \text{ and } (3). \tag{4}$$

3   Algorithm Design

In this paper, a multi-agent cooperative heuristic algorithm based on Jump point search (JMAC) is proposed, which can obtain the shortest non-collision path set of all agents' by the multi-tree search framework. Here, the multi-tree is expanded by the JPS algorithm to solve the collision problem. First, the path set will be stored in the root node by JPS algorithm. Second, a new child node is created after detecting a collision event, and then the replaned-path set is stored into the new child. This procedure is conducted iteratively until there is no collision path. Each node of the multi-tree stores the path sequences, constraints and corresponding costs of all agents. The detailed algorithm, i.e., the improved CBS algorithm based on JPS, can be found in Algorithm 1.

Noted that the terms 'point' and 'node' used in this paper are w.r.t. the map and the multi-tree, respectively.

Algorithm 1. Improved CBS algorithm based on JPS.

1: **Input** : Agent sets, pre-processed data map
2: **Output** : collision-free path set
3: **while** Tree is not empty **do**
4:    **if** P is Root node **then**
5:       plan unconstrained paths for node P according to JPS
6:    **else**
7:       plan constrained paths for node P according to constrained JPS
8:    **end if**
9:    **if** P has no collision **then**
10:       return $P.solution$
11:    **else**
12:       **if** P has vertex collision $(a_i, a_j, v, t) \in P$ **then**
13:          $A \leftarrow$ new node
14:          $A.constraints \leftarrow P.constraints + (a_i, v, t)$
15:          $P.cost$=SITC $(P.solution)$
16:       **end if**
17:       **if** P has edge collision $(a_i, v_1, v_2, t) \in P$ **then**
18:          $A \leftarrow$ new node
19:          $A.constraints \leftarrow$ P.constraints $+ (a_i, v, t) + (a_i, v, t+1)$
20:          $P.cost$=SITC $(P.solution)$
21:       **end if**
22:    **end if**
23: **end while**

In Algorithm 1, P denotes the multi-tree node, $P.constraints$ denotes the constraint of P. The vertex constraint (a_i, a_j, v, t) represents that the agents a_i and a_j can not appear at the same position v at the same time t. The edge constraint (a_i, v_1, v_2, t) represents that the agent a_i can not move to v_2 from vertex v_1 at time t. $P.solution$ represents a collection of non-collision paths stored in P. $P.cost$ represents the total time costs of the path sets stored in P. Besides, $SITC$ $(P.solution)$ represents a function to calculate the total time costs of the path sets included in the vertex P.

In Algorithm 1, the following improvements are achieved in comparison to the original one [12]. Firstly, a heuristic method based on JPS is adopted to reduce the number of expanded points and improve the search efficiency. Secondly, in order to improve the accuracy of the planned path, we store $h(n)$ during the initial low-level search, including reverse search and forward search. The reverse search is used to record the real distance $(h(n))$ from the point n to the end point and store it as a table ($EffecTable$ table). In addition, the collisions among agents are detected by comparing next jump points and constrained points.

In Algorithm 1, each point has 8 neighbors in the pre-processed data map, including the north, west, south, east, northwest, southwest, southeast, and northeast points. Each point has a cardinal direction identifier and diagonal identifier. The cardinal direction includes the east, south, west, and north directions, and the diagonal direction include the northwest, southwest, southeast, and northeast directions. Data map processing before planing collision-free paths using JPS algorithm is particularly critical. First, to check whether one point has a forced neighbor, it is necessary to traverse all points in the map. If this point has a $ForceNeighbor$, it is set to be a $PrimePoint$, and placed into the Primary Jump point set. For example, the current point is cur, its parent node is $pare$, the neighbor points of cur have $neighbor1$ and $neighbor2$, and $neighbor2$ is an obstacle point. If the distance calculation from $pare$ to $neighbor1$ is affected by $neighbor2$, then $neighbor1$ is regarded as the forced neighbor of cur. Second, if this point eventually run into a $PrimePoint$ during traversing the cardinal points, the distance from this point to $PrimePoint$ can be calculated and then placed into the StraightPoint set. Here, $Straightpoint$ denotes some points will eventually run into a $PrimePoint$ traversing in a cardinal direction (before running into a wall). Thereafter, if the point will reach either a $PrimePoint$ or a $Straightpoint$ during traversing in a diagonal direction, the distance from the point to $PrimePoint$ or a $Straightpoint$ can be calculated and placed into the $Diagonalpoint$ set. Here, $Diagonalpoint$ is a specific point which can reach either a $PrimePoint$ or a $Straightpoint$ along a diagonal direction. Last, to calculate the distance from these remaining points to wall or obstacles, we need traverse all the points in the map again. The remaining points are not calculated to the $Straightpoint$ or $Diagonalpoint$ in the direction of the cardinal direction or the diagonal direction. More details is shown in Algorithm 2.

To solve collisions among agents, it is necessary to add constraints to multi-tree nodes. For two conflicting agents A and B, it is necessary to avoid the conflict by adding a waiting state to the agent A or agent B under certain circumstances. For example, there always exist collisions between the path of A and B. First, during the path traversal, when there exist a conflicting point between the current point and the expanded one, the current point is set to waiting state. Second, we need to add the waiting state of all agents to the Open table, which is used to store the point to be expanded, and $f(n) = f(n) + 1$,

Algorithm 2. Map generating

1: **Input** : indoor map
2: **Output** : the preprocessed data map
3: **initinal** : input map file MF
4: **for** each point $P \in$ MF **do**
5:    **if** point P has ForceNeighbor **then**
6:       set node P as PrimePoint and place point P to the PrimePointSet set
7:    **end if**
8: **end for**
9: **for** each point P in a cardinal direction **do**
10:    **if** point P eventually run into a PrimePoint traversing in a cardinal direction **then**
11:       calculate the distance from point P to PrimePoint and place point P to the StraightPoint set
12:    **end if**
13: **end for**
14: **for** each point P in a diagonal direction **do**
15:    **if** point P will reach either a PrimePoint or a StraightPoint traversing in a diagonal direction **then**
16:       calculate the distance from point P to PrimePoint or a StraightPoint and place point P to the DiagonalPoint set
17:    **end if**
18: **end for**
19: **for** each point P direction that is not calculated to a StraightPoint or Diagonal-Point **do**
20:    calculate the distance from P to the surrounding walls or obstacles
21: **end for**

---

where $f(n)$ is a evaluation function, denoting the estimated cost from the start point to the end point via point n. $f(n)$ can be calculated by $g(n)$ and $h(n)$, i.e., $f(n) = g(n) + h(n)$, where $g(n)$ denotes the actual cost from the start point to n, and $h(n)$ denotes the estimated cost of the best path from point n to the end point. The reason why $f(n)$ is increased by one is that the distance from the start point to point n increased by one, that is, the value of $g(n)$ increases by one, but the value of $h(n)$ remains unchanged.

To solve collisions among agents, it is necessary to use the JPS algorithm to plan a collision-free path under constraints. The most critical step in the process is to get the successor points of the current one. Note that, the successor are points that must be subject to the constraints, which can be determined by the time of point. If the constraints hold, the current expanded point cannot be used as a successor point, and then the next expanded point is continuously to be checked. Otherwise, the current expanded point will be added to the Open table. The specific steps are as follows:

(1) The time of the current jump point < that of the constraint point, return false;

(2) The time of the current jump point = that of the constraint point, and then we should determine whether the agent can exactly match the coordinate. If there exists one matching pair, it will return true; otherwise, it will return false.

(3) The time of the current jump point > that of the constraint point. First, we should calculate the coordinate of a new point along the direction from the current point to successor point. Thereafter, we should determine whether the coordinate and the agent of points can match, including the points of the new and constraint ones. If it matches, it will return true; otherwise, it will return false.

4 Numerical Results

In this paper, to compare the efficiency of the JPS-based and the original A*-based [12] approaches, we choose the number of expanded points and system runtime as the main metrics. The number of expanded points also reflects the efficiency of the search algorithm, that is, the fewer the number of expanded nodes, the shorter the system runtime. The numerical results are as follows.

Figures 2 and 3 illustrate the expanded points and system runtime versus different map sizes, respectively. To calculate the average number of expanded points and average runtime, we set 50 different start and end points in each map. It can be seen that the number of expanded points are proportional to the running time when there are the same map size. Besides, the number of expanded points or map size larger, the system runtime larger. And the obstacles fewer, the difference between the number of expanded points and system runtime greater. In addition, the expanded points of the JPS is 3 times lower than that of A*.

Figures 4 and 5 compare the number of expanded points and system runtime between A* algorithm and the proposed one under different number of agents. The size of map is 20*20 and there are 50 sets of different start and end points. When the number of agents are equal, and each agent has the same start and end point, the number of expanded points generated by the proposed algorithm

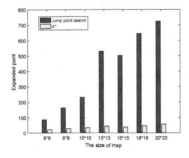

Fig. 2. The number of expanded node with different map sizes.

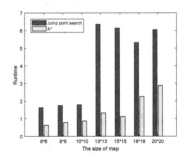

Fig. 3. The runtime with different map sizes.

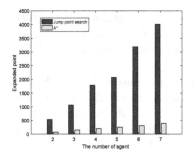

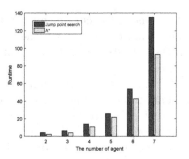

Fig. 4. The number of expanded points with different agents.

Fig. 5. The runtime with different agents.

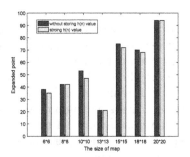

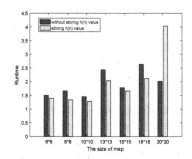

Fig. 6. The number of expanded points whether to store $h(n)$ value.

Fig. 7. The runtime whether to store $h(n)$ value.

is reduced by 8% than that of A* based CBS algorithm. And the system runtime is increased by more than 19%. Furthermore, it is observed that as the number of agents increase, the expanded points, the system runtime and the number of collisions also increase.

Figures 6 and 7 illustrate the relationship among the expanded points, the system runtime and the $h(n)$ value, respectively. It can be observed that there are larger number of expanded points and longer system runtime without storing $h(n)$ values. Specifically, the distance from the point n to the end point can be obtained by traversing the stored $EffecTable$ table when the $h(n)$ value is stored. It makes the planing path closer to the real path. Moreover, since the $EffecTable$ is directly traversed, a large amount of time for calculating the distance from point n to the end point can be reduced.

5   Conclusion

In this paper, we mainly study the problem how to efficiently find collision-free paths for multi-agent under an overloaded warehouse scenario. We aim at minimizing the running time of all agents. First, we propose an improved multi-agent collision avoidance algorithm based on JPS, which is more efficient than the traditional ones. Second, by using the method of reverse search, it also improves the efficiency and accuracy of during the processing. Moreover, the collisions are significantly reduced by comparing successor and constrained points during collision detection. Finally, we select the set of effective paths with the shortest total running time. Numerical results show that the proposed algorithm improves the efficiency of the warehouse system significantly.

Acknowledgement. This work is supported by the Natural Science Foundation of China (No. 61502118), the Natural Science Foundation of Heilongjiang Province in China (No. F2016009), the Fundamental Research Fund for the Central Universities in China (No. HEUCF180602 and HEUCFM180604) and the National Science and Technology Major Project (No. 2016ZX03001023-005).

References

1. Liu, M., Sivakumar, K., Omidshafiei, S., Amato, C., How, J.P.: Learning for multi-robot cooperation in partially observable stochastic environments with macro-actions, pp. 1853–1860 (2017)
2. Azprua, H., Freitas, G.M., Macharet, D.G., Campos, M.F.M.: Multi-robot coverage path planning using hexagonal segmentation for geophysical surveys. Robotica, 1–23 (2018)
3. Megalingam, R.K., Nagalla, D., Kiran, P.R., Geesala, R.T., Nigam, K.: Swarm based autonomous landmine detecting robots. In: 2017 International Conference on Inventive Computing and Informatics (ICICI), pp. 608–612 (2017)
4. Jeon, S., Lee, J.: Framework and modeling of a multi-robot simulator for hospital logistics. In: Kim, J.-H., Karray, F., Jo, J., Sincak, P., Myung, H. (eds.) Robot Intelligence Technology and Applications 4. AISC, vol. 447, pp. 213–219. Springer, Cham (2017). https://doi.org/10.1007/978-3-319-31293-4_17
5. Hönig, W., et al.: Multi-agent path finding with kinematic constraints. In: ICAPS, pp. 477–485 (2016)
6. Silver, D.: Cooperative pathfinding. In: AIIDE 1, pp. 117–122 (2005)
7. Yokoo, M., Kitamura, Y.: Multiagent real-time-A* with selection: introducing competition in cooperative search. In: Proceedings of the Second International Conference on Multiagent Systems (ICMAS-96), pp. 409–416 (1996)
8. Bnaya, Z., Stern, R., Felner, A., Zivan, R., Okamoto, S.: Multi-agent path finding for self interested agents. In: Sixth Annual Symposium on Combinatorial Search (2013)
9. Standley, T.S.: Finding optimal solutions to cooperative pathfinding problems. In: AAAI, vol. 1, Atlanta, GA, pp. 28–29 (2010)
10. Felner, A., et al.: Adding heuristics to conflict-based search for multi-agent path finding. In: ICAPS (2018)
11. Yu, J., LaValle, S.M.: Structure and intractability of optimal multi-robot path planning on graphs. In: AAAI (2013)
12. Sharon, G., Stern, R., Felner, A., Sturtevant, N.R.: Conflict-based search for optimal multi-agent pathfinding. Artif. Intell. **219**, 40–66 (2015)

An Improved Opportunistic Sensor Networks Connectivity Monitoring Model Based on Network Connectivity

Jian Shu[1]([✉]), Jiajun Xiong[1], Lei Xu[1], Xiaotian Geng[1], and Linlan Liu[2]

[1] School of Software, Nanchang Hangkong University, Nanchang 330063, China
liulinlan@nchu.edu.cn
[2] School of Information Engineering, Nanchang Hangkong University, Nanchang 330063, China

Abstract. The connectivity of opportunistic sensor networks (OSNs) is changing all the time with the movement of nodes. Finding a way to monitor connectivity can help researchers response to situations faster such as the node offline. This paper uses evolving graph to describe the snapshots of OSNs, redefines the connectivity parameters, and analyses the disadvantages of traditional network monitoring model. Then the paper proposes four different ways to improve the performance of the connectivity monitoring model of OSNs with the methods such as minimum node degree and sliding time window. The paper utilizes the multiple attribute decision tree to improve the connectivity monitoring model in the end. The experimental results show that the connectivity calculated by the model is in good agreement with actual message delivery rate, and can be used to monitor the connectivity of OSNs.

Keywords: Opportunistic Sensor Networks · Connectivity monitoring model · Evolving graph · Multiple attribute decision tree

1 Introduction

Opportunistic Sensor Networks (OSNs) are kinds of self-organization networks in which nodes can communicate with each other by nodes movement, they do not require stable links between source and target nodes [1]. The intelligent device with low-cost and short-distance communication capability can make wireless sensor network achieve great improvements and create new opportunities across almost every industries, e.g. communication science [2], energy consumption [3], data gathering [4] and Information attacking [5]. However, it is difficult to retain a stable topology in OSNs and hard to predict the network topology which has large communication range and

This paper is supported by the National Natural Science Foundation of China (61762065, 61363 015), the Natural Science Foundation of Jiang Province (20171ACB20018, 20171BBH80022).

S. Shen et al. (Eds.): CWSN 2018, CCIS 984, pp. 64–76, 2019.
https://doi.org/10.1007/978-981-13-6834-9_7

frequent nodes mobility. Furthermore, the whole network may have been divided into different parts called island and it means that they cannot exchange data directly as shown in Fig. 1. So the communication range of nodes is limited, and need Ferry [6] nodes to transport data between islands.

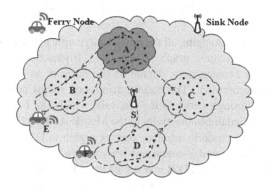

Fig. 1. The scenario of OSNs

The movement of nodes cause the connectivity opportunistic, discontinuous, and dynamic. The quality of data can be improved by the meeting opportunities of nodes and the associated strategies of message delivery. In order to study the connectivity of OSNs, we need study the movement pattern of nodes including the location and direction of nodes. As the critical parameter for network performance, OSNs' connectivity is significant different from traditional networks. So constructing connectivity monitoring model to evaluate network connectivity is necessary and important for network design and monitoring.

2 Related Work

In traditional sensor networks, sensors are statistically deployed and the topology does not change frequently. A description in [5] indicates this kind of network as a static graph, and a representation of its connectivity model as a 3-connected graphs, shows that each vertex in this graph can find an edge connecting to another vertex, with the property that the distance between them is smaller than the transmission range. In Wireless Sensor Networks (WSNs), the life span of networks is enhanced by methods depending on the energy dissipation of the sensor devices. Patil et al. [7] introduce an idea about improving network connectivity, by reducing the energy dissipation of sensor devices. To overcome energy inefficiency in selecting the cluster head, which results in loss of connectivity, they propose a PS-LEACH algorithm which selects the cluster head by calculating the node connectivity. Through this algorithm we can improve the lifetime of the network over 88.73% and improve the connectivity of network about 34.3%. In [8] a method is proposed to simulate network connectivity and hidden-terminal effects on network topology, following the hypothesis that the network connectivity can been optimized when n denotes the Network Scale, r denotes the Transmitting Range and l denotes the side length of the 2-dimensional square monitoring region, so we have the relationship that $n * r^2 = l^2 * \log_2 l$. A neighbor-assisted connectivity recovery protocol (NACRP) is introduced in [9]. NACRP automatically selects a subset of sensor nodes to act as relays for the nodes which lack connectivity. It relies a subset of relay nodes and the necessary transmitted power to restore network connectivity.

But topology has been changing all the time in a dynamic network, so it is difficult to model such network as a static graph. Zhao et al. [10] take a snapshot of network topology, and use the average node degree of the network to improve the network connectivity in mobile network. The node transmission radius and the network connectivity is obtained through curve fitting analysis, which can be used to deploy the nodes. Sheng et al. studied the connectivity of the Mobile Ad Hoc Networks (MANETs) under the RWP mobility mode in arbitrary convex region in [11]. The MANETs have certain transmitting ranges and k-connected networks, which can achieve high fault-tolerance in MANETs. Guo et al. [12] investigate three fundamental characteristics (the node degree distribution, the average node degree and the maximum node degree) of MANETs in the presence of radio channel fading. The results are very useful in the study of connectivity and algorithm complexity of incentive protocols. The premise of the connectivity research in MANETs is to ensure a complete end-to-end path which makes the connectivity and the node degree of the network are unsuitable in OSNs.

For OSNs, Yu Wang et al. [13] introduce a connectivity analytical model for vehicular ad hoc networks. The model considers different cases according to the location distribution of the entrance/exit. In order to calculate the connectivity probability, it considers the vehicle arrival rates, vehicle speeds, and the probability of the vehicle node travels through the entrance/exit. Also, the work in [14] predicts the connectivity of a vehicle-to-vehicle network base on the assumption that n vehicles randomly arrive according to a Poisson Process. Vehicular ad hoc networks have the characteristics of general self-organizing network distributed, centerless, multi-hop networking, dynamic topology and so on. OSNs can be applied to scenarios such as intermittent connectivity, large delays, and high error rates. This paper uses suitable connectivity monitoring model to analysis network connectivity in OSNs.

3   Connectivity Modeling

3.1   Connectivity Parameters Definition

In this chapter we introduce some parameters to describe network connectivity, some of which have been given in our previous work [15]. To research the connectivity of OSNs in dynamic way, we use a time slice to record the status of the network topology. Taking the network in Fig. 1 as an example, we use four ordered time slices, namely $T1, T2, T3, T4$, and take snapshots for each of these time slices. Then the results of snapshots are shown in Fig. 2.

In Fig. 2 A, B, C and D are the areas which send messages, and we call them area nodes. E, F are the ferry nodes which transport messages. S is the sink node which processes the messages and get snapshots.

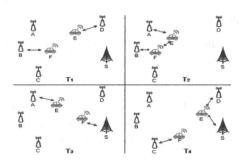

Fig. 2. The evolution of OSN over time

Definition 1: Evolving Graph θ

Given a graph $G = (V,E)$, where V is a node, E is a side. Given an ordered sequence of its subgraph $S_G = G_1, G_2, \ldots, G_T$ where $U_{i=1}^T G_i = G$. Given $S_T = t_0, t_1, t_2, \ldots, t_T$ is the series of an ordered sequence of time instance and G_i is a subgraph of (t_{i-1}, t_i). Finally we define $\theta = (G, S_G, S_T)$ as an evolving graph.

Definition 2: Connected Journey CJ

Given a set of unrepeated vertices $V_T = V_1, V_2, V_3, \ldots V_T$, let $V_{t=1,2,3,4,\ldots,T} = \theta$. Then θ represent evolution graph. Thus a set of corresponding time slices $S_T = t_1, t_2, t_3, \cdots, t_{T-1}$ where $t_1 < t_2 < t_3 < \cdots < t_{T-1}$ determines a decreasing sequence. Then we can define $CJ_{(v_1,v_k)} = (V_T, S_T)$ as a connected journey from V_1 to V_T.

Definition 3: Node Degree d

If the number of connected journeys between node V_i and the Sink node V_s is d, so d is the node degree of V_i.

Correspondingly, the definition of average node degree, minimum node degree and k-connectivity can be proposed. The average node degree of this OSNs is $\bar{d} = \frac{1}{N-1} \sum_{i=1}^{N-1} d_{V_i}$, where N is the number of nodes and d_{v_i} is the node degree of V_i. The minimum node degree of this OSNs is $d_{\min} = \min(d_1, d_2, \ldots, d_{N-1})$, the OSNs is k-connected if the minimum node degree of this network is $d_{\min} = k$.

Definition 4: Connectivity Degree P_Θ^1

The connectivity degree of θ can be defined as

$$P_\Theta^1 = \frac{1}{N-1} \sum_{i=1}^{N-1} \frac{\min(d_{V_i}, L_{V_i})}{T_n}, T_n = 1, 2, \ldots, n \tag{1}$$

where N is the number of nodes in the network, d_{V_i} is the node degree of V_i, L_{V_i} is the time series length accumulation of V_i, $\min(d_{V_i}, L_{V_i})$ represents the number of messages received by Sink nodes in N time slices, and the messages are produced by V_i.

3.2   Experimental Setup

In this section, we will introduce the detail of the experimental scene, and the experimental result obtained by applying formula (1). First, we will introduce the scene and some detail about parameters in this experiment. Then we will verify the network connectivity model based on its average degree.

The experimental scene is shown in Fig. 3. Figure 3(a) is the distribution of nodes in this experiment, which is based on satellite images of a school. The green area is the communication range of the Sink node and the red areas are the communication range of sensor nodes.

There are two tourist buses in the school to take students from one place to another place. As shown in Fig. 3(c) above, we deploy the ferry nodes on the tourist buses and seven sensor nodes in the school, as Fig. 3(a) shows. It indicates that the distribution of node is so widespread and the node cannot exchange data directly. It means that a node can only exchange data with another node by Ferry nodes. The Fig. 3(b) shows one of the possible movement paths of the Ferry nodes. There are three kinds of sensor nodes in this experiment: (i) Sink node, (ii) Sensor node and (iii) Ferry node. We put GPRS mode within the Ferry node in order to help us track its path, set the experimental period from 9:00 am to 7:00 pm. The parameters detail for this experiment is shown in Table 1.

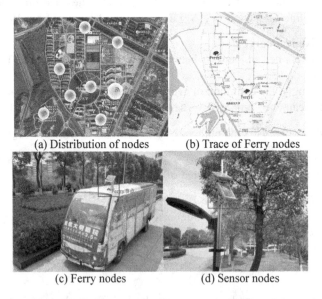

(a) Distribution of nodes   (b) Trace of Ferry nodes

(c) Ferry nodes   (d) Sensor nodes

Fig. 3. Schematic diagram of the experiment

Table 1. Parameters detail for the experiment

Parameters	Values
The number of areas	7
The number of Ferry nodes	2
The number of sink nodes	1
Area node sampling cycle	30 s
Modeling cycle	5 min
The length of sliding window	30 s
Sampling time	10 h
Message's time to life (TTL)	100 s

3.3 The Verification of Network Connectivity Degree

In order to verify network connectivity, we do the experiment and get the time related curves of network connectivity and success delivery rate as shown in Figs. 4 and 5.

Figure 4 indicates the trend of connectivity and the rate of successful package delivery within 10 h. It can be seen that connectivity gets peaks at about 10:15 and gradual declines after that. Then the next four peaks, coming in the following hours are between 11:30–12:00, 13:35–14:00, 15:30–15:50 and 17:00–18:00. From these results, these peaks appear when the students either attend or out of class. This coincides with known facts, because the activity of Ferry nodes becomes more frequent, and the communication range becomes larger, during these time periods.

On the other hand, it can be seen that success rate of package delivery keeps growing, and reaches 100% at the time of 10:15. This is because students are off the class and the Ferry nodes become active, and this rate gradual declines after 11:15. As classes begin, and Ferry nodes become inactivity. One thing need to mention is that the success rate should grow during 15:00–15:40 period, because it is the time going off-class, and the Ferry nodes should start to become more active at that point. The reason is that we manually removed an antenna in an area, preventing data exchange with the Ferry node.

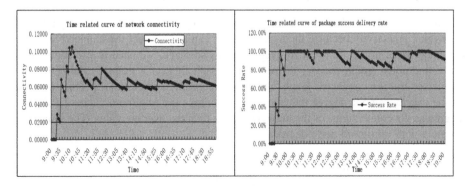

Fig. 4. Time related curves of network connectivity and success delivery rate from 9:00 to 19:00

Figure 5 indicates that there are two disadvantages within formula (1). The first is the connectivity of the network increased rather than decreased after we remove the antenna in one area. However, the success rate of package delivery is declining as excepted. Second, the tourist bus stops running during the 12:40–13:20 period, it means that the Ferry nodes neither communicate with nodes of other areas nor exchange data with them. So, the network connectivity should be zero instead of some value around 0.06. Therefore, the connectivity calculated by formula (1) cannot reflect the network connectivity in zero.

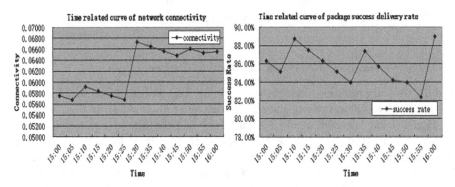

Fig. 5. Time related curves of network connectivity and success delivery rate from 15:00 to 16:00

4   Analysis and Improvement

In formula (1), the network connectivity is calculated by average node degree. Therefore, the other regions' connectivity is increasing while the connectivity of a sensor region is reduced to zero, the connectivity of the whole network may remain the same, or reduce. So that's the reason why the trend of connectivity is not as described in Fig. 5. To improve the formula (1), several further methods are proposed in this chapter.

4.1   The Connectivity Degree Based on Minimum Node Degree

As mentioned above, the average node degree failed to indicate the changing trend of network connectivity because the average value can only reflect the connectivity over the majority of nodes. In order to overcome this shortage, we need to use some ideas from traditional graph theory. In traditional graph theory, a graph is defined as k-connected if it is a connected graph, and if the minimum degree is k [12]. The relevance of the minimum node degree indicates that it can take the minimum value of the node degree as the connectivity of the network, rather than the average value. The improved formula with minimum node degree is:

$$P_\Theta^2 = \min\left(\frac{\min(d_{V_i}, L_{V_i})}{T_n}\right), T_n = 1, 2, \ldots, n \qquad (2)$$

where d_{V_i} is the node degree of node V_i, L_{V_i} is the summation of all time series corresponding to V_i and T_n is the number of snapshots from start to end.

This chapter recalculate the network connectivity using formula (2) and the result is shown in Fig. 6. It indicates that connectivity is increasing during the periods 10:00–10:15, 11:30–12:00, 13:20–13:45 and 17:00–17:20, while showing a decreasing trend at other times. Furthermore, the connectivity starts to decrease after 15:00, since one area cannot communicate with others due to remove an antenna.

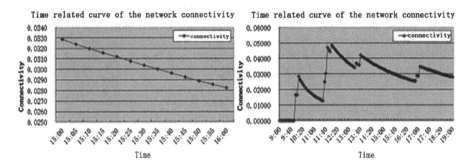

Fig. 6. The network connectivity measured by the minimum node degree

In this way, when the connectivity of a region falls or even paralysis, the network connectivity is bound to decline, which solves the problem that the network connectivity proposed by the formula (1) cannot reflect the decline of network connectivity caused by the paralysis of a few regions. So there are two problems: First, it cannot reflect the paralysis of network when the connectivity of the network is zero. Second, in this method the connectivity is only related to the area where the node degree is minimum in the current network according to formula (2). So we describe the network connectivity by this method is one-sided and cannot reflect the overall network connectivity. In order to solve the above problems, we will continue to improve the method.

4.2   The Sliding Window and the Minimum Node Degree

Besides the minimum node degree, L_{V_i} represents the summation of all time series corresponding to V_i which means that $\min(d_{V_i}, L_{V_i})$ is always greater than zero when V_i establishes a successful link to another node. Thus the network connectivity will become a decreasing hyperbolic rather than zero, even when all the nodes in the network are paralysis by this method. To solve this problem, this paper uses sliding window to pick off a part of the network snapshots. Therefore, we will confine T_n to be a stable number, so it can get rid of the influences coming from outdated snapshots. In conclusion, the computing formula will have been updated to:

$$P_\Theta^3 = \min\left(\frac{\min(d_{V_i}, L_{V_i})}{T_\Delta}\right), T_\Delta = n - \Delta + 1, n - \Delta + 2, \ldots, n \qquad (3)$$

where $T_\Delta = n - \Delta + 1, n - \Delta + 2, \ldots, n$, Δ is the width of the sliding window, and T_Δ is the number of snapshots within it. So the network connectivity have been confined to a time period of the sliding window, and it will reflect the status of network connectivity within this period of the sliding window.

From Fig. 7, it indicates formula (3) can not only show the status of network connectivity appropriately, when the node is working normally well, but also shows no network connectivity during the period 12:40–13:20. In that time the antenna has been removed. However during the 15:00–16:00 period, when we removed the antenna of one area and the rest of networks can work well, but the network connectivity is zero. This is because the network connectivity is calculated by the minimum node degree and the sliding window in formula (3). It means that if there is just one node which cannot establish connection with any other nodes and the whole network will be paralysed which is contrary to actual situation.

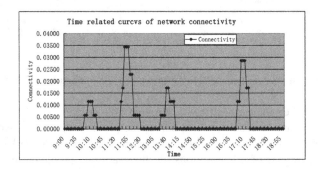

Fig. 7. The connectivity based on sliding window and minimum node degree

4.3   Further Improvement of the Sliding Window

To solve that problem, this paper uses the average node degree instead of minimum node degree to make the model more robust. So the network connectivity will decrease when there are some nodes paralysis, but it will not become zero. Here is the resulting formula, where N denotes the number of nodes in the network:

$$P_\Theta^4 = \frac{1}{N-1} \sum_{i=1}^{N-1} \frac{\min(d_{V_i}, L_{V_i})}{T_\Delta}, T_\Delta = n - \Delta + 1, n - \Delta + 2, \ldots, n \qquad (4)$$

In Fig. 8, during 5:00–16:00, the successful delivery rate of the network message is lower than the other four peak periods, because during that time we removed an antenna of one area which results in the successful delivery rate decreased. While in Fig. 9 there is a higher peak and the connectivity is obviously better than other time during 15:00–16:00, which is not in line with the actual.

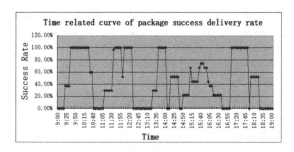

Fig. 8. Success delivery rate based on using average node degree and sliding window

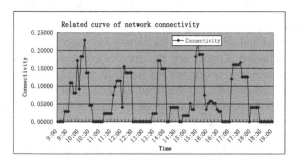

Fig. 9. Experimental data based on using average node degree and sliding window

4.4 The Connectivity Model Based on Multiple Attribute Decision Tree

Given the formulas above, it can be inferred that the connectivity of OSNs is complex and changeable. It is hard to describe every characteristic with a simple formula. Therefore, to achieve a comprehensive model for calculating connectivity, the paper proposes a method based on a multiple attribute decision tree and consider each characteristic of network connectivity as an attribute of the tree. First of all, the status of OSNs can been divided into three major situations below: "completely disconnected network", "partially connected network", or "fully connected network".

1. Completely disconnected network: No network connectivity means that the whole network is paralyzed completely. We could verify it by using formula (4) to see if the final result of connectivity is 0. Having zero connectivity means no network connectivity;
2. Partially connected network: Part of nodes being connected means some areas of the network are workable, and we could use formula (3) to prove that. If the result of applying formula (3) is greater than zero, then the network is fully functional without any broken nodes, otherwise there would be some areas unable to exchange data with each other. In order to research this kind of situation more specifically, we could use formula (5) to evaluate if the final result is greater than or equal zero:

$$d_{P_\Theta^i} = d\left(\frac{1}{N-1}\sum_{i=1}^{N-1}\frac{\min(d_{V_i}, L_{V_i})}{T_\Delta}\right), T_\Delta = n - \Delta + 1, n - \Delta + 2, \ldots, n \qquad (5)$$

The formula (5) is different from the formula (4) because it represents the trend of connectivity of the network. If the result of formula (5) is above zero. It can be inferred that the trend of connectivity is positive and increasing; the connectivity is stable when the result is zero; otherwise this paper considers that the connectivity is substandard if the result is below zero.

3. Fully connected network: Having fully connected network means that all nodes in the network are activated, and every pair of distinct vertices are connected by a unique node. As the situations above, the paper still use formula (5) to classify the network status as 'good', 'common' or 'substandard'.

To summarize, the status of connectivity can been classified from zero to six:

- S0: Completely disconnected network—0;
- S1: Partially connected network and the trend of connectivity is 'substandard'—1;
- S2: Partially connected network and the trend of connectivity is 'common'—2;
- S3: Partially connected network and the trend of connectivity is 'good'—3;
- S4: Fully connected network but the trend of connectivity is 'substandard'—4;
- S5: Fully connected network but the trend of connectivity is 'common'—5;
- S6: Fully connected network but the trend of connectivity is 'good'—6;

According the P_Θ^3 calculated by formula (3), P_Θ^4 calculated by formula (4) and $d_{P_\Theta^4}$ calculated by formula (5), the multiple attribute decision tree as shown in Fig. 10 and the experimental data based on a multiple attribute decision tree as shown in Fig. 11:

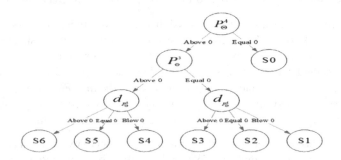

Fig. 10. Multiple attribute decision tree

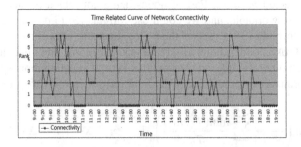

Fig. 11. Experimental data based on a multiple attribute decision tree

In order to prove the accuracy of the multiple attribute decision tree model, this paper extends the experiment to 10 days and collects data for 100 h based on the multiple attribute decision tree. The experimental results in Fig. 12.

From Fig. 12, we can find that the connectivity of network on second day is fewer than other days. It is because of the node with insufficient voltage in an area. And we can find that the number of peak on seventh day is fewer than other days. It is because there are only one tourist bus on work, but there are two buses on work in other days. So Fig. 12 is in line with the actual. It means the multiple attribute decision tree can reflect the connectivity of network more realistically and comprehensively than other methods.

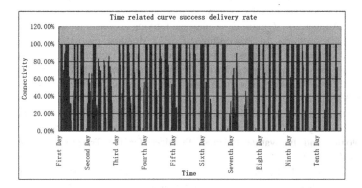

Fig. 12. Experimental data based on multiple attribute decision tree.

5 Conclusion

The connectivity of OSNs is time correlative and evolutionary. This paper points out the disadvantages of traditional connectivity models and proves it by experiments. Then, it proposes four different ways to improve the connectivity model at the same time compare their advantages and disadvantages. Finally the paper uses the model of a multiple attribute decision tree to improve the connectivity model and achieve a satisfactory result with this method. The experiment proves that the multiple attribute decision tree model can reflect some of the different status levels of connectivity, and minimize the error during the monitoring process. In the future, this paper will examine the accuracy of the multiple attribute decision tree model and further refine the classification in terms of the same priority levels.

References

1. Bulusu, N., Estrin, D., Girod, L., et al.: Scalable coordination for wireless sensor networks: self-configuring localization systems. In: Proceedings of International Symposium on Communication Theory & Applications, Ambleside Lake District, vol. 88, pp. 78–90 (2001)
2. Cheng, S., Yuan, F.: Coverage control for mobile sensor networks with limited communication ranges on a circle. Automatica **92**, 155–161 (2018)
3. Sangeetha, M., Sabari, A.: Prolonging network lifetime and optimizing energy consumption using swarm optimization in mobile wireless sensor networks. Sens. Rev. **6**(9), 238 (2016)
4. Song, X., Li, Y.: Data gathering in wireless sensor networks via regular low density parity check matrix. IEEE/CAA J. Autom. Sin., 1–9 (2017)
5. Finogeev, A.G., Finogeev, A.A.: Information attacks and security in wireless sensor networks of industrial SCADA systems. J. Ind. Inf. Integr. **5**, 6–16 (2017)
6. Zhao, W., Ammar, M., Zegura, E.: A message ferrying approach for data delivery in sparse mobile ad hoc networks. In: Proceedings of ACM Mobihoc, pp. 187–198 (2004)
7. Patil, M., Sharma, C.: Energy efficient cluster head selection to enhance network connectivity for wireless sensor network. In: Proceedings of IEEE International Conference on Recent Trends in Electronics, Information & Communication Technology, pp. 175–179. IEEE (2017)
8. Ke, L., Hu, X., Li, W., et al.: Joint analysis of connectivity and hidden-terminal effects for network topology in WSNs. In: Proceedings of IEEE International Conference on Emerging Technologies and Innovative Business Practices for the Transformation of Societies, pp. 153–157. IEEE (2016)
9. Goratti, L., Baykas, T., Rasheed, T., et al.: NACRP: a connectivity protocol for star topology wireless sensor networks. IEEE Wirel. Commun. Lett. **5**(2), 120–123 (2016)
10. Zhao, J.L., Shang, R.Q., Sun, Q.X., et al.: Study of the relationship between mobility model of ad hoc network and its connectivity. J. Comput. **9**(4), 49–56 (2006)
11. Min, S., Yan, S., Ye, T., et al.: On the k-connectivity in mobile ad hoc networks. Acta Electron. Sin. **36**(10), 1857–1861 (2008)
12. Guo, L., Xu, H., Harfoush, K.: The node degree for wireless ad hoc networks in shadow fading environments. In: Proceedings of Industrial Electronics and Applications, pp. 815–820. IEEE (2011)
13. Wang, Y., Zheng, J.: A connectivity analytical model for a highway with an entrance/exit in vehicular ad hoc networks. In: Proceedings of IEEE International Conference on Communications, pp. 1–6. IEEE (2016)
14. Kwon, S., Kim, Y., Shroff, N.B.: Analysis of connectivity and capacity in one-dimensional vehicle-to-vehicle networks. IEEE Trans. Wirel. Commun. **15**(12), 8182–8194 (2016)
15. Shu, J., Jiang, S., Liu, Q., et al.: A connectivity monitoring model of opportunistic sensor network based on evolving graph. Comput. Sci. Inf. Syst. **12**(2), 895–909 (2015)

Positioning and Location

Near Ground UWB Channel Modeling for Relative Localization

Shihong Duan$^{(\boxtimes)}$, Jiacan Si, and Jie He

University of Science and Technology Beijing, Beijing 100083, China
duansh@ustb.edu.cn

Abstract. Ultra-Wideband (UWB) technology has great potential to solve the cooperation and relative localization among near ground mobile robots in GPS-denied environments. Our goal is to build a computationally efficient near-ground field UWB channel model for facilitating realistic mobile robots network simulation and designing accurate relative positioning algorithm. In this paper, with considering the UWB multipath condition in very near-ground environment, field measurement with antenna height of 0 cm–20 cm, and signal frequency from 3 GHz to 8 GHz are conducted. The antenna height-dependent near-ground path loss channel model is put forward based on statistical computation and enhancement by introducing because the key near ground features such as diffraction loss due to obstruction of the first Fresnel zone. The proposed models comply with the logarithmic normal shadow path attenuation model, and there exists a logarithmic function relationship between the path loss parameter and the antenna height. The model is validated against several experimental datasets obtained in open and grassed areas. Correction of relative range between robots based on channel model is also confirmed to be effective.

Keywords: Near ground channel modeling · Path loss · Mobile robot swarm · Relative localization

1 Introduction

Mobile near-ground robots with local sensing and communication capabilities have recently drawn the attention of the robotics community, especially situated in a possibly unknown environment performing a collective action [1] . In robots swarming, knowledge of one's own location and/or that of neighboring teammates is required. For most robot swarm application task shown in Fig. 1, only relative distance and bearing information is needed; although this information could also be obtained with an absolute positioning system (GPS-like system or overhead camera system) and an effective communication channel, the communication overhead resulting from this solution might be much higher and less scalable than a solution based on a relative localization system [2]. Also, robots will work in an unknown environment with no GPS reception. In order to extract the distance and bearing information in all kinds of situation, Ultra-wideband (UWB) signal is employed for ranging and finding direction. UWB technology is characterized by the transmission of extremely short duration pulses, has become a candidate technology for diverse ranging and positioning

© Springer Nature Singapore Pte Ltd. 2019
S. Shen et al. (Eds.): CWSN 2018, CCIS 984, pp. 79–88, 2019.
https://doi.org/10.1007/978-981-13-6834-9_8

applications [3], which stands out in accurate ranging and fine angle resolution capability due to its ability to alleviate multi-path effects [4]. Knowing the channel characteristics of UWB is the premise and basis of correcting the ranging error and designing the rotational direction-finding algorithm.

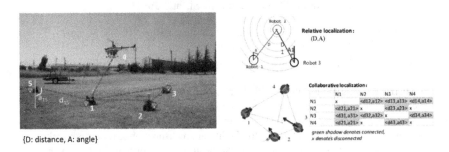

{D: distance, A: angle}

Fig. 1. Near-ground UWB communication and localization application

Mobile robots in military, agriculture monitoring, and landslides monitoring of-ten operate at the ground level with antenna height less than 20 cm; for example, the Self-Healing Minefield system has an antenna phase-center height of 7 cm above the ground [5]. However, near-ground channel models are scarce [6]. Some researches just concluded that lowering the antennas shrinks the range of entire system [7], and the ground reflection in near-ground environment is the main factor affecting the signal transmission [8]. But no quantified channel model is proposed or only tailored empirical statistical models for low-altitude communication is offered in that references. This paper created measurement dataset with very low antenna height and deduced accurate channel model for simulation scalability in mobile robot networks.

There are a few researches focused on revealing the theory of near-ground UWB signal attenuation. [9] described the near-ground radio waves by using the formula: Ground Wave = Direct Wave + Reflected Wave + Surface Wave. Surface waves mainly associated with the diffraction of electromagnetic waves [10], which is considered in the long-distance communications. Because of near-ground multi-path effect, the ground reflected wave is the main influence on the receiving end signal. So, we can conclude that in near ground short distance communication with very low antenna height, the said different waves will affect the channel significantly in different geometric relationship of distance and height pairs. Traditional two-ray path loss model [11] is impossible to take into account the statistical characteristics of ground roughness [12]. [13] explained excess path loss in terms of Fresnel zones and calculated the critical value for the antenna, but not verified in very near-ground mobile robots application scenario.

In our study, we built up Network-Analyzer based platform to take measurement of channel characteristics of very low antenna on grass ground and established statistical path loss model. The main works include:

(1) We established a near-ground path-loss channel model by using the method of statistical parameter estimation based on typical Log distance path loss model. The model provided the liner relationship of path loss parameters with antenna height.

(2) We established a more accurate segmented near-ground path-loss channel model. The model accuracy is compared and explained.

This paper is organized as follows. The measurement and multipath condition of near-ground UWB channel characteristics are introduced in Sect. 2. In Sect. 3, the near-ground path loss model are developed. The proposed models are verified in Sect. 4. Section 5 concludes the paper.

2   Multipath Conditions Analysis of Near-Ground UWB Channel

In near-ground scenarios, transmitted wave could be classified into three components, namely directed wave, ground reflected wave and surface wave as shown in Fig. 2. For a dipole antenna located at h above the ground, the generated magnitude of the electric field could be demonstrated as Eq. 1.

$$E_{total} = \frac{E_0}{d}\left[\underbrace{\cos^3(\phi_0)e^{-\gamma_0 R_0}}_{Direct\ Wave} + \underbrace{\Gamma_{f,\text{л}}\cos^3(\phi_1)e^{i2\pi R_1/\lambda}}_{Ground-reflected\ Wave} + \underbrace{(1-\Gamma_{f,\text{л}})F(P,B)\cos^2(\phi_1)e^{i[2\pi(\frac{R_1}{\lambda})+\varphi]}}_{Surface\ wave}\right] \quad i \equiv \sqrt{-1} \quad (1)$$

The quantities d, R0, R1, Φ_0, Φ_1 are defined in following Fig. 2, which show the different transmission paths. E0 means free-space field intensity at a unit distance, λ is the wavelength. Γ is the plane-wave reflection coefficient of the ground and related with antenna height h and frequency f. P and B are the values of "numerical distance" p and the angle b corresponding to elevated transmitting and receiving antennas. The function F(P, B) eiφ is the surface-wave attenuation function.

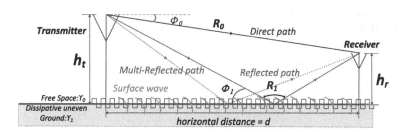

Fig. 2. Multi-reflected paths between near-ground transmitter and receiver.

According to Fresnel zone theory and transmit wave composition theory, the near-ground path loss E_{total} is defined as the sum of free-space path loss (E_f) and near-ground diffraction loss (E_{NG}) that accounts for the region of the first Fresnel zone obstructed by the ground. In said Fresnel Zone based Near Ground channel model (FZNG), E_{total} is described to be

$$E_{\text{total}} = \begin{cases} E_f, & d_1 + d_2 < d_b \\ E_f + E_{NG}, & d_1 + d_2 \geq d_b \end{cases}$$

$$E_{NG} = -20 \log_{10}\left(\frac{5h}{3\sqrt{(d_1 + d_2)\lambda}} + \frac{35h^2}{6\sqrt{(d_1 + d_2)\lambda}}\right) \qquad (2)$$

$$E_f = 32.44 + 20 \log_{10}(f \times 10^{-6}) + 20 \log_{10}(d \times 10^{-3})$$

$$d = d_1 + d_2$$

3 Near-Ground Channel Measurement and Statistical Model

In this section, near-ground UWB channel measurements are performed in open and synthetic turf rooftop field, using vector network analyzer (VNA, Agilent E8363). Next, the empirical UWB channel model is investigated.

3.1 Measurement Setup and Scenario

The measurement system employed in this paper consists of a VNA, a pair of low loss cable, a 30 dB power amplifier and a pair of small size UWB patch antenna (Skycross SMT-3TO10M). The power amplifier is employed to guarantee the peak detection at the Rx side due to the huge pathloss of the near ground channel. The Tx and Rx antenna tied to liftable wooden poles with same height.

The S parameter S21, which is also known as the channel transfer function has been measured by the VNA in frequency domain. A symmetric hamming window has been applied to the frequency domain at the cost of time resolution in order to limit the sidelobe and enable detection of more multipath components. The frequency domain profile is transferred to time domain by a base band complex inverse fast Fourier transform (IFFT). Typical recorded time domain channel profile has been shown in Fig. 3 in which proper threshold has been established to detect the first path, thus determine the first path pathloss.

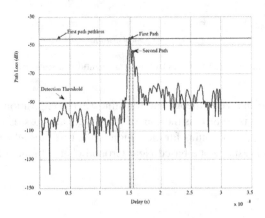

Fig. 3. Sample time domain channel profile with detection threshold.

From the perspective of scenario-based approach, a measurement case set denoted by:

$$Case = \{h, d\}$$

is composed of a subset h which is the antenna height of Tx and Rx, and subset d which is the distance between Tx and Rx. Settings of h and d are shown in Table 1. In order to guarantee accuracy and validity of measurement and channel modelling, over 500 snapshots are obtained in each case.

Table 1. Settings of near-ground channel measurement.

h (cm)	d (m)
{2, 4, 8, 15, 20}	{0.25, 0.5, 0.75, 1, 2, 3, 4, 5, 6, 8}

Total path loss with different d is the integration of path loss on the whole frequency band, instead of recording the time domain channel profile. We abstained the total path loss according to the following equation:

$$P_{total}(d) = -20 \log_{10}(\frac{1}{N}\frac{1}{N}\sum_{i=1}^{N_s}\sum_{n=1}^{N_f}|H_i^p(n)|) \tag{3}$$

where $P_{total}(d)$ denotes the total path loss at distance d; Ns is number of snapshots in each case (hi, dj) which is 500 in this paper in each case, N_f is number of frequency sample points in each snapshot which is 1601 here, and $H_i^p(n)$ is the S21 reading at each sample in i_{th} point from the VNA.

3.2   Empirical Statistical Channel Model

In this section, we first discuss the propagation characteristic of the near ground UWB channel based on slow fading model, which is the superposition of path loss and random shadow variation. Typical Log distance path loss model is a generic model, which is used to predict the propagation loss for a wide range of environment. The path loss is the average of the signal attenuation related to the distance d between the Tx and Rx, with path loss exponent related to different environment. Shadowing effect on channel is described by a zero-mean Gaussian distributed random variable (in dB) with standard deviation (σ), which can produce signal fluctuation. Therefore, first path loss model and total path loss model can be unified by the following Eq. (4)

$$PL(d) = PL(d_0) - 10n \log_{10}\frac{d}{d_0} + X_\sigma \tag{4}$$

where PL(d) is path loss in dB at an arbitrary distance d. PL(d0) is path loss in dB at a distance d0. N is path loss exponent for modelling the slope. X_σ is random shadow variation with standard deviation σ. N and X_σ are all related to various environment factors. Least squares method is employed to estimate N and X_σ, that is minimizing the sum of the squared deviations of the measured path loss from the estimated path loss given by fitting formula. Figure 4 show the fitting results of the first path loss and total path loss with different antenna height.

From Fig. 4, we can see antenna height is major factor to affect path loss in the near-ground application scenario. The lower of the antenna, the greater of the slope of the fitting curve, and the bigger of the N. The optimal fitting value of N_{first} and N_{total} with different antenna height is shown in Table 2. We use least squares fitting method to get the relationship between path loss exponent and antenna height, which is described by Eqs. 5 and 6.

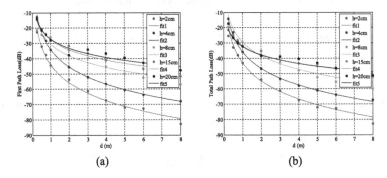

(a)   (b)

Fig. 4. Statistical summary of signal path loss at different antenna heights. (a) The first path loss (b) the total path loss

Table 2. Path loss exponent with different antenna height.

h (cm)	2	4	8	15	20
N_{first}	3.879	3.768	2.933	2.171	1.941
N_{total}	3.932	3.616	2.969	1.906	1.848

$$N_{first} = -2.107 * \log_{10}(h) + 0.5397 \tag{5}$$

$$N_{total} = -2.277 * \log_{10}(h) + 0.2507 \tag{6}$$

From analyzing our sampling data, we found Random shadow variation does obey Gaussian distribution with different standard deviation σ because of different antenna height, as shown in Fig. 5 and Table 3. σ_{first} and σ_{total} respectively describe random shadow variation of first path loss or total path loss. We use least squares fitting method to get the relationship between σ and antenna height.

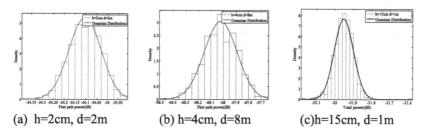

(a) h=2cm, d=2m   (b) h=4cm, d=8m   (c)h=15cm, d=1m

Fig. 5. Gaussian distribution of random shadow variation with standard deviation σ.

Table 3. Standard deviation of random shadow variation with different antenna height.

h (cm)	2	4	8	15	20
σ_{first}	0.1679	0.0925	0.0551	0.0489	0.035
σ_{total}	0.0796	0.0699	0.0669	0.0606	0.0515

According to the above statistical analysis, the first path loss model can be defined as

$$PL_{first}(d) = PL_{first}(d_0) - 10N_{first}\log_{10}\frac{d}{d_0} + \chi_{\sigma_{first}}$$
$$N_{first} = -2.107 * \log_{10}(h) + 0.5397 \tag{7}$$
$$\chi_{\sigma_{first}} = G(0, \sigma_{first})$$
$$\sigma_{first} = -0.1231 * \log_{10}(h) - 0.0609$$

total path loss model can be defined as,

$$PL_{total}(d) = PL_{total}(d_0) - 10N_{total}\log_{10}\frac{d}{d_0} + \chi_{\sigma_{total}}$$
$$N_{total} = -2.277 * \log_{10}(h) + 0.2507 \tag{8}$$
$$\chi_{\sigma_{total}} = G(0, \sigma_{total})$$
$$\sigma_{total} = -0.0247 * \log_{10}(h) + 0.0375$$

3.3   Fresnel Zone Based Near Ground Channel Model

We compared sampling path loss data with generated data from FZNG model defined in Eq. 2, there exists an deviation PLc, as shown in Fig. 6. Deviation PLc is different with different antenna height (h) in our data analysis. With the increase of antenna height, the change of deviation PLc is getting smaller, we choose fitting function PLc = a*log(h) + b to depict the relationship with h. The coefficients (with 95%

confidence bounds) is deduced as a = −0.8395, b = 18.12. The sum of squares due to error (SSE) is 0.4634, and the coefficient of determination (R-square) is 0.8448, so the fitting works well. The FZNG model is modified as the following Eq. 9.

$$E_{total} = PL_c + \begin{cases} E_f, & d_1 + d_2 < d_b \\ E_f + E_{NG}, & d_1 + d_2 \geq d_b \end{cases}$$ (9)

$$PL_c = -0.8395 * \log_{10}(h) + 18.12$$

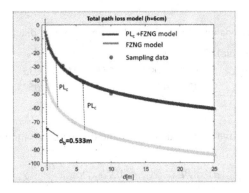

Fig. 6. Deviation between data from FZNG model and sampling data.

4   Near-Ground Channel Measurement and Statistical Model

In this section, prediction ability of the proposed model is verified by comparing it to the near-ground measurements in open grassed areas discussed in Sect. 3.1, the data for verification is not used for modeling.

4.1   Statistical Channel Model Validation

In Sect. 3.1, over 500 snapshots are obtained in each measurement case. 400 snapshots are used to build the channel model, the other 100 snapshots are used for verification. Also, the 500 snapshots in the case of antenna height is 6 cm are used for verification. Predicated path loss data by the empirical model shown in Eqs. 11, 12 are compared with measurement data. The results are shown in Fig. 7. The high degree of coincidence of test data and model data indicates that our model has credibility and good predictability.

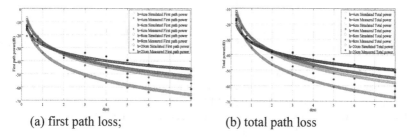

(a) first path loss;   (b) total path loss

Fig. 7. Statistical channel model validation results.

4.2   Modified FZNG Model Validation

Similar with the validation scheme stated in Sect. 4.1, we produce the total path loss data by employed the modified FZNG model shown in Eq. 13, then we compare the data with measurement data for verification and predicated data from statistical model. The sample results are described in Fig. 8.

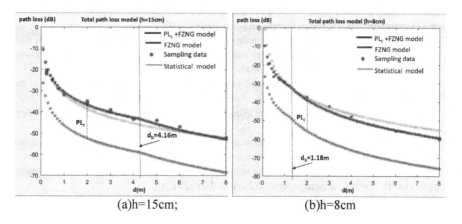

(a)h=15cm;   (b)h=8cm

Fig. 8. Modified FZNG channel model validation results.

5   Conclusion

Empirical near-ground and modified Fresnel-zone-based field prediction model are presented to facilitate highly accurate near ground network simulations. It is observed that the proposed models are accurate and feasible for very near ground applications (antenna height is less than 20 cm). In our future work, we will focus on research of impact of different terrain surface roughness on channel signal attenuation characteristics.

References

1. Chamanbaz, M., Mateo, D., Zoss, B.M., et al.: Swarm-enabling technology for multi-robot systems. Front. Robot. AI **4**, 12 (2017)
2. Pugh, J., Martinoli, A.: Relative localization and communication module for small-scale multi-robot systems. In: Proceedings 2006 IEEE International Conference on Robotics and Automation, ICRA 2006, pp. 188–193. IEEE (2006)
3. Mani, V.V., Bose, R.: Direction of arrival estimation of multiple UWB signals. Wireless Pers. Commun. **57**(2), 277–289 (2011)
4. Guo, K., Qiu, Z., Meng, W., et al.: Ultra-wideband based cooperative relative localization algorithm and experiments for multiple unmanned aerial vehicles in GPS denied environments. Int. J. Micro Air Veh. **9**(3), 169–186 (2017)
5. Merrill, W.M., Liu, H.L.N., Leong, J., et al.: Quantifying short-range surface-to-surface communications links. IEEE Antennas Propag. Mag. **46**(3), 36–46 (2004)
6. Torabi, A., Zekavat, S.A.: Near-ground channel modeling for distributed cooperative communications. IEEE Trans. Antennas Propag. **64**(6), 2494–2502 (2016)
7. Hugine, A., Volos, H.I., Gaeddert, J., et al.: Measurement and characterization of the near-ground indoor ultra wideband channel. In: 2006 IEEE Wireless Communications and Networking Conference, WCNC 2006, vol. 2, pp. 1062–1067. IEEE (2006)
8. Landolsi, M.A., Muqaibel, A.H., Al-Ahmari, A.S., et al.: Performance analysis of time-of-arrival mobile positioning in wireless cellular CDMA networks. In: Christos, J. (ed.) Trends in Telecommunications Technologies. InTech, Paris (2010)
9. Parameswaran, A.T., Husain, M.I., Upadhyaya, S.: Is RSSI a reliable parameter in sensor localization algorithms an experimental study. In: Field Failure Data Analysis Workshop (F2DA), New York, NY, September 2009
10. Dagefu, F.T., Sarabandi, K.: Analysis and modeling of near-ground wave propagation in the presence of building walls. IEEE Trans. Antennas Propag. **59**(6), 2368–2378 (2011)
11. Pahlavan, K., Krishnamurthy, P.: Principles of Wireless Access and Localization. Wiley, Chichester (2013)
12. Xu, C., He, J., Zhang, X., et al.: Toward near-ground localization: modeling and applications for TOA ranging error. IEEE Trans. Antennas Propag. **65**(10), 5658–5662 (2017)
13. Aslam, M.I., Zekavat, S.A.R.: New channel path loss model for near-ground antenna sensor networks. IET Wireless Sensor Syst. **2**(2), 103–107 (2012)

Sensor Location Verification Scheme Based on Range-Free Localizations in WSNs

Keji Mao, Xiannian Zhou[(⊠)], Zhikai Yang, and Weiyuan Shi

Zhejiang University of Technology, Liuhe Road 288, Hangzhou, China
maokeji@zjut.edu.cn, 920046045@qq.com

Abstract. Localization is a pivotal technology in wireless sensor networks and location information of sensor nodes is essential to location-based applications. In the beacon-based localization, the reliability of beacons' location information is critical to the quality of network service. In this paper, we study the influences of drifting beacons and malicious beacons in the network localization. So according to this scenario mentioned above, we propose a distributed and lightweight beacons locations verification algorithm based on neighborhood-similarity (BLVNS), which utilizes similarity of the beacons' neighborhood in different time slot to recognize drifting beacons. Then, we propose a distributed and lightweight unreliable beacons verification algorithm based on trust-model (BLVTM). The whole algorithms can be applied to the static and dynamic WSNs to improve the accuracy of range-free localization. Experiment results show that our algorithms can recognize unreliable beacons with detection rate higher than 90%.

Keywords: WSNs · Reliable localization · Drifting beacons · Malicious beacons

1 Introduction

Localization is one of the most essential research issues in WSNs. Because predefine nodes' positions manually is not available for large scale WSN, we always predefine a small part of nodes' locations manually in deployment, which are called beacon nodes. And other nodes are called unknown nodes. Take the location of beacons as reference, the normal sensor nodes can estimate their locations using some certain localization algorithms. These localization algorithms can be divided into Range-Based localization algorithms and Range-Free localization algorithms [1]. The former assumes the distances between sensors and beacons can be estimated by using different measurements, such as TDoA, ToA, AoA and RSSI [2–5], While the latter estimates location of normal nodes based on the features of networks, such as hop counts [6], topology of network [7], etc.

In [8] it proposed a range-based point to point location verification algorithm, but the checked node need GPS receiver. He et al. proposed a location verification algorithm based on TOA to eliminate abnormal range value, which is used in Range-Based localization algorithms [9]. Kuo et al. proposed beacon movement detection (BMD) algorithm to detect the unexpected movements of beacons [10]. However, all of above methods can't be suitable for Range-Free algorithms and solve single problem.

© Springer Nature Singapore Pte Ltd. 2019
S. Shen et al. (Eds.): CWSN 2018, CCIS 984, pp. 89–98, 2019.
https://doi.org/10.1007/978-981-13-6834-9_9

To solve these problems mentioned above, we proposed a distributed and light-weight beacons locations verification algorithm based on neighborhood-similarity, which use the similarity of the beacons' neighborhood in different time slot to verify which beacons are drifting. On this basis, we propose a distributed and lightweight unreliable beacon verification algorithm based on trust-model, which utilizes similarity of the location trust from beacons to their neighborhoods in different time slot to recognize unreliable beacons.

2   BLVNS Algorithm

2.1   Neighborhood Relationship

When one node is moved, its neighbors are changed. As an example, Fig. 1 shows a scenario where B_2 is moved in the (t_0, t_1). At time t_0, its neighbors are S_5, S_4 and S_6. But at time t_1, its neighbor is only S_5. Its neighbors are changed obviously. We denote sensor S_i's change of neighbors by $IDSame(i)_{(t,t+1)}$ in the $(t, t+1)$, using the formula (1).

$$IDSame(i)_{(t,t+1)} = \frac{|ID(i)_t \cap ID(j)_t|}{|ID(i)_t \cup ID(j)_t|} \tag{1}$$

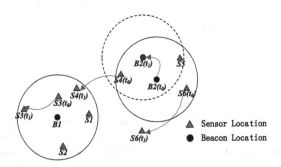

Fig. 1. The process of drifting nodes

Neighborhood relationship of S_i and S_j's at time t is defined as $Relation(i,j)_t$. $Relation(i,j)_t$ and $Relation(i,j)_{t+1}$ are computed by

$$Relation(i,j)_t = \begin{cases} DisRank(i,j)_t \cdot IDSame(j)_{(t,t+1)} & j \in (ID(i)_t \cap ID(i)_{t+1}) \\ DisRank(i,j)_t \cdot \left(1 - IDSame(i)_{(t,t+1)}\right) & j \in (ID(i)_t / ID(i)_{t+1}) \\ 0 & j \in (ID(i)_{t+1} / ID(i)_t) \end{cases} \tag{2}$$

Table 1. The BLANS algorithm

Algorithm BLANS algorithm

For Sensors

1. At time t, for $i = 1$: Sensors

2.   Get $ID(i)_t$

3. end

4. At time $t+1$, for $i = 1$: Sensors

5.   Get $ID(i)_{t+1}$

6.   Calculate and broadcast $IDSame(i)_{(t,t+1)}$

7. end

For Beacons

1. At time t, for $j = 1$: Beacons

2.   Get $ID(j)_t$ and $DisRank(j,n)_t, n \in ID(j)_t$

3. end

4. At time $t+1$, for $j = 1$: Beacons

5.   Get $ID(j)_{t+1}$ and $DisRank(j,m)_{t+1}, m \in ID(j)_{t+1}$

6.   Calculate and broadcast $IDSame(j)_{(t,t+1)}$

7. end

8. for $k = 1$: Beacons

9.   Calculate $RelationV(k)_t$ and $RelationV(k)_{t+1}$

10.   Calculate $NeiSim(k)$

11.   if $NeiSim(k) <$ threshold

12.   Beacon B_k is drifting

13. end

$$Relation(i,j)_{t+1} = \begin{cases} DisRank(i,j)_t \cdot IDSame(j)_{(t,t+1)} & j \in ID(i)_{t+1} \\ 0 & j \in (ID(i)_t / ID(i)_{t+1}) \end{cases} \quad (3)$$

We use cosine law to calculate the similarity of $RelationV(i)_t$ and $RelationV(i)_{t+1}$ by

$$NeiSim(i) = \frac{RelationV(i)_t \cdot RelationV(i)_{t+1}}{\left\| RelationV(i)_t \right\| \cdot \left\| RelationV(i)_{t+1} \right\|} \quad (4)$$

2.2   Procedures of BLVNS

The procedure of BLANS is shown in Table 1. Considering sensors' energy consumption, we only need to recognize and filter out drifting beacons. For the normal nodes only calculate $IDSame(j)_{(t,t+1)}$ and send it to neighbor beacons. Each beacon calculates and transfers $IDSame(j)_{(t,t+1)}$ and calculates $Relation(i,j)_t$ and $Relation(i,j)_{t+1}$ of its each neighbor. Then, each beacon gets $RelationV(i)_t$ and $RelationV(i)_{t+1}$. Finally, each beacon calculates the similarity of neighborhood relationship by the formula (4). If B_i's $NeiSim(i)$ is lower than threshold value, B_i is a drifting Beacon.

3   BLVTM Algorithm

3.1   Trust Model

In the trust model, we denote estimated distance between S_i and S_j by $EstDis(i,j)_t$, which is normalized by using the formula (5), where $EstDisRank(i,j)_t$ reflects the estimated distance coefficient between S_i and S_j at time t.

$$EstDisRank(i,j)_t = \begin{cases} 1 - \frac{EstDis(i,j)_t}{R} & EstDis(i,j)_t \leq R \\ 0 & EstDis(i,j)_t > R \end{cases} \quad (5)$$

In this paper, the trust model is consisted of three components: direct trust, recommendation trust and integrated trust, which are defined as follows.

Direct trust is a kind of trust calculated based on the direct neighborhood observation of sensors. We define direct trust by $DT(i,j)_t$, calculated by the formula (6).

$$DT(i,j)_t = 1 - \frac{\left| DisRank(i,j)_t - EstDisRank(i,j)_t \right|}{DisRank(i,j)_t + EstDisRank(i,j)_t} \quad (6)$$

Recommendation trust is a kind of trust from other sensors. It is needed to improve the trust evaluation. We define recommendation trust as $RT(i,j)_t$, calculated by the formula (7).

$$RT(i,j)_t = \frac{\sum DT(i,m)_t \cdot DisRank(i,m)_t}{\sum DisRank(i,m)_t} \left(m \in Nei(i,j)_t \right) \tag{7}$$

Integrated trust synthesizes the direct trust and recommendation trust, reflecting trust between neighbor nodes and defined as $IT(i,j)_t$, calculated by the formula (8).

$$IT(i,j)_t = DT(i,j)_t \cdot DisRank(i,j)_t + RT(i,j)_t \cdot \left(1 - DisRank(i,j)_t\right) \tag{8}$$

We denoted S_i and S_j's trust relationship at time t by $Trust(i,j)_t$. $Trust(i,j)_t$ and $Trust(i,j)_{t+1}$ are computed by

$$Trust(i,j)_t = \begin{cases} IT(i,j)_t \cdot IDSame(j)_{(t,t+1)} & j \in \left(ID(i)_t \cap ID(i)_{t+1}\right) \\ IT(i,j)_t \cdot \left(1 - DSame(i)_{(t,t+1)}\right) & j \in \left(ID(i)_t / ID(i)_{t+1}\right) \\ 0 & j \in \left(ID(i)_{t+1} / ID(i)_t\right) \end{cases} \tag{9}$$

$$Trust(i,j)_{t+1} = \begin{cases} IT(i,j)_{t+1} \cdot IDSame(j)_{(t,t+1)} & j \in ID(i)_{t+1} \\ 0 & j \in \left(ID(i)_t / ID(i)_{t+1}\right) \end{cases} \tag{10}$$

We use Jaccard similarity coefficient to replace the cosine law coefficient in (11).

$$NeiTVSim(i) = \frac{NeiTV(i)_t \cdot NeiTV(i)_{t+1}}{\left\|NeiTV(i)_t\right\|^2 + \left\|NeiTV(i)_{t+1}\right\|^2 - NeiTV(i)_t \cdot NeiTV(i)_{t+1}} \tag{11}$$

3.2   Procedures of BLVTM

The procedure is shown in Table 2. For reducing sensors' energy consumption, we only need to recognize unreliable beacons. Both of sensors and beacons calculate $IDSame(i)_{(t,t+1)}, DT(i,j)_t, RT(i,j)_t, IT(i,j)_t, j \in ID(i)_t$ and $DT(i,m)_{t+1}, RT(i,m)_{t+1}, IT(i,m)_{t+1}, m \in ID(i)_{t+1}$. Then, beacons calculate $NeiTV(i)_t$ and $NeiTV(i)_{t+1}$. At last, beacons utilizes the Jaccard similarity coefficient $NeiTVSim(i)$.

Table 2. The BLVTM algorithm

Algorithm BLVTM algorithm

For Sensor node

1. At time t, for $i = 1$:SensorNum

2. Get $ID(i)_t$, $DisRank(i,j)_t$, $EstDisRank(i,j)_t$, $j \in ID(i)_t$

3. Calculate $DT(i,j)_t$, $RT(i,j)_t$, $IT(i,j)_t$, $j \in ID(i)_t$

4. end

5. At time $t+1$, for $i = 1$:SensorNum

6. Get $ID(i)_{t+1}$, $DisRank(i,m)_{t+1}$, $EstDisRank(i,m)_{t+1}$, $m \in ID(i)_{t+1}$.

7. Calculate $DT(i,m)_{t+1}$, $RT(i,m)_{t+1}$, $IT(i,m)_{t+1}$, $m \in ID(i)_{t+1}$.

8. Calculate and broadcast $IDSame(i)_{(t,t+1)}$.

9. end

For Beacon node

1. At time t, for $j = 1$:Beacons

2. Get $ID(j)_t$, $DisRank(j,n)_t$, $EstDisRank(j,n)_t$, $n \in ID(j)_t$

3. Calculate $DT(j,n)_t$, $RT(j,n)_t$, $IT(j,n)_t$, $n \in ID(j)_t$

4. end

5. At time $t+1$, for $j = 1$: Beacons

6. Get $ID(j)_{t+1}$, $DisRank(j,m)_{t+1}$, $EstDisRank(j,m)_{t+1}$, $m \in ID(j)_{t+1}$.

7. Calculate $DT(j,m)_{t+1}$, $RT(j,m)_{t+1}$, $IT(j,m)_{t+1}$, $m \in ID(j)_{t+1}$.

8. Calculate and broadcast $IDSame(j)_{(t,t+1)}$

9. end

10. for $k = 1$: Beacons

11. Calculate $NeiTV(k)_t$, $NeiTV(k)_{t+1}$

12. Calculate $NeiTVSim(k)$

13. if $NeiTVSim(k) <$ threshold

14. Beacon B_k is unreliable.

15. end

4 Experiment and Analysis

The network configuration of our simulation is set as follows: 150 nodes, including 15 beacons and 135 sensors, are deployed randomly in a 150 m × 150 m region. The transmission range of each nodes equals to 30 m. We use the signal attenuation model to simulate the RSSI value between nodes, by using the formula (12). d_{kl} is the distance between sender S_k and receiver S_l. d_0 is a reference distance and equals to 1 m. n_p is an exponent of path loss. ε is an error coefficient.

We use success detection rate R_s and error rate R_e to evaluate the detection performance. The calculation of R_s and R_e is given in (13) and (14), in which B_u is the set of unreliable beacons, B_{du} is the set of unreliable beacons detected by algorithms.

$$p_{kl} = \left(p_0 - 10 n_p lg \left(\frac{d_{kl}}{d_0} \right) \right) \cdot (1 - \varepsilon) \tag{12}$$

$$R_s = \frac{Num(B_u \cap B_{du})}{Num(B_u)} \tag{13}$$

$$R_e = \frac{Num((B - B_u) \cap B_{du})}{Num(B_u)} \tag{14}$$

4.1 Performance of BLANS and BLATM with Drifting Beacons

At first, the measurement of RSSI does not exist any error, $\varepsilon = 0$, and the thresholds of BLANS and BLATM are 0.6 and 0.45 respectively. Figure 2 shows the performance of the verification algorithms with the drifting beacons. For example, when exponent of path loss is 1.5, 2, and 2.5, respectively, R_s of two algorithms is maintained at about 95% and R_e is under the 20% with the drifting nodes increasing. The influences of drifting sensors are small. When the measurements of RSSI exist errors, we set $\varepsilon = 0$, $\varepsilon \in (-0.05, 0.05)$ and $\varepsilon \in (-0.1, 0.1)$ respectively. Figure 3 shows the performances of the verification algorithms with measuring errors. The experiment shows that BLVNS and BLVTM are robust.

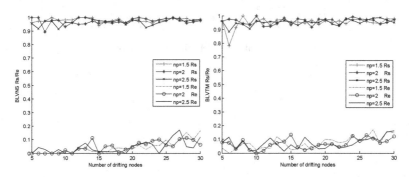

Fig. 2. Performance of BLVNS and BLVTM with different drifting nodes and environments

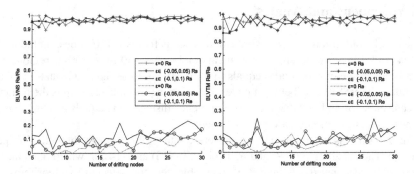

Fig. 3. Performance of BLVNS and BLVTM with different drifting nodes and measuring errors

4.2   Performance of BLVTM with Malicious Beacons

When the measurements of RSSI don't exist any error $\varepsilon = 0$. The threshold is 0.45. The number of drifting sensors is set as 15. Figure 4(a) shows the performance of BLVTM with the malicious beacons. For example, when exponent of path loss is 1.5, 2, and 2.5, respectively, R_s is maintained at 95% and R_e is closed to 0 with the malicious beacons increasing. However, when the measurements of RSSI exist errors, we set exponent of path loss as 2. Figure 4(b) shows the performance of BLVTM with different RSSI measuring errors. Compare Fig. 4(b) with Fig. 4(a), we can find their performances are similar. The experiment shows that BLVTM is robust.

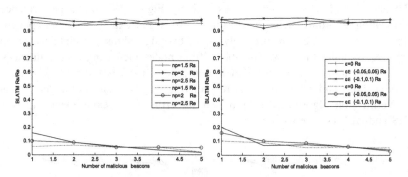

Fig. 4. Performance of BLVTM with the malicious beacons

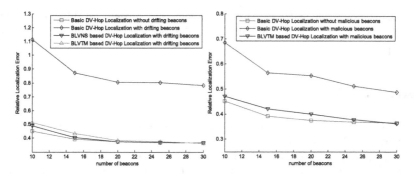

Fig. 5. Comparison of relative localization error

4.3 Applicability of BLVNS and BLVTM Based on Range-Free Localizations

We choose DV-Hop algorithm [11] localization to verify our proposed algorithms' applicability. The relative localization error is used to indicate the accuracy of localization.

Reliable DV-Hop Algorithm with Drifting Beacons

The simulation configure is set as follow: the measurements of RSSI error $\varepsilon \in (-0.1, 0.1)$, exponent of path loss $n_p = 1.5$. The number of drifting nodes is set as 20, including drifting sensors and beacons. The impacts of the drifting nodes on the DV-Hop localization and the performance of our proposed algorithms are shown in Fig. 5(a). We can see that when drifting beacons exist, the relative localization error for the DV-Hop localization increases obviously. However, when the drifting beacons are filtered out by BLVNS and BLVTM, the relative localization error is gradually close to that the basic DV-Hop localization without drifting beacons, especially when the number of beacons is larger than 20.

Reliable DV-Hop Algorithm with Malicious Beacons

The simulation configure is similar with the above. The number of drifting sensors is set as 20. The malicious beacons ratio is 1/3. The impacts of the malicious beacons on the DV-Hop localization and the performance of BLVTM are shown in Fig. 5(b). We also can find that when malicious beacons exist, the relative localization error for the DV-Hop localization increases obviously. However, the performance of BLVTM based DV-Hop is close to basic DV-Hop.

5 Conclusion

In this paper, we analyze the several impacts of the unreliable beacons on Range-Free localization algorithms. To eliminate the influences on localization arisen from these unreliable beacons, we propose two distributed and lightweight algorithms BLVNS and BLVTM. They can efficiently recognize and filter out the drifting beacons. In addition, the latter can detect the malicious beacons. Simulation results show they can minimize the re-localization error and have strong anti-jamming capacity in different environments and networks. Future study will extend the location verification model to real-world experiments.

References

1. Safa, H.: A novel localization algorithm for large scale wireless sensor networks. Comput. Commun. **45**, 32–46 (2014)
2. Gezici, S., Tian, Z., Giannakis, G.B., et al.: Localization via ultra-wideband radios: a look at positioning aspects of future sensor networks. IEEE Signal Process. Mag. **22**(4), 70–84 (2005)
3. Patwari, N., Ash, J.N., Kyperountas, S., et al.: Locating the nodes: cooperative localization in wireless sensor networks. IEEE Signal Process. Mag. **22**(4), 54–69 (2005)
4. Vempaty, A., Ozdemir, O., Agrawal, K., et al.: Localization in wireless sensor networks: Byzantines and Mitigation techniques. IEEE Trans. Signal Process. **61**(6), 1495–1508 (2013)
5. Shao, H.J., Zhang, X.P., Wang, Z.: Efficient closed-form algorithms for AOA based self-localization of sensor nodes using auxiliary variables. IEEE Trans. Signal Process. **62**(10), 2580–2594 (2014)
6. Wang, Y., Wang, X., Wang, D., et al.: Range-free localization using expected hop progress in wireless sensor networks. IEEE Trans. Parallel Distrib. Syst. **20**(10), 1540–1552 (2009)
7. Zhou, Y., Xia, S., Ding, S., et al.: An improved APIT node self-localization algorithm in WSN based on triangle-center scan. J. Comput. Res. Dev. **46**(4), 566–574 (2009)
8. Liu, D., Lee, M.C., Wu, D.: A node-to-node location verification method. IEEE Trans. Ind. Electron. **57**(5), 1526–1537 (2010)
9. He, D., Cui, L., Huang, H., et al.: Design and verification of enhanced secure localization scheme in wireless sensor networks. IEEE Trans. Parallel Distrib. Syst. **20**(7), 1050–1058 (2009)
10. Kuo, S.P., Kuo, H.J., Tseng, Y.C.: The beacon movement detection problem in wireless sensor networks for localization applications. IEEE Trans. Mob. Comput. **8**(10), 1326–1338 (2009)
11. Niculescu, D., Nath, B.: DV based positioning in ad hoc networks. Telecommun. Syst. **22**(1–4), 267–280 (2003)

The Improvement of Indoor Localization Precision Through PCA-Based Channel Combination Method

Xiaochao Dang[1,2]⊙, Jiaju Ren[1]⊙, Zhanjun Hao[1,2(✉)]⊙, Yan Yan[1]⊙, and Yili Hei[1]⊙

[1] College of Computer Science and Engineering, Northwest Normal University,
Lanzhou 730070, China
dangxc@nwnu.edu.cn, renjiaju@vip.sina.com, zhanjunhao@126.com
[2] Gansu Province Internet of Things Engineering Research Center,
Lanzhou 730070, China
http://www.nwnu.edu.cn

Abstract. At present, the traditional indoor localization system based on Received Signal Strength (RSS) cannot provide high efficiency, high precision and high adaptability due to the instability of the RSS. For improving the locating problem preferably, Channel State Information (CSI) replacing RSS as a more fine-grained signal. However, its merits of perception of the surrounding environment are also its defects, not all CSI raw data can be fully qualified for positioning. In this paper, we proposed a novel method of Wi-Fi indoor localization. At first, the localization system assembles the unified feature dataset after channel combination processing. then it uses a two-stage method, Principal Component Analysis (PCA) plus Spearman Rank Correlation Coefficient (SRCC) to select and compress the sub-sampled CSI data. Finally, it adopts Weighted K nearest neighbor (WKNN) classifier to recognize the corresponding physical position. The experimental verification results show that proposed method, which named PCA-CC, compared with other RSS-based location systems, can improve the accuracy of the positioning results in real environment effectively.

Keywords: Indoor localization · Fingerprint database ·
Channel State Information · PCA · Spearman factor

1 Introduction

Ubiquitous Wi-Fi technology has fostered a broad range of applications beyond a vehicle for communication [1]. According to surveys, people spend over 80% of their time in indoor environments [2]. Therefore, indoor localization services and related applications in current environment need to be addressed urgently. Indoor localization is very practical for many applications, such as regional monitor, disaster emergency responses, expensive devices prevention, patients care in

© Springer Nature Singapore Pte Ltd. 2019
S. Shen et al. (Eds.): CWSN 2018, CCIS 984, pp. 99–113, 2019.
https://doi.org/10.1007/978-981-13-6834-9_10

hospital, location of cars in parking lot, etc. In recent years, numerous of indoor positioning methods have been proposed with off-the-shelf hardware, such as Intel 5300 NIC and Atheros NICs in wireless sensing field. At the same time, ZigBee, Wi-Fi and Bluetooth became more and more mature in indoor localization. But in the outdoor environment, one of the best ways for positioning is GPS, which is in the line of sight transmission (LOS) conditions in a wider area and with no building blocks. In general, it can provide a more accurate positioning in outdoor environment, but not effectively enough in indoor environments [3]. To satisfy the urgent needs of the high accuracy in indoor, localization system must be low-budget, and it also needs to be less complex and highly effective. Wi-Fi indoor localization method, based on fingerprint database, has become a new positioning method gradually without adding any special hardware devices. With the development of Wi-Fi supporting IEEE 802.11n standard protocol, it is possible to obtain values of CSI directly and precisely. Compared with the RSSI, CSI contains more fine-grained information, which can reflect the multipath effect in indoor environment comprehensively. Therefore, CSI-based methods, attract more attention in this field.

The localization system based on CSI in indoor conditions can be divided into two types, one of them is geometrical location method [4], it includes trilateraion localization algorithm and triangulation localization algorithm. For example, FIFS [5] exploits a weighted average of CSI amplitudes over three antennas to achieve fine-grained location information, while CSI amplitudes and calibrated phase information are exploited in DeepFi [6] and PhaseFi [7], respectively. The reference [8] has proposed an indoor signal propagation model based on CSI to estimate the distance between transmitter and receiver. Spot-Fi [9] conducts the trilateraion localization through multi-receivers. The geometrical location has the characteristics of low algorithm complexity and fast computing speed, but it needs at least two nodes to assist the localization and its accuracy is fully depend on the line of sight transmission' distance (the quality of distance accuracy). While another type is the localization method using fingerprint, it is not depended on the LOS transmission measurement and only needs one Wi-Fi access point to finish the localization. Positioning method based on fingerprint is divided into two phases: the offline phase and the online phase. The offline phase builds the fingerprint information in the database and compares it with the test point. In online phase, real-time sampling values are used to match the fingerprint database, it enables us to calculate their precise location.

For instance, some indoor localization systems use RSSI to complete the indoor positioning, Youssef et al. [10], designed Horus system, using location-clustering techniques to enhance the accuracy. PinLoc [11] system uses eigenvalues of CSI for training and classification. Lei et al. [12] proposed a coordinate difference correction and weighted KNN method (DC-WKNN), This method first builds an RSS-based fingerprint database, then uses the weighted KNN method to find K-nearest points from the test points.

In this paper, the proposed method attempts to preprocess CSI raw data by merging three channels into one channel, and then uses principal component analysis to extract main features from data of combined channel and building robust fingerprint database. In the online phase, the WKNN algorithm is used to estimate more accurate position after achieving the Spearman Rank Correlation Coefficient with combined channels. The merging and extension within a certain range is a preprocess step. The factor of the Spearman has been regarded as weight for better computing distance from sampling data to fingerprint data. Experimental results demonstrate the validity of localization accuracy, compared with other methods, the proposed method improves the positioning precision significantly.

2   System Model and Relevant Definitions

2.1   Channel State Information

The localization methods based on fingerprint database refer to achieve the accurate localization results through finding one-to-one correspondence between physical location and the fingerprint database which is constructed by the signal features in real-time sampling. Device-free fingerprint localization means positioning without carrying any devices. Therefore, it increased signal processing requirements. PCA is applied into this method for an extraction of fingerprint features, which includes an array of mapping collection $L = \{L_1, L_1, \cdots, L_N\}$ between sampling signal and physical locations, and many transmission targets $CSI_i (i \in \{1, 2, \cdots, M\})$ in which exist the communication links from transmitter to receiver have been addressed. The targets are the CSI data sets received by the signal transmitter. Alternatively, modify the Atheros-CSI-tool [13] driver source code to support NIC which supported the IEEE 802.11n standard at the kernel level and rewrite applications to take more advanced extraction of Channel State Information. CSI refers to the channel characteristics of a link between communication of transmitters which shows how the signal propagates in the space [14,15]. The frequency domain model of the CSI is represented by this formula:

$$Y = HX + N \tag{1}$$

Where matrix N represents additive gaussian white noise. H represents the channel frequency response, which is regarded as CSI matrix. CSIs are capable of estimating the X and Y at the receiver. All CSI of the subcarriers can be expressed as:

$$CSI = \frac{Y}{X} \tag{2}$$

According to the IEEE 802.11n protocol, the CSI is divided into different index groups. At 40 mHz bandwidth, the number of subcarriers are 114, and CSI matrix can be expressed as:

$$H = \begin{bmatrix} H_{11} & H_{12} & \cdots & H_{1M} \\ H_{21} & H_{22} & \cdots & H_{2M} \\ \vdots & \vdots & \ddots & \vdots \\ H_{N1} & H_{N2} & \cdots & H_{NM} \end{bmatrix} \tag{3}$$

Where M and N denote the number of the transmitting antenna and the receiving antenna respectively, and H denotes the CSI from the ith receiving antenna and the jth transmitting antenna. The signal propagation paths in the indoor environment are different, received signal from diverse antennas at the channel are also different. Compared with the RSSI, CSIs describe the features after the signal propagating in the indoor space. A single subcarrier of CSIs can be expressed as:

$$csi = |csi|\, e^{j \sin \angle csi} \tag{4}$$

$|csi|$ and $\angle csi$ are the amplitude response and the phase response respectively [16]. An example of CSI collections in diverse points are shown in Fig. 1. Figure 1(a) for the changes of amplitude at location 1 and Fig. 1(b) for the fluctuations of signal amplitude at location 2. For these figures, the different lines of signal amplitude are extremely similar in the same location. The diverse degree of signal attenuation between different locations shows that the inconsistent phenomena of channels can reflect the changes of location, and it proves the possibility of positioning through the CSI amplitudes.

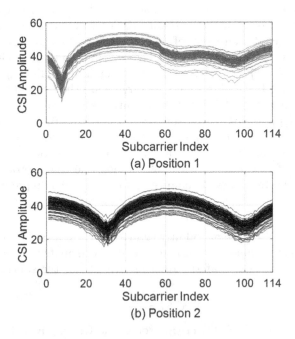

(a) Position 1

(b) Position 2

Fig. 1. Raw CSI amplitudes obtained in location 1 and location 2.

2.2   Spearman Rank Correlation Coefficient

Spearman Rank Correlation Coefficient is a non-parametric measure of statistical dependence between two observational sequences [17]. To pursue the most similar sampling data, it computes the real-time value of CSI by retrieving the fingerprint database in an actual positioning phase. In the process of calculation, the factor of spearman characterizes the relationship among the sequences, and the coefficient can be depicted using a monotonic function as:

$$\rho = 1 - \frac{6 \sum d^2}{n(n^2 - 1)} \tag{5}$$

Where ρ denotes the Spearman Rank Correlation Coefficient, d is the difference between the sequences, and n is the number of the sequences., it requires the same number of the observational sequences for this method.

Definition 1: Suppose $\phi_{\omega,v} = [\phi_1 \; \phi_2 \; \cdots \; \phi_j]$ is the amplitude when there are j subcarriers, so ω represents the measurement times, and v represents the subcarrier serial numbers.

Definition 2: Define $\theta_{m,n}, m = 1 \cdots \mu, j = 1 \cdots \tau$ as the amplitude gained from actual measurement, so m is the measurement times and n is the subcarrier total serial numbers.

Definition 3: Define the ωth measurement phase value as: $\theta_\omega = [\theta_{1,1} \; \theta_{1,2} \; \cdots \; \theta_{1,n}]$.

3   PCA-CC Indoor Localization System

The proposed method is a step-by-step process, including PCA-based channel combination preprocessing and precise positioning respectively. The PCA preprocessing method is the basic premise of the positioning, it organized the information of three channels into one channel after the completion of the basic combination method, it uses a rough set of locations by computing the Spearman Rank Correlation Coefficient between test CSIs and the fingerprint in database. On the basis of the location discrimination, the method put the factor of the Spearman as the weight and used a WKNN based on Spearman Correlation Coefficient algorithm to obtain precise positioning.

3.1   PCA-Based CSI Preprocessing

The fingerprint information characterized by the single channel is less than multiple channels. One drawback of the single channel approach is that it probably has no wealthy information, and it is unable to express its characteristics sufficiently. We combined the amplitude values of the three channels into one and put their head and tail connected respectively. The illustration of the channel combination is shown in Fig. 2. Figure 2(a), (b) and (c) represent the amplitude values of three different channels, Fig. 2(d) shows the amplitudes of combined channel. The amplitudes of the channel 1, channel 2 and channel 3 are combined to integrated data. In this way, the method achieves an extended value of CSI

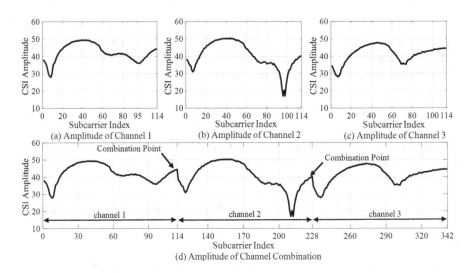

Fig. 2. CSI amplitudes combination within channel 1, channel 2 and channel 3

amplitude which has more information effectively. The combined channel can be extracted more valid data for calculation, and it is also realistic in reflection of the relationship between three lines of channels. After processing the value of combined channel, PCA is used to reduce the dimensionality of raw data before storing the values of combined channel in the database as a fingerprint first, and its dimensionality reduction steps are as follows:

Step 1: Achieve the pre-processed whole fingerprint data matrix, a total of L locations, each sample size is $M \times N$, then each training sample matrix is $L = [l_1, l_2, \cdots, l_n]^T$, Where l_i is the ith phase of subcarrier, the size of the entire data matrix is $n \times (M \times N)$, n is the number of the index of subcarriers. Map the original feature vector to the p-dimensional subspace.

Step 2: Calculate the training average and difference:

$$\Psi = \frac{1}{n}\sum_{i=1}^{n} l_i, d_i = l_i - \Psi \tag{6}$$

Step 3: Construct a covariance matrix:

$$C = \frac{1}{n}\sum_{i=1}^{n} d_i d_i^T = \frac{1}{n}AA^T \tag{7}$$

Where the A expressed as $[d_1, d_2, \cdots, d_n]$.

Step 4: Solve the eigenvalues and eigenvectors of the covariance matrix and obtain the eigenvalues and eigenvectors by computing the eigenvalues and eigenvectors of AA^T.

Step 5: Select the appropriate principal components, sort the obtained eigenvalues, and take the top p eigenvectors and eigenvalues. Find the original eigenvector of the covariance matrix:

$$D_i = \frac{1}{\sqrt{\lambda}} A v_i (i = 1, 2, \cdots, p) \tag{8}$$

Then the linear transformation matrix composed of the first P largest eigenvectors can be obtained as W:

$$W = [D_1, D_2, \cdots, D_p] \tag{9}$$

Step 6: Projecting the original input feature vector into a P-dimensional subspace:

$$\Omega_i = W^T d_i (i = 1, 2, \cdots, n) \tag{10}$$

The dimension of P determines the feature extraction effect of the data. However it becomes larger or smaller, it is always a matter of uncertainty, and the accuracy of the positioning is not linear. It is necessary for us to verify by actual experiments and find the most suitable P value.

3.2   Factor Search and Sample Classification

The online phase is to get the coordinates of the location estimation, it compares the samples of CSI eigenvalues and the real-time data. After calculation with above steps, it will obtain a factor represents similarity degree between reference eigenvalue of CSI and fingerprint in database. The elements in the collection represent the aggregation of similar points, and they also complete the division of the region. However, these points are not unique. The divided area is a collection of position points, each CSI fingerprint set is written as a matrix of $N_c \times 2$:

$$D = \begin{bmatrix} C_1 & CSI_1 \\ \vdots & \vdots \\ C_{Nc} & CSI_i \end{bmatrix} \tag{11}$$

Where N_c is the number of the channels. In the MIMO communication system in 802.11n protocol, three transmitting antennas will make up N_c which the maximum is 9. The value of each CSI represents the set of CSI in the diverse channels, as shown in the following equation:

$$CSI = [csi_1 \ csi_2 \quad \cdots \quad csi_k] \tag{12}$$

The value of the k depends on the bandwidth, in the 20 MHz bandwidth $k = 56$ and in 40 MHz bandwidth the $k = 114$. The reference fingerprint database R can be written as:

$$R = \begin{bmatrix} L_1 & D_1 \\ \vdots & \vdots \\ L_{Th} & D_t \end{bmatrix} \tag{13}$$

L_{Th} is the coordinate position of the reference position, and D_t represents the fingerprint set of the CSIs. Each element in $R(t,2)$ represents the different fingerprint information. Spearman Rank Correlation Coefficient is used to calculate the relevance of the target CSI fingerprint and it sets D and fingerprint database R. Each element in $D(i,2)$ is unique, therefore the target CSI eigenvalue and the elements in the fingerprint database can use this method correctly [16]. We define matrix V_T, the first column K_i is the original sequence of CSI, the second column N_{ti} represents sequence of the Spearman rank. By exploiting the spearman rank correlation of CSI measurements from the following equation:

$$\rho = 1 - \frac{6\sum_{i=0}^{k} d_i{}^2}{n(n^2 - 1)} \tag{14}$$

Where $d_i{}^2 = (V_T(i,1) - V_T(ti,2))^2$ Subsequently, the Spearman Rank Correlation Coefficient can be given as ρ. In generally $\rho = [-1,1]$.

Algorithm 1. Factor Calculation(A, B)

1: $A\ location = x_A\ B\ location = x_B$
2: $s =$ *the mumber of subcarriers*
3: **for** $i = 1$ to s **do**
4:    *sort* A, B
5: **end for**
6: **for** $i = 1$ to s **do**
7:    *compute spearman factor*
8: **end for**
9: **if** $A[j] <= 0$ **then**
10:    $swap(A[i], A[j])$
11:    $i = i + 1$
12: **end if**
13: **if** $B[j] <= 0$ **then**
14:    $swap(B[i], B[j])$
15:    $i = i + 1$
16: **end if**
17: *Return factor sequence*

To obtain the set of region location, it compares the eigenvalues of the reference CSI values which pre-stored in the database respectively in computing Spearman Rank Correlation Coefficient factor. In the process of calculating the factor, it estimated one position from other positions one by one, listing all factors in a set. It presents that we had achieved several positions and the positions are more relevant than other positions. Thus, location of the nearest correlation is obtained. These points served as a set of V_T. The proposed method using the WKNN algorithm on the basis of KNN. Firstly, select the largest initial distance. We calculated the distance from the unknown sample and each training sample *dist* in the second step. Then got the maximum distance *maxdist* in the current *K*-nearest sample. If *dist* was less than *maxdist*, the training sample was used as the K-nearest neighbor sample. Repeated the above steps until the distance between the unknown sample and all the training samples was calculated. In addition, we calculated the number of occurrences of each class label in the nearest neighbor of *K*, then selected the class label with the highest frequency as the class label for the unknown sample. In order to refine the final positioning result from the set of the regional position estimation location, we used the previously obtained factor as the weight according to the Spearman Rank Correlation Coefficient ρ, we can obtain a vector T. The location information of the fingerprint is pre-built, and the position vector can be expressed as:

$$T = (r_{t1}, r_{t2}, \cdots r_{ti}) \tag{15}$$

Where r_{t1} presents reference position. Meanwhile the correlation factor for each position reference point is ρ_i. The weight of the element in vector R is $W_{\rho i}$ and final positioning result can be given as:

$$x = \frac{1}{n} \sum_{i=1}^{n} w_{pi} r_{ti} \tag{16}$$

Finally, the obtained value x is an effective result for localization.

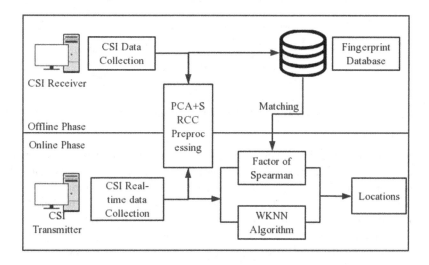

Fig. 3. System framework

4   Experimental Study

4.1   Localization System Design

In this section, the follows will introduce the methodology of positioning system and experimental environment. The experimental testbed is composed of two desktop computers. The overall framework of system in indoor positing is illustrated in Fig. 3. The values of the CSI collected from commercial Wi-Fi devices is prepared for processing, and at the different positions in the localization region and the scene feature; it has different values. Diverse positions in the processing of the fingerprinting-based localization present different eigenvalue, which can be compared with real-time reference values. The whole process of the system is divided into two main phases: offline sampling phase and online positioning phase [18, 19].

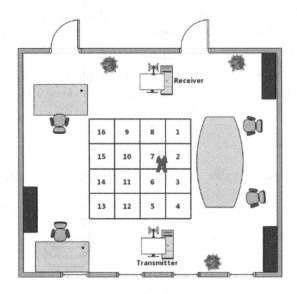

Fig. 4. Experimental site actual scene

The transmitter and receiver are installed with Atheros AR9380 NIC, which supports IEEE802.11n protocol, and it is easy to collect CSI from device. We installed the external antenna with the length of 1.5 m. All Transmitters are equipped with Ubuntu 16.04 LTS, 32-bits system and 4.1.10 Linux kernel version. The driver modules make it possible to obtain CSI from Linux kernel when it receives signals and save them for other processing. One of the desktop computers equipped with Intel Core i3-4150 CPU works as a sender while another computer works as a receiver. In our system, the obtained data is processed using C programmer. Real-time program of the display implemented by QT 5.8. Figure 4 depicts the layout sketch of the environment and lists the location of the transmitter and receiver. The experimental scenario is shown in Fig. 5.

4.2   Experimental Analysis

Comparison for the Number of Channels. Single-channel indoor positioning results and multi-channel fusion of indoor positioning results are different.

Fig. 5. Experimental site actual scene

The single channel characterizes the attenuation of a link in space, but the multi-channels portrayed more detailed information. The advantage of this method is determined by the combination of channels, it facilitates the implementation and the application of spearman rank correlation coefficient. As shown in Fig. 6, in order to obtain the experimental result. the rate of the CSI is set at 50 packets per second. The positioning accuracy of multi-channel data in a minute of time stabilizes near 1.5 m, but other single-channel data links of accuracy is lower than the multi-channel's. There is a great fluctuation in signal channel 3. Although the performance of the channel 1 is better than that in channel 3, their overall positioning accuracy level is lower than the accuracy of the mixing channel.

Impact for the Number of Sampling Points. As shown in Fig. 7, the number of different sampling value determines the system's positioning error. When the number of sampling value increases from 500 to 2000, the positioning error of the system gradually decreases, but the positioning error starts increasing slowly when the number of sampling values gradually increases from 2000. At the same time, when the number of sampling values is 2000, the positioning error of the system is minimized. When the number of sampling values is 500, the positioning error is 1.42 m. Compared to the number of samples, the positioning error is reduced by 9.8% at the time of 2000. Among them, when the number of samples is 1000 to 1500, the degree of localization error is the largest, which is 5.71%. When the number of samples is greater than 2,000, the positioning error will increase by different degrees for every 1000 additional samples. Compared to the sampling time of 2000. The positioning error increasing 0.77%,

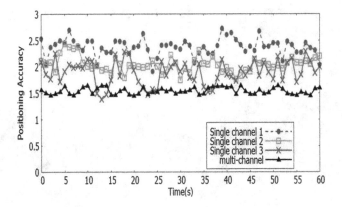

Fig. 6. Comparison for the number of channels

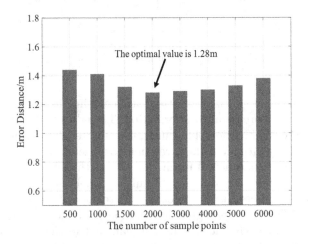

Fig. 7. Diverse number of sample points

0.78%, 2.25% and 3.62%. Experimental results show that when the number of samples increasing, the error of distance gradually increases, when the samples are optimal, the system obtains the minimum error of distance.

Impact for Different Grids of Experimental Site. The number of sampling points has a significant impact on location positing while building a fingerprint database. The relationship is shown in Figs. 8, 9 and 10. We divided the test area into 16 cells, 25 cells and 36 cells. In each sampling number of cells experiment, the experimenter (height 1.88 m, weight 71 kg) stood at least 20 s in each cell for 2000 packets as location fingerprint information, in order to obtain a stable eigenvalues of CSI. Through the experiment we concluded that the region divided into 16 cells obtained the lowest positioning accuracy about 1.32 m. While the

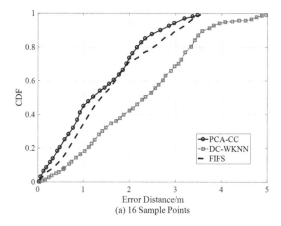

Fig. 8. The CDF of dividing the experimental site into 4×4 grids

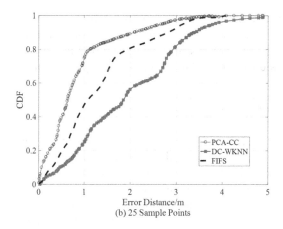

Fig. 9. The CDF of dividing the experimental site into 5×5 grids

region was divided into 25 cells, the positioning accuracy increased to 1.28 m. Subsequent experiments continued to expand the number of cell division in the region, and we found that the experimental results on the impact of changes gradually stabilized when it was divided to 25 cells as shown in Fig. 8. In the case of three types of grids divisions, the distance error of PCA-CC algorithm is better than that of WC-KNN and FIFS system. In the case of 25 meshes, the PCA-CC algorithm has a 80 percent probability of positioning error less than 1 m. At the same time, WC-KNN and FIFS system only has 50.4% and 26.6%, respectively. FIFS system has the probability of 78.8% less than 2 m, while there is small degree of improvement at this point using PCA-CC algorithm. The more cells divided, the smaller length of the rectangle obtained. The reduced grids do not really improve the positioning accuracy. While the grids becomes

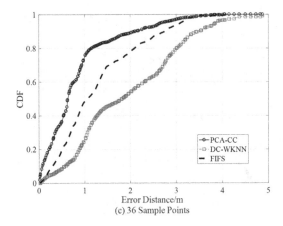

(c) 36 Sample Points

Fig. 10. The CDF of dividing the experimental site into 6×6 grids

smaller, the accuracy of the unit measurement increases, but the error probability increases, which affects the positioning performance of the system. The experimental results show that when the area is divided into 25 cells, the length of the rectangle is 0.9 m and 1.1 m, the minimum positioning error is 1.28 m.

5   Conclusions

In this paper, we proposed a WKNN indoor positioning matching algorithm based on PCA and Spearman Rank Correlation Coefficient. We preprocessed eigenvalues of CSI and store it into database that effectively reduces the CSI noise and improves the positioning accuracy. The correlation factor between the reference point and the fingerprint database is calculated, and the original location estimation position is obtained, also the correlation factor is used as the weight to obtain the exact position with WKNN. Meanwhile we setup a experimental environment in the laboratory. The WKNN algorithm based on Spearman Correlation Coefficient is verified by the actual location data. It achieved the positioning error which is 1.28 m; the maximum is 2.936 m, and 91.4% of the test distance error less than 2 m.

References

1. Zhuo, Y., et al.: Perceiving accurate CSI phases with commodity Wi-Fi devices. In: IEEE Conference on Computer Communications, INFOCOM 2017, pp. 1–9. IEEE (2017)
2. Shi, S., Sigg, S., Ji, Y.: Probabilistic fingerprinting based passive device-free localization from channel state information. In: 2016 IEEE 83rd Vehicular Technology Conference (VTC Spring). IEEE (2016)

3. Felix, G., Siller, M., Alvarez, E.N.: A fingerprinting indoor localization algorithm based deep learning. In: 2016 Eighth International Conference on Ubiquitous and Future Networks (ICUFN). IEEE (2016)
4. Wu, K., et al.: CSI-based indoor localization. IEEE Trans. Parallel Distrib. Syst. **24**(7), 1300–1309 (2013)
5. Xiao, J., et al.: FIFS: fine-grained indoor fingerprinting system. In: 2012 21st International Conference on Computer Communications and Networks (ICCCN). IEEE (2012)
6. Wang, X., Gao, L., Mao, S., Pandey, S.: CSI-based fingerprinting for indoor localization: a deep learning approach. IEEE Trans. Veh. Technol. **66**(1), 763–776 (2017)
7. Wang, X., Gao, L., Mao, S.: CSI phase fin-gerprinting for indoor localization with a deep learning approach. IEEE Internet Things J. **3**(6), 1113–1123 (2017)
8. Xie, H., Lin, L., Jiang, Z., Xi, W., Zhao, K., Ding, M., et al.: Accelerating crowd-sourcing based indoor localization using CSI. In: IEEE International Conference on Parallel and Distributed Systems, pp. 274–281. IEEE (2016)
9. Kotaru, M., Joshi, K., Bharadia, D., Katti, S.: SpotFi: decimeter level localization using Wi-Fi. ACM SIGCOMM Comput. Commun. Rev. **45**(4), 269–282 (2015)
10. Youssef, M., Agrawala, A.: The horus WLAN location determination system. In: Proceedings of the 3rd International Conference on Mobile Systems, Applications, and Services. ACM (2005)
11. Sen, S., et al.: You are facing the Mona Lisa: spot localization using PHY layer information. In: Proceedings of the 10th International Conference on Mobile Systems, Applications, and Services. ACM (2012)
12. Yen, L., et al.: A modified WKNN indoor Wi-Fi localization method with differential coordinates. In: 2017 International Conference on Applied System Innovation (ICASI). IEEE (2017)
13. Xie, Y., Li, Z., Li, M.: Precise power delay profiling with commodity Wi-Fi. In: Proceedings of the 21st Annual International Conference on Mobile Computing and Networking. ACM (2015)
14. Li, J., Li, Y., Ji, X.: A novel method of Wi-Fi indoor localization based on channel state information. In: 2016 8th International Conference on Wireless Communications & Signal Processing (WCSP). IEEE (2016)
15. Wu, Z., Zhou, Y.: Device-free passive localization based on channel state information. J. Transducer Technol. **28**(5) (2015)
16. Qian, K., et al.: PADS: passive detection of moving targets with dynamic speed using PHY layer information. In: 2014 20th IEEE International Conference on Parallel and Distributed Systems (ICPADS). IEEE (2014)
17. Liu, D., et al.: A spearman correlation coefficient ranking for matching-score fusion on speaker recognition. In: TENCON 2010–2010 IEEE Region 10 Conference. IEEE (2010)
18. Alhmiedat, T., Samara, G., Abu Salem, A.O.: An indoor fingerprinting localization approach for ZigBee wireless sensor networks. arXiv preprint arXiv:1308.1809 (2013)
19. Koyuncu, H., Yang, S.H.: Improved fingerprint localization by using static and dynamic segmentation. In: 2014 International Conference on Computational Science and Computational Intelligence (CSCI), vol. 1. IEEE (2014)

Neural Network

Event-Triggered Fault Estimation
for Nonlinear State-Delay Systems
with Saturations in Both State and Sensor

Xu Liu, Yunji Li, and Li Peng$^{(\boxtimes)}$

Engineering Research Center of Internet of Things Technology Applications (Ministry of Education), Jiangnan University, Wuxi 214122, People's Republic of China
jnpengli@126.com

Abstract. In this paper, an event-triggered communication mechanism and fault estimator are co-designed for the nonlinear stochastic system with time-varying delays, both state and sensor saturations. The mean-square boundedness of the error dynamics of state and fault is guaranteed by using stochastic Lyapunov stability. At the same time, a linear matrix inequality technique is exploited to derive the estimator gains and the corresponding event-triggered condition. On the other hand, a strong nonlinear characteristic on measurement is approximated by the radial basis function of neural network. Experimental results demonstrate the potential and effectiveness of the theoretical results.

Keywords: Event-triggered fault estimator · Time-varying delays · State saturations · Sensor saturations

1 Introduction

Motivated by recent achievements in sensor technology and wireless communication, networked dynamics systems (NDSs) have attracted much attention in the past decades. Compared with traditional wired dynamics systems, the advantages of NDSs are less wiring, lower installation cost, and greater operation flexibly in diagnosis and maintenance. However, the increased use of battery-powered wireless sensors in NDSs has some inherent merits, especially power limitation [1–3]. In general, energy consumption for wireless nodes can be utilized via reducing communication actions, which also may decrease the estimation accuracy. Thus, taking estimation performance and energy conservation into consideration is essential in NDSs. An event-triggered communication mechanism has provided an inspiring opportunity for trade-off between estimation performance and energy consumption of nodes in literature [3]. In addition, model-based fault diagnosis is accepted as a powerful tool because of the demand for operation safety and reliability [4]. It was declared in literature that the purpose of fault diagnosis was to detect and estimate system faults when they occurred,

© Springer Nature Singapore Pte Ltd. 2019
S. Shen et al. (Eds.): CWSN 2018, CCIS 984, pp. 117–130, 2019.
https://doi.org/10.1007/978-981-13-6834-9_11

and to identify the fault types and their locations. Recently, the idea of event-triggered communication mechanism has been applied to fault diagnosis to balance between security and energy efficiency. For example, the work [1] focused on how to derive an event-triggered estimator of state and fault against both randomly occurring nonlinearities and randomly occurring packet dropouts.

It is well recognized that most real systems are unknown nonlinear systems. Several excellent results on the state/fault estimation for stochastic nonlinear systems were given in [1, 2]. According to the research about neural network, it has great ability to approximate unknown nonlinear functions. In [5], the problem of distributed adaptive synchronization was solved for unknown nonlinear multi-agent systems in pure-feedback form by utilizing neural networks to approximate the unknown nonlinear dynamics. On the other hand, the state or sensor saturation behaviors for all kinds of systems have attracted much attention in recent years, and some preliminary results related to this emerging topic of research have been reported in the literature, see for example [6,7]. Compared with the existing literature [7,8], the results on state saturation are rare. It is worth mentioning that the nonlinear systems with simultaneous presence of state and sensor saturations have not been fully investigated, although such a phenomenon is quite typical in engineering practice.

In this paper, we aim to address the design problem of event-triggered fault estimator for nonlinear stochastic systems subject to time-varying delays, state and sensor saturations. The contributions of this paper lie in that:

(1) A unified framework is established within which the event-triggered fault estimator for nonlinear stochastic systems can be practical handled against time-varying delays, state and sensor saturations. The proposed event-triggered fault estimator is to estimate system states while simultaneously identifying time-varying actuator faults.

(2) The estimator gains and event conditions are co-derived by using the random Lyapunov operator and linear matrix inequality technique so as to guarantee the mean-square boundedness of estimation error dynamics. Furthermore, the generated event-triggered transmission mechanism can reduce the communication actions for energy conversation.

(3) Radial basis function neural network (RBFNN) is utilized to carry out effective approximation and analysis for strong nonlinear terms in the considered system.

Notations: $\mathbb{N}$ and $\mathbb{R}$ denotes the sets of natural and real numbers respectively. $\mathbb{R}^{m \times n}$ denotes the sets of m by n real-valued matrices, whereas $\mathbb{R}^n$ is short for $\mathbb{R}^{n \times 1}$; $\mathbb{R}_+^{n \times n}$ and $\mathbb{R}_{++}^{n \times n}$ are the sets of $n \times n$ positive semi-definite and positive definite matrices respectively. When $X \in \mathbb{R}_+^{n \times n}$, we simply write $X \geq 0$ (or $X > 0$ if $X \in \mathbb{R}_{++}^{n \times n}$). For $X \in \mathbb{R}^{m \times n}$, X^{T} denotes the transpose of X and $E\{\cdot\}$ denotes the mathematical expectation. For $s \in \mathbb{N}$ and $X \in \mathbb{R}^{m \times n}$, X^s denotes the X to the power s.

2   Problem Statement and Some Preliminaries

2.1   System Description

Consider the following discrete-time stochastic nonlinear systems with time-varying delays

$$
\begin{cases}
x_{k+1} = \sigma_x(x_k^s) + Ff_k + w_k + D\phi(x_k) \\
x_k^s = Ax_k + A_d x_{k-d_k} \\
y_k^s = \sigma_y(y_k) + v_k + N(x_k) \\
y_k = Cx_k
\end{cases}
\tag{1}
$$

where $x_k \in \mathbb{R}^n$ and $f_k \in \mathbb{R}^n$ are the state and fault signals to be estimated, respectively. Measurement output $y_k \in \mathbb{R}^m$, state saturation function $\sigma_x(\cdot) \in \mathbb{R}^n$, and $x_k^s \in \mathbb{R}^n$ represents the ideal system state before the state saturation. $\sigma_y(\cdot) \in \mathbb{R}^m$ is the sensor saturation function and $y_k^s \in \mathbb{R}^m$ represents the ideal sensor measurement output before the sensor saturation. $\phi(\cdot) \in \mathbb{R}^n$ and $N(\cdot) \in \mathbb{R}^m$ are nonlinear terms. A, A_d, C and D are known matrices with appropriate dimensions. Time-varying delay d_k satisfies the following condition:

$$
d_{\min} \le d_k \le d_{\max}
\tag{2}
$$

where $d_{\min}$ and $d_{\max}$ are known scalars. The noise signals, w_k and v_k, satisfy Gaussian with zero-mean and known variance as follows:

$$
w_k \sim N(0, Q_w), \; v_k \sim N(0, R_v)
\tag{3}
$$

Definition 1. *A nonlinear function $\psi : \mathbb{R}^q \rightarrow \mathbb{R}^q$ satisfies the following sector condition if $H_1 \in \mathbb{R}^{r \times r}$ and $H_2 \in \mathbb{R}^{r \times r}$ are real matrices, and H is positive-definite symmetric matrix.*

$$
(\psi(v) - H_1 v)^T (\psi(v) - H_2 v) \le 0, \forall v \in R^r
\tag{4}
$$

where $H = H_2 - H_1 \ge 0$.

In this case, it is concluded that ψ belongs to $[H_1, H_2]$. If there exist diagonal matrices $0 \le K_1 < I \le K_2$ and $0 \le R_1 < I < R_2$; then, the saturation functions $\sigma_x(x_k^s)$ and $\sigma_y(y_k)$ in system (1) can be decomposed into a linear and a nonlinear part as

$$
\sigma_x(x_k^s) = K_1 x_k^s + \psi_x(x_k^s)
\tag{5}
$$

and

$$
\sigma_y(y_k) = R_1 C x_k + \psi_y(y_k)
\tag{6}
$$

where $\psi_x(x_k^s)$ and $\psi_y(y_k)$ satisfy the sector condition mentioned in (4), respectively. For technical convenience, $\psi_x(x_k^s)$ and $\psi_y(y_k)$ can be further described as follows:

$$
\begin{aligned}
\psi_x^T(x_k^s)[\psi_x(x_k^s) - K x_k^s] \le 0 \\
\psi_y^T(y_k)[\psi_y(y_k) - R C x_k] \le 0
\end{aligned}
\tag{7}
$$

where $K = K_2 - K_1 \ge 0$ and $R = R_2 - R_1 \ge 0$.

Before giving the main results, the following assumption is introduced.

Assumption 1. *Nonlinear function $\phi(x_k) \in \mathbb{R}^n$ satisfies the following condition:*

$$\|\phi(S_1) - \phi(S_2)\| \leq \|W(S_1 - S_2)\| \tag{8}$$

Assumption 2. *Fault vector f_k satisfies that*

$$\|f_k\| \leq \sigma_2, \ \forall k \geq 0 \tag{9}$$

where σ_2 is an appropriate positive scalar.

2.2   Radial Basis Function Neural Network

In this paper, the radial basis function neural network (RBFNN) can be employed to approximate sensor nonlinearities, $N(X) : R^n \rightarrow R^m$, as follows:

$$\hat{N}(X) = \hat{W}^T \Phi(X) \tag{10}$$

where $X \in R^n$ and $\hat{N}(X)$ are the input vector and the approximation of unknown nonlinear function $N(X)$; n denotes the neural networks input dimension. $W \in R^{l \times m}$ represents weight matrix, $\hat{W}$ is the estimation of the optimal weight matrix. l denotes the number of neurons, and $\Phi(X) = \begin{bmatrix} \varphi_1 & \varphi_2 & \cdots & \varphi_l \end{bmatrix}$ is the basis function vector with

$$\varphi_i = \exp[\frac{-(X - c_j)^T(X - c_j)}{\delta_i^2}] \ i = 1, 2, \ldots, l \tag{11}$$

where c_j is the center of the receptive field and $(\sqrt{2}\delta_i)/2$ is the width of the Gaussian function. It has been proved that the above RBFNN can approximate any smooth function over a compact set $\Omega_X \subset R^n$ to arbitrarily accuracy [9–11]. For any given positive constant τ providing sufficient neurons, there exists the weight matrix W^* such that

$$N(X) = (W^*)^T \Phi(X) + \tau \tag{12}$$

where τ is the bounded function approximation error satisfying $\|\tau\| \leq \tau_N$.

The optimal matrix W^* is required for analytical purpose, which can be expressed as follows:

$$W^* = \arg \min_{W \in R^{l \times m}} \left\{ \sup_{X \in \Omega_X} \|N(X) - W^T \Phi(X)\| \right\} \tag{13}$$

In system (1), the estimation $\hat{W}$ is used for the function approximation. The estimation of sensor nonlinearities $N(x_k)$ can be given as follows

$$\hat{N}(x_k) = \hat{W}^T \Phi(x_k) \tag{14}$$

For any given positive constant σ_1, training network with sufficient data and providing sufficient neurons, the $N(x_k)$ can achieve the rule:

$$\left\| N(x_k) - \hat{N}(x_k) \right\| \leq \sigma_1 \tag{15}$$

3   Fault Estimation Based on an Event-Triggered Fault Estimator

In this section, an event-triggered fault estimator will be presented and its stability, as well as convergence of fault estimation, will be proven.

3.1   Co-design of a Fault Estimator and an Event Condition

For the purpose of estimating system states and actuator faults, the fault estimator is designed in the following form.

$$\begin{cases} \hat{x}_{k+1} = K_1 A \hat{x}_k + D\phi(\hat{x}_k) + F\hat{f}_k + L_1(y^s_{k,l} - R_1 C \hat{x}_k - N(\hat{x}_k)) \\ \hat{f}_{k+1} = \hat{f}_k + L_2(y^s_{k,l} - R_1 C \hat{x}_k - N(\hat{x}_k)) \end{cases} \tag{16}$$

where $\hat{x}_k$ and $\hat{f}_k$ are the estimated system states and actuator faults, respectively. The matrices L_1 and L_2 are estimator gains to be determined. The previous measurement information $y^s_{k,l}$ is transmitted from sensor to remote fault estimator when new measurement information is not transmitted. In the event-triggered transmission framework, sensor information is not transmitted at each time instant, but transmitted only at the transmission times that are denoted by k_i $i \in \mathbb{N}$. As a result, actual measurement sent to the remote fault estimator module can be described as follows:

$$y^s_{k,l} = y^s_{k_i}, \; k \in [k_i, k_{i+1}), \; k \in \mathbb{N} \tag{17}$$

Furthermore, the event-triggered condition can be expressed as follows

$$(y^s_{k,l} - y^s_k)^T (y^s_{k,l} - y^s_k) \le \delta_1 \tag{18}$$

where δ_1 is the threshold of event-triggered condition. The events are triggered as long as the condition is satisfied. According to (1) and (16), the fault and state estimation errors dynamics can be expressed as follows:

$$\begin{aligned} e_{k+1} &= x_{k+1} - \hat{x}_{k+1} \\ &= K_1(Ax_k + A_d x_{k-d_k}) + \psi_x(x^s_k) + Ff_k \\ &\quad + w_k + D\phi(x_k) - K_1 A\hat{x}_k - D\phi(\hat{x}_k) \\ &\quad - L_1(y^s_k + \Delta_k - R_1 C\hat{x}_k - N(\hat{x}_k)) - F\hat{f}_k \\ &= K_1 Ae_k + K_1 A_d x_{k-d_k} + Fe^f_k + D\phi(e_k) \\ &\quad + w_k + \psi_x(x^s_k) - L_1(\Delta_k + R_1 Ce_k \\ &\quad + \psi_y(y_k) + \Omega_k + v_k) \\ &= (K_1 A - L_1 R_1 C)e_k + Fe^f_k + K_1 A_d x_{k-d_k} \\ &\quad + D\phi(e_k) + w_k + \psi_x(x^s_k) - L_1 \psi_y(y_k) \\ &\quad - L_1 \Omega_k - L_1 v_k - L_1 \Delta_k \end{aligned} \tag{19}$$

where $e_k = x_k - \hat{x}_k$, $\Omega_k = N(x_k) - N(\hat{x}_k)$ and $\Delta_k = y^s_{k,l} - y^s_k$, and

$$
\begin{aligned}
e^f_{k+1} &= f_{k+1} - \hat{f}_{k+1} \\
&= f_{k+1} - \hat{f}_k - L_2(y^s_k + \Delta_k - R_1 C\hat{x}_k) \\
&= f_{k+1} - f_k + e^f_k - L_2(R_1 C x_k + \psi_y(y_k) \\
&\quad + \Delta_k - R_1 C\hat{x}_k - N(\hat{x}_k) + v_k) \\
&= \Delta_{f,k} + e^f_k - L_2 R_1 C e_k - L_2 \psi_y(y_k) - L_2\Delta_k \\
&\quad - L_2\Omega_k - L_2 v_k - L_2\Delta_k - L_2\Omega_k - L_2 v_k
\end{aligned}
\tag{20}
$$

where $e^f_k = f_k - \hat{f}_k$, $\Delta_{f,k} = f_{k+1} - f_k$.

3.2 Stability Analysis

Here, the stability and convergence of the event-triggered fault estimator (16) are proved, and detailed design of estimator gain matrices L_1 and L_2 are discussed.

Theorem 1. *Consider the nonlinear stochastic system (1) subject to time-varying delays, state and sensor saturations. For a given scalar ε_2, if there exist positive definite symmetric matrices $P_i(i = 1,\ldots,4)$ and matrices J_1 J_2 such that the following condition is held*

$$
\Xi = \begin{bmatrix} \Lambda_1 & \Lambda_2 & \Lambda_3 & \Lambda_4 \\ * & -P_1 & 0 & 0 \\ * & * & -P_2 & 0 \\ * & * & * & -P_3 \end{bmatrix} \leq 0
\tag{21}
$$

where

$$
\Lambda_1 = \begin{bmatrix} \Xi_{11} & \Xi_{12} & 0 \\ * & \Xi_{22} & 0 \\ * & * & -I \end{bmatrix}
\tag{22}
$$

$$
\Xi_{11} = \begin{bmatrix} -P_1 & 0 & 0 & 0 & 0 \\ * & -P_2 & 0 & 0 & 0 \\ * & * & -P_4 & 0 & 0 \\ * & * & * & -P_3 & 0 \\ * & * & * & * & -I \end{bmatrix}
\tag{23}
$$

$$
\Xi_{12} = \frac{1}{2}\begin{bmatrix} 0 & 0 & 0 & 0 & 0 \\ 0 & 0 & 0 & 0 & 0 \\ 0 & 0 & C^T R^T & A^T K^T & 0 \\ 0 & 0 & 0 & A^T_d & 0 \\ 0 & 0 & 0 & 0 & 0 \end{bmatrix}
\tag{24}
$$

$$
\Xi_{22} = \begin{bmatrix} -\frac{1}{\delta_1}I & 0 & 0 & 0 & 0 \\ * & -I & 0 & 0 & 0 \\ * & * & -I & 0 & 0 \\ * & * & * & -I & 0 \\ * & * & * & * & -I \end{bmatrix}
\tag{25}
$$

$$\Lambda_2 = [P_1 K_1 A - J_1 R_1 C, \ P_1 F, \ 0, \ P_1 K_1 A_d,$$
$$-J_1, \ -J_1, \ P_1 D, \ 0, \ -J_1, \ P_1, \ 0, \ 0]^T \tag{26}$$

$$\Lambda_3 = [-J_2 R_1 C, \ P_2, \ 0, \ 0, \ -J_2, \ -J_2, \ 0, \ 0, \ -J_2, \ 0, \ 0, \ P_2]^T \tag{27}$$

$$\Lambda_4 = [0, \ 0, \ P_3 K_1 A, \ P_3 K_1 A_d, \ 0, \ 0, \ 0, \ P_3 D, \ 0, \ P_3, \ P_3 F, \ 0]^T \tag{28}$$

and $\varepsilon_2 = \sigma_1^2 + 2\sigma_2^2 + trace\,(Q_w P_1) + trace\,(R_v L_1^T P_1 L_1) + trace\,(R_v L_2^T P_2 L_2) + \delta_1$. *Then the presented event-triggered fault estimator (16) can realize that state estimation error and fault estimation error are mean-square bounded. Moreover, the estimator gains can be calculated by $L_1 = P_1^{-1} J_1$ and $L_2 = P_2^{-1} J_2$.*

Proof. The proof is given in the Appendix.

4 Experimental Simulation

Now we are in a position to verify the effectiveness of proposed event-triggered fault estimation involving a water-tank system. The dynamic model of the water-tank system borrowed from [3] is obtained as follows

$$\begin{bmatrix} h_{k+1}^{(1)} \\ h_{k+1}^{(2)} \end{bmatrix} = \begin{bmatrix} 0.99016 & 0.0024 \\ 0.0024 & 1.12047 \end{bmatrix} \begin{bmatrix} h_k^{(1)} \\ h_k^{(2)} \end{bmatrix} + \begin{bmatrix} 0.0145 \\ 0 \end{bmatrix} q^{(in)} + w_k \tag{29}$$

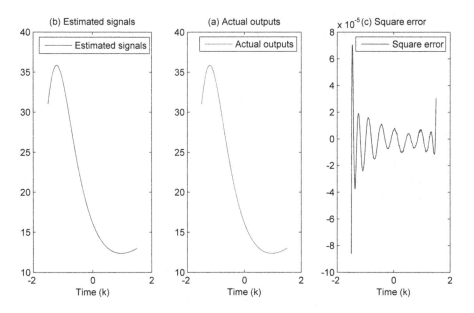

Fig. 1. Actual and estimated curves for nonlinear term $N(x_k)$. (Color figure online)

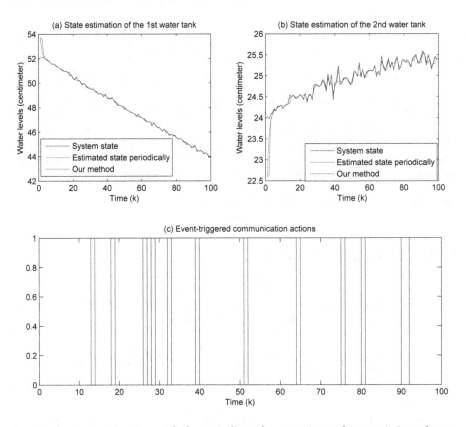

Fig. 2. The state estimation with the periodic and event-triggered transmission scheme.

$$\begin{bmatrix} y_k^{(1)} \\ y_k^{(2)} \end{bmatrix} = \begin{bmatrix} 1 & 0 \\ 0 & 1 \end{bmatrix} \begin{bmatrix} h_k^{(1)} \\ h_k^{(2)} \end{bmatrix} + v_k \tag{30}$$

where $h_k^{(1)}$ and $h_k^{(2)}$ are the water level of two tanks, $y_k^{(1)}$ and $y_k^{(2)}$ are the measurement outputs of the water level transmitters, $q^{(in)}$ represents input water flow, w_k and v_k are mutually independent zero mean white noise. According to the technical specifications of water level sensors [3], the error covariances of noise are specified as follows

$$Q_w = \begin{bmatrix} 1 & 0 \\ 0 & 1 \end{bmatrix}, \ R_v = \begin{bmatrix} 0.25 & 0 \\ 0 & 0.25 \end{bmatrix} \tag{31}$$

The saturation functions $\sigma_x\left(x_k^s\right)$ and $\sigma_y\left(y_k\right)$ are described as follows

$$\sigma_x\left(x_k^s\right) = \begin{cases} x_{\max}^s, & if \ 0.8x_k^s > x_{\max}^s \\ 0.8x_k^s, & if \ -x_{\max}^s \le 0.8x_k^s \le x_{\max}^s \\ -x_{\max}^s, & if \ 0.8x_k^s < -x_{\max}^s \end{cases} \tag{32}$$

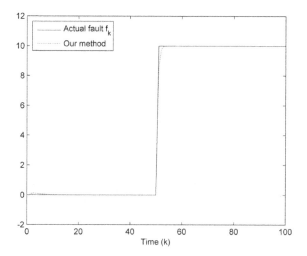

Fig. 3. Estimated signals of a constant fault.

and

$$\sigma_y\left(y_k\right) = \begin{cases} y_{\max}, & if\ 0.75y_k > y_{\max} \\ 0.75y_k, & if\ -y_{\max} \leq 0.75y_k \leq y_{\max} \\ -y_{\max}, & if\ 0.75y_k < -y_{\max} \end{cases} \tag{33}$$

The nonlinear functions are chosen to be

$$\phi(x_k) = 0.12sin\left(3e^{-2k}\right)$$
$$N\left(x_k\right) = 20 + k^2 - 10\cos\left(e^{-k}\right) + e^{-k} + \frac{1}{k+2} \tag{34}$$

Furthermore, other parameters are taken as $A_d = \begin{bmatrix} 0.1 & 0 \\ 0.12 & 0.3 \end{bmatrix}$, $F = D = \begin{bmatrix} 1 \\ 1 \end{bmatrix}$, $d_{\min} = 1$, $d_{\max} = 3$ and $K = R = 0.2$. We provide one solution by solving LMI (21) and obtain the estimator gains as follows:

$$L_1 = \begin{bmatrix} 0.6162 & 0.0014 \\ 0.0014 & 0.8123 \end{bmatrix}, \ L_2 = \begin{bmatrix} 0.628 & 0.573 \end{bmatrix} \tag{35}$$

Following radial basis function neural network, the reconstructed nonlinear term $N\left(x_k\right)$ is illustrated in Fig. 1 where the red, blue and black lines are the actual outputs, the estimated signals and the square estimation error, respectively. It means that the presented RBFNN can accurately track original nonlinear signals.

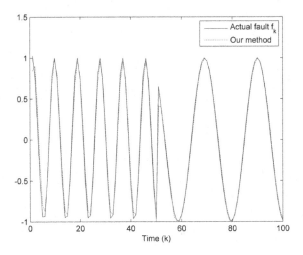

Fig. 4. Estimated signals of a time-varying fault.

For the system without actuator faults, the state estimation with the periodic and event-triggered transmission are shown in Fig. 2 who also depict the corresponding event-triggered communication actions. It can be observed from Fig. 2 that the proposed event-triggered fault estimator can achieve state estimation robustly. Compared with the periodic transmission scheme, the proposed event-triggered mechanism can reduce the use of resources by 10%.

In order to verify the performance of fault estimation, two fault scenarios are created as follows:

$$f_k = \begin{cases} 0 & k < 50 \\ 10 & k \geq 50 \end{cases} \tag{36}$$

$$f_k = \begin{cases} \cos{(0.7k)} & k < 50 \\ \sin{(0.3k)} & k \geq 50 \end{cases} \tag{37}$$

The simulated curves are described in Figs. 3 and 4 for the system subject to constant fault (36) and time-varying fault (37). One can see that two lines are almost coincident as time increases. Obviously, the fault estimation accuracy is not affected by the proposed communication mechanism which is not aperiodical transmission of data.

Making comparison among Figs. 2, 3 and 4, one can see that the state estimation performance are always desired no matter whether the event is triggered or not. This point is also supported by comparing the fault estimation curves under different fault environments. Consequently, the fault estimator can work well via our algorithm.

5   Conclusion

In this work, an event-triggered fault estimator were designed for the nonlinear stochastic system with time-varying delays, saturations in both state and sensor. With the help of the stochastic Lyapunov function and linear matrix inequality technique, the mean-square boundedness of the error dynamics of state and fault was ensured, while the estimator gains and event condition were also derived. On the other hand, a strong nonlinear characteristic on measurement was approximated via the radial basis function of neural network. Experimental simulations demonstrated the potential and effectiveness of the theoretical results. These researches in this work will suggest a new way for event-triggered fault estimation, which has an important theoretical references and practical significance.

Acknowledgments. This work is supported by National Key R&D Program of China (No. 2018YFD0400900); Video Big Data Analysis and IoT Interaction Technology Research (No. MCM20170204), respectively.

Appendix A

Proof of Theorem 1

Define the following Lyapunov function

$$
V_k = V_{k_1} + V_{k_2} + V_{k_3} + \sum_{i=k-d_k}^{k-1} x_i^T P_3 x_i
$$

$$
+ \sum_{j=k-d_{\max}+1}^{k-d_{\min}} \sum_{i=j}^{k-1} x_i^T P_3 x_i
\tag{38}
$$

where

$$
V_{k_1} = e_k^T P_1 e_k \tag{39}
$$

$$
V_{k_2} = (e_k^f)^T P_2 e_k^f \tag{40}
$$

$$
V_{k_3} = x_k^T P_4 x_k \tag{41}
$$

and $P_i (i = 1, \ldots, 4)$ are positive definite symmetric matrices. Along the trajectories of (19) and (20), we have

$$
\begin{aligned}
E\{\Delta V_k\} &= E\{V_{k+1} - V_k\} \\
&= E\{\Delta V_{k_1} + \Delta V_{k_2} + \Delta V_{k_3} - x_{k-d_k}^T P_3 x_{k-d_k} \\
&\quad + (d_{\max} - d_{\min} + 1)x_k^T P_3 x_k\}
\end{aligned}
\tag{42}
$$

where,

$$
\begin{aligned}
\Delta V_{k_1} &= e_{k+1}^T P_1 e_{k+1} - e_k^T P_1 e_k \\
&= -e_k^T P_1 e_k + e_k^T (K_1 A - L_1 R_1 C)^T P_1 (K_1 A - L_1 R_1 C) e_k \\
&\quad + (e_k^f)^T F^T P_1 F e_k^f + x_{k-d_k}^T A_d^T K_1^T P_1 K_1 A_d x_{k-d_k} + \phi^T (e_k) D^T P_1 D \phi(e_k) \\
&\quad + \psi_x^T (x_k^s) P_1 \psi_x(x_k^s) + \psi_y^T (y_k) L_1^T P_1 L_1 \psi_y(y_k) + \Omega_k^T L_1^T P_1 L_1 \Omega_k \\
&\quad + \Delta_k^T L_1^T P_1 L_1 \Delta_k + w_k^T P_1 w_k + v_k^T L_1^T P_1 L_1 v_k \\
&\quad + 2(e_k^f)^T F^T P_1 (K_1 A - L_1 R_1 C) e_k + 2 x_{k-d_k}^T A_d^T K_1^T P_1 (K_1 A - L_1 R_1 C) e_k \\
&\quad + 2\phi^T (e_k) D^T P_1 (K_1 A - L_1 R_1 C) e_k + 2\psi_x^T (x_k^s) P_1 (K_1 A - L_1 R_1 C) e_k \\
&\quad - 2\psi_y^T (y_k) L_1^T P_1 (K_1 A - L_1 R_1 C) e_k - 2\Omega_k^T L_1^T P_1 (K_1 A - L_1 R_1 C) e_k \\[6pt]
&\quad - 2\Delta_k^T L_1^T P_1 (K_1 A - L_1 R_1 C) e_k + 2 x_{k-d_k}^T A_d^T K_1^T P_1 F e_k^f \\
&\quad + 2\phi^T (e_k) D^T P_1 F e_k^f + 2\psi_x^T (x_k^s) P_1 F e_k^f - 2\psi_y^T (y_k) L_1^T P_1 F e_k^f \\
&\quad - 2\Omega_k^T L_1^T P_1 F e_k^f - 2\Delta_k^T L_1^T P_1 F e_k^f + 2\phi^T (e_k) D^T P_1 K_1 A_d x_{k-d_k} \\
&\quad + 2\psi_x^T (x_k^s) P_1 K_1 A_d x_{k-d_k} - 2\psi_y^T (y_k) L_1^T P_1 K_1 A_d x_{k-d_k} \\
&\quad - 2\Omega_k^T L_1^T P_1 K_1 A_d x_{k-d_k} - 2\Delta_k^T L_1^T P_1 K_1 A_d x_{k-d_k} \\
&\quad + 2\psi_x^T (x_k^s) P_1 D \phi(e_k) - 2\psi_y^T (y_k) L_1^T P_1 D \phi(e_k) \\
&\quad - 2\Omega_k^T L_1^T P_1 D \phi(e_k) - 2\Delta_k^T L_1^T P_1 D \phi(e_k) \\
&\quad - 2\psi_y^T (y_k) L_1^T P_1 \psi_x(x_k^s) - 2\Omega_k^T L_1^T P_1 \psi_x(x_k^s) - 2\Delta_k^T L_1^T P_1 \psi_x(x_k^s) \\
&\quad + 2\Omega_k^T L_1^T P_1 L_1 \psi_y(y_k) + 2\Delta_k^T L_1^T P_1 L_1 \psi_y(y_k) + 2\Delta_k^T L_1^T P_1 L_1 \Omega_k
\end{aligned}
\tag{43}
$$

$$
\begin{aligned}
\Delta V_{k_2} &= (e_{k+1}^f)^T P_2 e_{k+1}^f - (e_k^f)^T P_2 e_k^f \\
&= -(e_k^f)^T P_2 e_k^f + \Delta_{f,k}^T P_2 \Delta_{f,k} + (e_k^f)^T P_2 e_k^f + e_k^T C^T R_1^T L_2^T P_2 L_2 R_1 C e_k \\
&\quad + \psi_y^T (y_k) L_2^T P_2 L_2 \psi_y(y_k) + \Delta_k^T L_2^T P_2 L_2 \Delta_k + \Omega_k^T L_2^T P_2 L_2 \Omega_k \\
&\quad + v_k^T L_2^T P_2 L_2 v_k + 2(e_k^f)^T P_2 \Delta_{f,k} - 2 e_k^T C^T R_1^T L_2^T P_2 \Delta_{f,k} \\
&\quad - 2\psi_y^T (y_k) L_2^T P_2 \Delta_{f,k} - 2\Delta_k^T L_2^T P_2 \Delta_{f,k} - 2\Omega_k^T L_2^T P_2 \Delta_{f,k} \\
&\quad - 2 e_k^T C^T R_1^T L_2^T P_2 e_k^f - 2\psi_y^T (y_k) L_2^T P_2 e_k^f - 2\Delta_k^T L_2^T P_2 e_k^f - 2\Omega_k^T L_2^T P_2 e_k^f \\
&\quad + 2\psi_y^T (y_k) L_2^T P_2 L_2 R_1 C e_k + 2\Delta_k^T L_2^T P_2 L_2 R_1 C e_k + 2\Omega_k^T L_2^T P_2 L_2 R_1 C e_k \\
&\quad + 2\Delta_k^T L_2^T P_2 L_2 \psi_y(y_k) + 2\Omega_k^T L_2^T P_2 L_2 \psi_y(y_k) + 2\Omega_k^T L_2^T P_2 L_2 \Delta_k
\end{aligned}
\tag{44}
$$

and

$$
\begin{aligned}
\Delta V_{k_3} &= x_{k+1}^T P_4 x_{k+1} - x_k^T P_4 x_k \\
&= -x_k^T P_4 x_k + x_k^T A^T K_1^T P_4 K_1 A x_k + x_{k-d_k}^T A_d^T K_1^T P_4 K_1 A_d x_{k-d_k} \\
&\quad + \phi^T(x_k) D^T P_4 D \phi(x_k) + \psi_x^T(x_k^s) P_4 \psi_x(x_k^s) + f_k^T F^T P_4 F f_k + w_k^T P_4 w_k \\
&\quad + 2 x_{k-d_k}^T A_d^T K_1^T P_4 K_1 A x_k + 2 \phi^T(x_k) D^T P_4 K_1 A x_k + 2 \psi_x^T(x_k^s) P_4 K_1 A x_k \\
&\quad + 2 f_k^T F^T P_4 K_1 A x_k + 2 \phi^T(x_k) D^T P_4 K_1 A_d x_{k-d_k} \\
&\quad + 2 \psi_x^T(x_k^s) P_4 K_1 A_d x_{k-d_k} + 2 f_k^T F^T P_4 K_1 A_d x_{k-d_k} \\
&\quad + 2 \psi_x^T(x_k^s) P_4 D \phi(x_k) + 2 f_k^T F^T P_4 D \phi(x_k) \\
&\quad + 2 f_k^T F^T P_4 \psi_x(x_k^s)
\end{aligned}
\tag{45}
$$

With the help of Gaussian noise (3), state and sensor saturation conditions (7), fault assumption (9), nonlinear approximation function (15) and event condition (18), one can obtain that

$$
\begin{aligned}
E\{\Delta V_k\} &\le \sigma_1^2 + 2\sigma_2^2 + 1 + \eta_k^T \Xi \eta_k \\
&\le \varepsilon_2 + \eta_k^T \Xi \eta_k
\end{aligned}
\tag{46}
$$

where
$\varepsilon_2 = \sigma_1^2 + 2\sigma_2^2 + trace\,(Q_w P_1) + trace\,(R_v L_1^T P_1 L_1) + trace\,(R_v L_2^T P_2 L_2) + \delta_1$.
The vector η_k can be written in the following form:

$$
\begin{aligned}
\eta_k = \Big[& e_k^T,\ (e_k^f)^T,\ x_k^T,\ x_{k-d_k}^T,\ \Omega_k^T,\ \Delta_k^T,\ \phi^T(e_k), \\
& \phi^T(x_k),\ \psi_y^T(y_k),\ \psi_x^T(x_k^s),\ f_k,\ \Delta_{f,k} \Big]
\end{aligned}
\tag{47}
$$

It follows that $E\{\Delta V_k\} < 0$ for $\lambda_{\min}(-\Xi)\,\hat{\eta}_k^T \hat{\eta}_k > \varepsilon_2$. It means that the trajectory of $\hat{\eta}_k$ that is outside of a small set $\Theta = \left\{ \hat{\eta}_k \,\middle|\, \hat{\eta}_k^T \hat{\eta}_k \le \frac{\varepsilon_2}{\lambda_{\min}(-\Xi)} \right\}$ will converge to this set Θ according to the stochastic Lyapunov stability theory; thus, $\hat{\eta}_k$ is mean-square bounded.

References

1. Li, Y.J., Peng, L.: Event-triggered fault estimation for stochastic systems over multi-hop relay networks with randomly occurring sensor nonlinearities and packet dropouts. Sensors **18**(3), 731:1–731:22 (2018)
2. Li, Y.J., QingE, W., Peng, L.: Simultaneous event-triggered fault detection and estimation for stochastic systems subject to deception attacks. Sensors 18(2), 321:1–321:25 (2018)
3. Li, Y.J., Peng, L., Chen, W.: An energy-efficient data transmission scheme for remote state estimation and applications to a water-tank system. ISA Trans. **70**, 494–501 (2017)
4. Mahdi Alavi, S.M., Saif, M.: Fault detection in nonlinear stable systems over lossy networks. IEEE Trans. Control Syst. Technol. **21**(6), 2129–2142 (2013)

5. Cui, G., Zhuang, G., Lu, J.: Neural-network-based distributed adaptive synchro-nization for nonlinear multi-agent systems in pure-feedback form. Neurocomputing **218**, 234–241 (2016)
6. Ding, D., Wang, Z., Jun, H., et al.: Dissipative control for state-saturated discrete time-varying systems with randomly occurring nonlinearities and missing measure-ments. Int. J. Control **86**(4), 674–688 (2013)
7. Wen, C., Wang, Z., Hu, J., et al.: Recursive filtering for state- saturated systems with randomly occurring nonlinearities and missing measurements. Int. J. Robust Nonlinear Control **28**(5), 1715–1727 (2017)
8. Wang, Z., Ho, D.W.C., Dong, H., et al.: Robust H∞ finite-horizon control for a class of stochastic nonlinear time-varying systems subject to sensor and actuator saturations. IEEE Trans. Autom. Control **55**(7), 1716–1722 (2010)
9. Cheng, L., Hou, Z.G., Tan, M., et al.: Neural-network-based adaptive leader-following control for multiagent systems with uncertainties. IEEE Trans. Neural Netw. **21**(8), 1351 (2010)
10. Wen, G.X., Chen, C.L.P., Liu, Y.J., Liu, Z.: Neural network-based adaptive leader-following consensus control for a class of nonlinear multiagent state-delay systems. IEEE Trans. Cybern. **47**(8), 2151–2160 (2017)
11. Wen, G.X., Chen, C.L.P., Liu, Y.J., Liu, Z.: Neural-network-based adaptive leader-following consensus control for second-order non-linear multi-agent systems. IET Control Theor. Appl. **9**(13), 1927–1934 (2015)

Research on Human Behavior Recognition Based on Convolutional Neural Network

Pengkun Ma$^{(\boxtimes)}$, Tong Zou, and Yuejie Wang

School of Information Science and Technology,
Northwest University, Xi'an, China
mpk980126@qq.com, 894155838@qq.com, 454917996@qq.com

Abstract. The traditional human behavior recognition technology mainly includes sign point action recognition technology and recognition technology based on motion sensor parameters. The former's error is very large and the latter's recognition speed is slow as well as the accuracy is very low. In this paper, a method of recognition of depth learning behavior based on convolutional neural network is proposed to identify different behaviors (jogging, walking, running, upstairs, downstairs, sitting) with different location of mobile phone (arm, waist, pocket, wrist), collecting a large amount of data by using the built-in sensor of the mobile phone. The data are standardized, normalized and window segmentation, and then the data are divided into testing set and training set. Establish a convolutional neural network learning model to extract local feature structure and combine supervised learning mode, use training set for training, and then use testing set for classifying and evaluating. Through experiments, in the common movements and different placement positions, the accuracy is more than 94%, and the effect of high speed and high accuracy to identify human behavior is achieved.

Keywords: Behavior recognition · Deep learning ·
Convolutional neural network · Feature extraction

1 Introduction

With the progress and development of science and technology, human behavior recognition technology is used in various research fields, such as video image processing [1], intelligent monitoring [2], medical health [3], driving safety [4] and so on. Because of the diversity and complexity of human behavior, the identification results are also uncertain. Nowadays, smart phones have been widely popularized, and human behavior recognition technology based on mobile phone built-in sensors arises at the historic moment. Because of the small size of the mobile phone, it is convenient to carry, and its built-in sensors are becoming more and more diverse, such as acceleration sensor, gyroscope sensor, light sensor, temperature sensor, GPS [5] and so on. In recent years, because of the rise of artificial intelligence, neural network has shown amazing effects in the application of recognition and classification. Therefore, our research on human behavior recognition technology based on cell phone sensors and convolutional neural network has important practical value and scientific significance.

© Springer Nature Singapore Pte Ltd. 2019
S. Shen et al. (Eds.): CWSN 2018, CCIS 984, pp. 131–144, 2019.
https://doi.org/10.1007/978-981-13-6834-9_12

The main contributions of this article are as follows:

(1) We propose a deep learning behavior recognition method based on convolutional neural network, which has fast training speed and high training accuracy.
(2) For mobile phones, different placement methods and locations all have higher recognition accuracy and universality.

2   Related Work

We put the mobile phone in different positions and different posture on the body, and carry on different movements (jogging, walking, running, upstairs, downstairs, sitting), using the acceleration sensor, the gravity sensor and the gyroscope built in the mobile phone to obtain the large amount of motion data in the three directions of XYZ, use the convolutional neural network for training. By experiments, draw different classification training results.

There are a lot of methods for human behavior recognition. In 2016, Hiram Ponce and others proposed a method based on artificial hydrocarbon network (AHN) identification in literature [6]. The recognition accuracy is up to 98.29% under the condition of non noise interference and data integrity, but the process is complicated and difficult to understand and operate. In 2015 Liu [7] proposed a multi-layer model (Time Series Shapelets) using the shape of time series to identify complex human behavior such as playing basketball, but the accuracy of recognition is low and the highest accuracy rate of jumping action is 80.95%. In 2016, Cihang Liu and others adopted the Lasagna frame, the condition limited Boltzmann machine (CRBM) is used for depth learning and training [8]. The classification accuracy is up to 92%, but the parameters of the condition limited Boltzmann machine are difficult to adjust, and it is not easy to achieve a relatively ideal state. In 2016, Donghui Wu and others proposed a hybrid kernel based weighted limit learning machine (MK-WELM) method, with an average precision of more than 90%, which solved the problems caused by unbalanced data. However, a large number of balanced data in the normal environment were too complex and limited [9].

The method adopted in this paper has the characteristics of more simpler than AHN, stronger universality than MK-WELM, simpler parameter adjustment than Lasagna frame and higher recognition accuracy than the Time Series Shapelets model. Convolutional neural network is a kind of deep supervised training machine learning model [10], which is convenient to learning.

3   Conceptual Design

The general process of behavior recognition based on mobile sensor is as follows (Fig. 1). First, it preprocesses the collected sensor data, eliminates the noise influence, and facilitates the feature learning and model evaluation of the post sequence, and then studies the characteristics of the data of the sensors under different placement positions by neural network and classifies it. Finally, evaluate model and summary.

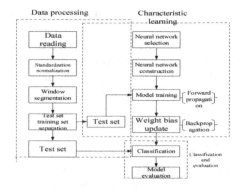

Fig. 1. Conceptual design

3.1 Data Preprocessing

Standard normalization: Because the collected data are influenced by the hardware equipment and the acquisition environment, it will produce data noise and disturb our experiment, so we need to standardize and normalize the data and eliminate the noise effect. The way of processing is as follows: after reading data, each axis data of each sensor set dataset is processed as follows:

$$dataset* = \frac{dataset - mu}{sigma} \tag{1}$$

In the formula (1), *mu* is the mean value of the axis, and *sigma* is the standard deviation of the axis. This method is used to standardize and normalize data.

Window segmentation: Due to the huge amount of data we have collected, and the labels are not uniform, all of them are put into the neural network at one time are easily confused. So we divide our data into one by one windows. The way of dividing the window is as follows: the normalized data set is divided into windows, each window contains three sensors, 90 consecutive data of three axes, in order to prevent the effect of data segmentation on the edge data, the window combines the combined window with the dynamic window, and slides in 50% overlapping ways (like Fig. 2).

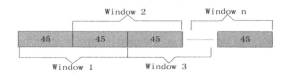

Fig. 2. Window segmentation

Finally, label the data with the most frequent occurrence in each window as the label of the group.

Data set separation: There are two uses for our data. One is used for training the model, the other is used for testing the performance of the model. In order to better training the model and evaluating the performance of the model, we will divide the data set in the windows, separate the training set and the testing set with the rate of 7:3 for subsequent use.

3.2   Characteristic Learning

Selection of neural networks: At present, several of the main neural networks are the following: the convolutional neural network (CNN), the recurrent neural network (RNN), the deep neural network (DNN) and the automatic encoder (AE) [11].

Considering that the amount of our data is great, the parameters are very large and all are labeled data, we need to use supervised learning, so we use the convolution neural network (CNN) with local connection, weight sharing and down sampling. It can reduce a lot of parameters, improve the learning rate and robustness of the model. It's very suitable for our experiments.

Neural network construction: The convolution neural network has a lot of super parameters, the structure and the number of layers also have a variety of combinations and changes. So we build the following structure convolution neural network (Fig. 3) by reading a lot of literature, drawing on the experience of the predecessors and combining our own test experiments.

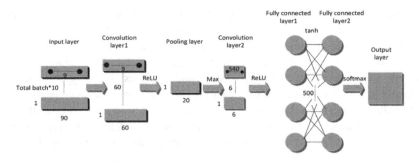

Fig. 3. Construction of CNN model

Input layer design: our input data is non picture type, without height, so the height of the input layer is set to 1, and the width (width) is set to the window size (width = 90). The number of channels (num_chennels) corresponds to the 3 axes of the 3 sensors, each axis is a channel and a total of 9 channels. Since the amount of data after the division is still much, and the labels are different, we will do batch processing, each of which contains 10 windows (that is, batch_size = 10). Then a batch of data are convoluted (Fig. 4).

Convolution layer design: the first convolution layer, the convolution kernel size (kernel_size) is defined as the 2/3 of the window (kernel_size = 60), and the number of convolution kernel (that is, the depth) is also fixed as 60, and the number of channels (num_chennels) is the same as the number of channels in the input layer. The kernel size and number of the second convolution layers are set to the first layer of 1/10, the number of channels is the product of the number of channels and numbers of the first layer (num_chennels*depth). The calculation here is related to convolution methods, The convolution methods often used in CNN is: common convolution: any number of convolution nuclear do convolution operations on different channels at the same time. Deep convolution: an arbitrary number of convolution nuclear do independently convolution operations on one's own channel; separation convolution: point by point convolution after the first deep convolution. Comparing the three convolution methods, we can find that when the common convolution method is used, first weighted to sum and then convoluted (or first convoluted then weighted to sum, and the result is the same). While the deep convolution is each channel independently use their own convolution nuclear do convolution operations without weighted and sum, the separation convolution is a convolution using several convolution kernel. First, do deep convolution, then use 1×1 convolution kernel again to do common convolution. The data used in our experiment are 3 axis data of 3 sensors. Each axis is a channel. There are no obvious connection between each axis and have independent features. Finally, the pool layer [12] can be used to reduce the dimension again. So this paper will use the deep convolution method. After convoluting, the total number of channels becomes num_chennels*depth.

After the convolution is completed, we need the activation function to activate. In the neural network, the function of the activation function is to add some nonlinear factors to the neural network, so that the neural network can better solve the more complex problems. At present, there are several common activation functions: Sigmoid function [13] tanh function [14] and ReLU function [15],in these three activation functions, ReLU has the fastest convergence speed, and can effectively alleviate the problem of gradient disappearance. It has good convergence performance, and it has good effect in unsupervised training and practice [16]. The sparse expression ability can fit well with the characteristics of the convolution neural network, while tanh and sigmoid are worse than ReLU in these aspects, but their optimization performance is relatively stable, and there is no neuron death, and no the weight can not be updated, but the ReLU could be in this situation. In the Convolution layer, the amount of input data is huge and the gradient is easy to disappear. In order to speed up the training speed of the model, we need faster convergence speed and better convergence performance, so we choose ReLU as the activation function of the Convolution layer. The calculation formula can be obtained as follows:

$$a^{i,l} = ReLU\left(\sigma\left(W^l * a^{i,l-1} + b^l\right)\right) \tag{2}$$

In the formula (2), a is the input data, i represents the i neuron, l represents the number of layers, w is the weight, and b is the bias. The formula in the latter part involves all these variables have same means.

Pool layer design: the pool operation uses a matrix window to scan the data entered in the convolution layer, and reduces the number of elements by taking the maximum value, average value or other methods in each matrix window, in order to achieve the effect of reducing parameter and feature extraction and maintaining invariance. The size of the matrix window for each pool operation is specified by ksize, and we set ksize as the 1/3 of the first convolution layer kernel convolution kernel size (that is, ksize = 20). The pooling operation determines the mobile step length according to the step length (strides). We set the strides to 2. The main ways of pooling are the following: average pooling: calculating the average of the elements in the pool area; maximum pooling: calculating the maximum of the elements in the pool area. Boureau and others put forward [17]. The error of feature extraction mainly comes from two aspects: the estimated value variance of the neighborhood size is increased; the convolution layer parameter error causes the offset of the estimated mean. The pool mode of the average pooling can reduce the error of the former, and the maximum pooling can reduce the latter. Because of the huge amount of our experimental parameters, second kinds of errors are mainly caused. In order to minimize the error, this paper will use the maximum pooling method to carry out the pool operation. The formula can be obtained as follows:

$$a^{i,l} = \max(a^{i,l-1}) \tag{3}$$

Fully Connected Layer [18] Design: The first fully connected is used to connect all the features, that is to expand and weight the previously learned features. The expansion formula is as follows:

$$a^{i,l} = \sigma(W^l a^{i,l-1} + b^l) \tag{4}$$

Owning to the number of neurons in this layer is large and does not share the weight reduction parameters, the probability of neuron death is larger. Based on the discussion of the activation function, we use a more stable method, tanh as the activation function, and then pass the data to second full connection layers. The second fully connected layer is equivalent to the classifier, and the result is output after the classification is finished. There are two kinds of activation functions commonly used for classification: softmax and logistic. Softmax is used with multi classification, logistic is used with binary classification. There are 6 kinds of motion patterns in our experimental data, which are multiple classifications, so softmax is used as the activation function of this layer. The output formula is:

$$a^{i,l} = soft\max(W^l a^{i,l-1} + b^l) \tag{5}$$

The hidden neurons (num_hiddens) of these two full connection layers are not well determined, because the more hidden neurons in the whole connection layer, the larger the model, the slower the speed, the higher the model fitting ability, the higher the accuracy of the training set, but the greater the risk of overfitting. On the contrary, the fewer neurons in the whole connection layer, the smaller the model and the faster the speed. The lower the model fitting ability, the lower the accuracy rate on the training set.

To solve this problem, we first set the num_hiddens to 1000. After the model is completed, we will test it and find out the appropriate num_hiddens.

3.3   Reverse Propagation

Weight and bias update: The data is input into the neural network and then convoluting, pooling, connecting and to the final output. This process is called the forward propagation process. If the value of the forward propagation output is not up to the desired output value, the forward propagation is turned back to the back propagation, and the error sensitivity is calculated layer by layer. If the current is a fully connected layer, the formula is:

$$\delta^{i,l} = (W^{l+1})^T \delta^{i,l+1} \sigma'(z^{i,l})$$

(6)

In the formula (6), the error sensitivity is δ, and the transposition is T, the z is input. If the current is a convolution layer, the formula is:

$$\delta^{i,l} = \delta^{i,l+1} * rot180(W^{l+1})\sigma'(z^{i,l})$$

(7)

In the formula (7), *rot180* represents the rotation of the matrix by 180°.
If the current is a pool layer, the formula is as follows:

$$\delta^{i,l} = upsample(\delta^{i,l+1})\sigma'(z^{i,l})$$

(8)

In the formula (8), upsample is the process of restoring the size of the matrix before pooling. Using error sensitivity as the basis for modifying weights, multiple iterations are repeated to modify weights and bias. The formula for modifying the weight and bias are:

Fully connected layer:

$$W^l = W^l - \alpha \sum_{i=1}^{m} \delta^{i,l}(a^{i,l-1})^T$$

(9)

$$b^l = b^l - \alpha \sum_{i-1}^{m} \delta^{i,l}$$

(10)

In the formula (10), α is iterative strides.

Convolution layer:

$$W^l = W^l - \alpha \sum_{i=1}^{m} \delta^{i,l} * \text{rot}180(a^{i,l-1})^T \tag{11}$$

$$b^l = b^l - \alpha \sum_{i=1}^{m} \sum_{u,v} (\delta^{i,l})_{u,v} \tag{12}$$

After modifying the weight and bias until the error reaches the desired value, or when the specified number of iterations is reached, the network learning is finished and the model training is completed.

Iterative method and learning rate: The iterative method is mainly used to reduce the loss between the model output and the real output. The good iteration method can reduce the number of iterations and the amount of calculation, so that we can find the optimal weight and the combination of bias faster. There are two iterative methods: Random gradient descent [19] and gradient descent [20]. The calculation of the cost function of the gradient descent method needs to traverse all the samples and traversing each iteration until the local optimal solution is reached. This method's amount of calculation is very large and the speed of convergence is slow when the sample size is large. Random gradient descent is a random sampling instead of a complete sample. That is to choose a point randomly to do gradient descent instead of traversing all samples. The main function of this method is to improve the speed of iteration and avoid getting into huge computation, but it can only be solved with the minimum value of the current sample point, and it usually can not reach the real local optimal solution, but it can be close. The amount of data used in our experiments is very large, for conveniently, the method of random gradient descent is more appropriate.

Learning rate controls the speed of adjusting neural network weights based on the loss gradient. The smaller the learning rate, the slower the descent along the gradient. On the contrary, if the rate of decline is too fast, it is easy to miss the optimal value. In order to be safe, we choose 0.0001 as the learning rate. In the follow-up experiment, we found that using 0.0001 learning rate could complete the module training in 30 min, so there was no need to improve the learning rate.

3.4   Classification and Model Evaluation

The previously separated test set is put into the trained model and classified. After sorting, the classification result is judged by the confusion matrix.

In the process of classification, there are four kinds of decisions:
TP: It is judged to be a positive sample, and in fact it is also a sample.
FP: It is judged to be a positive sample, but in fact it is a negative sample.
TN: It is judged to be a negative sample, and in fact it is also a negative sample.
FN: It is judged to be a negative sample, but in fact it is a positive sample

AS the formulas show:

$$precision = \frac{TP}{TP + FP} \tag{13}$$

$$recall = \frac{TP}{TP + FN} \tag{14}$$

$$accuracy = \frac{TP + TN}{TP + FP + TN + FN} \tag{15}$$

$$f1\_score = \frac{2 * precision * recall}{precision + recall} \tag{16}$$

These values are the performance evaluation index of the model. The closer the value is 1, the better the performance of the model. By calculating these values, we can well evaluate the performance of our trained models.

4   The Implementation and Evaluation of Experiments

In this section, the feasibility, practicability and universality of the network model are verified by different experiments. After the experiment is completed, the analysis and evaluation of the recognition method will be given. In order to facilitate the construction of the neural network, we will use the second generation artificial intelligence learning system: TensorFlow developed by Google in DistBelief. This is a system that transmissions complex data structures into artificial neural networks for analysis and processing. It is used in multiple machines, such as voice recognition [21] or image recognition [22]. There is a good performance in the field of machine learning and deep learning. Now TensorFlow is completely open source and can be used by anyone. This system will provide great convenience for our experiments.

4.1   Data Acquisition

The experimental data collected by Samsung Galaxy S2, the tester placed four same mobile phones in four parts: arms, pockets, belts and wrist, and carried out 6 regular and representative activities in a period of time: jogging, walking, running, upstairs, downstairs and sitting, each movement lasted 3–5 min, in which the jogging, walking, and running test sites were the school playground, the sitting test was the classroom, the upstairs and the downstairs were tested on the stairs in the teaching building. The number of test staffs are 10, their age was between 20 and 30. In order to conform to the reality of life, the way of placing mobile is arbitrary. All of our experiments are based on inter CORE i7 CPU and 8G memory of Dell laptop.

4.2 The Effect of the Number of Hidden Neurons on the Performance of the Model

Based on the discussion of the design of the fully connected layer in Sect. 3.2, this experiment mainly discusses the effects of hidden neurons on the model performance, and finds out the number of hidden neurons to carry out subsequent experiments.

Fig. 4. Training accuracy in different number of hidden neurons

Based on the 30 iteration, we used the data collected in pocket to test the results.

As a result, the training accuracy of num_hidden at over 1200 has been greatly reduced, the phenomenon of over fitting appears, so over fitting not appears below 1200, and the accuracy of the test is almost close. Under comprehensive consideration, 500 is chosen as num_hiddens, which has faster computation speed and higher accuracy under the same iteration number.

4.3 Experimental Results in Different Positions

We use the results obtained in the last experiment to change the number of hidden neurons in the fully connected layer to 500. On this basis, we experiment with the data collected at different parts. The Confusion matrix and related information are shown as follows: (0, 1, 2, 3, 4, 5 representing downstairs, running, sitting, jogging, upstairs, walking) (Tables 1, 2, 3 and 4).

Table 1. Confusion matrix for arm

	0	1	2	3	4	5
0	112	0	0	0	2	1
1	1	191	0	0	0	0
2	0	0	211	1	0	0
3	0	0	1	212	2	4
4	1	9	1	1	99	29
5	8	0	0	1	1	194

Data quantity: 160655
Training completion time: 5 min 2 s

Table 2. Confusion matrix for belt

	0	1	2	3	4	5
0	107	0	0	0	3	1
1	2	221	0	0	1	0
2	0	0	176	0	0	0
3	0	0	0	202	0	0
4	4	1	0	0	139	5
5	3	0	1	0	0	208

Data quantity: 161808
Training completion time: 5 min 3 s

Table 3. Confusion matrix for pocket

	0	1	2	3	4	5
0	126	5	0	0	3	1
1	4	188	0	0	2	0
2	0	0	190	0	0	0
3	0	0	3	205	0	1
4	2	3	0	0	128	8
5	2	0	2	0	3	221

Data quantity: 161958
Training completion time: 5 min 3 s.

Table 4. Confusion matrix for wrist

	0	1	2	3	4	5
0	124	0	0	1	1	2
1	1	195	0	1	0	0
2	0	0	218	0	0	0
3	0	0	1	198	0	0
4	0	2	1	0	86	37
5	4	0	0	1	1	202

Data quantity: 159992
Training completion time: 5 min 1 s

4.4   Experimental Results of Mixed Data

In real life, the location of the mobile phone is not the same, and sometimes it is possible to take the mobile phone frequently. Can this method be well identified at this time? In order to imitate this situation, we mixed the four parts data into the experiment and got the confusion matrix as follows (Table 5):

Table 5. Confusion matrix for mixture text

	0	1	2	3	4	5
0	444	3	0	9	29	13
1	7	751	0	3	25	2
2	0	0	650	141	0	0
3	4	0	15	750	9	3
4	3	1	0	3	528	48
5	56	0	0	3	22	815

Data quantity: 644412
Training completion time: 24 min 28 s.

Table 6. Model evaluation results

Position	Accuracy	Precision	Recall	F1. Score
Arm	95.07%	95.49%	95.07%	94.88%
Belt	96.44%	96.44%	96.44%	96.43%
Pocket	96.39%	96.52%	96.39%	96.37%
Wrist	94.17%	94.43%	94.17%	94.00%
Mixture	90.80%	91.38%	90.80%	90.85%

4.5   Assessment

Based on the confusion matrix obtained from the previous experiments, the results obtained from the experiments are evaluated. The results are as follows (Table 6):

It can be seen from the previous table that the model we have trained has good performance. The training time of the models in each position is about 5 min, and it can be completed in 25 min after mixing, the training time is faster. It has higher recognition accuracy which between 94% and 96.5% in different locations of mobile phones, the accuracy rate of identification at the belt was the highest, reaching 96%. After mixing the data in each position, the recognition accuracy can reach about 90%, and the universality is very strong. It can be a good solution to the difficulty of mobile phone's position in real life to the recognition of the motion behavior.

5 Summary and Prospect

In this paper, a method of deep learning behavior recognition based on convolutional neural network is proposed. This method simplifies and extracts the collected motion data through convoluting, pooling and back propagation, which makes the computer easier to deal with and learning, so as to judge the motion state of human being in various movements. On the mobile platform, the acceleration sensor, gravity sensor, gyroscope and other equipment can be used to judge the motion state of the human body, and the accuracy is more than 94%.

The method of this paper still has some limitations, and the more detailed and deeper behavior can not be identified accurately. In the follow-up work, we will join the unsupervised learning method and collect more situations to carry out experiments in more ways to improve our research.

References

1. Wei, C.: Classification and recognition of human behavior in video image sequences. Yanshan University (2012)
2. Mi, X., Li, X.: Study on the automatic monitoring method of elderly living alone based on internet of things intelligence. Comput. Simul. **31**(02), 378–381 (2014)
3. Liu, N.: Recognition and research of fall behavior based on multi-feature fusion. Hebei University of Technology (2015)
4. Xue, F.: Research and application of behavior detection based on smart phone sensor. Southwest University (2017)
5. Zhang, Y.: Human behavior recognition based on smart phone sensor data [OL], 21 February 2017. http://www.infoq.com/cn/articles/human-behavior-recognition-based-on-smart-phone-sensor-data?utm_source=tuicool&utm_medium=referral
6. Ponce, H., Martínez-Villaseñor, M.L., Miralles-Pechuán, L.: A novel wearable sensor-based human activity recognition approach using artificial hydrocarbon networks. Sensors (Basel, Switzerland) **16**(7), 1033 (2016)
7. Liu, L., Peng, Y., Liu, M., Huang, Z.: Sensor-based human activity recognition system with a multilayered model using time series shapelets. Knowl. Based Syst. **90**, 138–152 (2015)
8. Liu, C., Zhang, L., Liu, Z., et al.: Lasagna: towards deep hierarchical understanding and searching over mobile sensing data. In: International Conference on Mobile Computing and Networking, pp. 334–347. ACM (2016)
9. Wu, D., Wang, Z., Chen, Y., Zhao, H.: Mixed-kernel based weighted extreme learning machine for inertial sensor based human activity recognition with imbalanced dataset. Neurocomputing **190**, 35–49 (2016)
10. Zhang, X.: Deep learning algorithm and application based on convolutional neural network. Xidian University (2015)
11. Deng, J., Zhang, X.: Deep learning optimization method based on automatic encoder combination. Comput. Appl. **36**(03), 697–702 (2016)
12. Ji, S., Xu, W., Yang, M., Yu, K.: 3D convolutional neural networks for human action recognition. IEEE Trans. Pattern Anal. Mach. Intell. **35**(1), 221–231 (2013)
13. Zhang, H.Y.: Simulation line design and its FPGA realization based on bp neural network. J. Electron. Inf. Technol. **29**(5), 1267–1270 (2007)

14. Luo, P., Li, H.: Quantum neural network algorithm based on Tanh multilayer function and its application. Comput. Digit. Eng. **40**(1), 4–6 (2012)
15. Wang, D., Liu, S.: A new modified activation unit LogReLU using log function. J. Jilin Univ. (Sci. Ed.) **55**(3), 617–622 (2017)
16. Liu, Q., Tang, X., Zhang, N.: Structural optimization convolutional neural network based on unsupervised pre-training. Eng. Sci. Technol. **2017**(s2): 210–215 (2017)
17. Boureau, Y., Bach, F., Lecun, Y., et al.: Learning mid-level features for recognition. In: Computer Vision and Pattern Recognition, pp. 2559–2566. IEEE (2010)
18. Charalampous, K., Kostavelis, I., Gasteratos, A.: Robot navigation in large-scale social maps: an action recognition approach. Expert Syst. Appl. **66**(C), 261–273 (2016)
19. Wang, G., Duan, M., Niu, C.: A stochastic gradient descent algorithm based on convolutional neural network. Comput. Eng. Des. **39**(02): 441–445+462 (2018)
20. Liu, Q., Guo, J., Pu, H., Yan, Z.: Four-rotor UAV attitude estimation system based on gradient descent method [J/OL]. Electrooptics and Control, pp. 1–7, 11 April 2018. http://kns.cnki.net/kcms/detail/41.1227.TN.20171213.0935.020.html
21. Chen, S.: Research on deep learning neural network in speech recognition. South China University of Technology (2013)
22. Wang, Y.: Design and implementation of image recognition and text recommendation system based on deep learning. Beijing Jiaotong University (2017)

Energy Efficiency and Harvesting

Performance Analysis of UWB System in the Presence of the Narrowband Interference

Yanliang Jin[1] , Xue Wang[2(✉)] , Hong Nie[3] , and Xuetao Luo[2]

[1] Key Laboratory of Specific Optical Fiber and Light Access of Ministry of Education, Shanghai University, Shanghai, China
jinyanliang@staff.shu.edu.cn
[2] College of Communication and Information Engineering, Shanghai University, Shanghai, China
snowking1212@163.com, luoxuetao00100@163.com
[3] Department of Technology, University of Northern Iowa, Cedar Falls, IA, USA
hong.nie@uni.edu

Abstract. Impulse radio ultra-wideband (IR-UWB) is a radio technology transmitting information over a broad bandwidth which can take in narrowband signals from the existing wireless systems and have them as narrowband interference (NBI). The interference will definitely degrade the system performance. For better communication of Wireless Body Area Networks (WBANs), it is important to evaluate the performance of the system properly. In this paper, bit error rate (BER) and packet error rate (PER) are used to evaluate the performance of the IEEE 802.15.6 standard-based IR-UWB transmission systems in both additive white Gaussian noise and CM4 multipath channels with and without the NBIs respectively. And it is the first time to use variance-detection-based receivers in the IEEE 802.15.6 standard-based systems. Simulation results show that comparing with conventional energy-detection-based receivers, the variance-detection-based receivers have better interference tolerance in the IEEE 802.15.6 IR-UWB systems.

Keywords: Impulse radio ultra-wideband · Narrowband interference · Variance-detection-based receiver

1 Introduction

With the decreasing size and increasing capability of electronic devices, it becomes more and more convenient for people to remotely monitor health states with wearable data collecting devices [1]. Therefore, standards for wireless body area network (WBAN), such as the IEEE 802.15.6 standard, have been developed for connecting

© Springer Nature Singapore Pte Ltd. 2019
S. Shen et al. (Eds.): CWSN 2018, CCIS 984, pp. 147–156, 2019.
https://doi.org/10.1007/978-981-13-6834-9_13

portable medical devices. Impulse radio ultra-wideband (IR-UWB) signals can be radiated without a carrier, which simplifies the structure of wireless transceivers and makes it a strong candidate for low power and low complexity communication applications, at which WBAN exactly aims [2, 3]. Therefore, IR-UWB technology has attracted increasing research interests for its outstanding advantages, which can be employed in portable and wearable medical devices.

However, broad bandwidth, multipath channel, inter-symbol interference make it a challenge for IR-UWB systems to demodulate transmitted information accurately in the receiver end. Traditionally, there are mainly two kinds of demodulation technologies, coherent and non-coherent receivers [4]. The coherent receivers, like Rake receivers, have good performance but come with high system complexity [5]. The non-coherent receivers, such as energy-detection (ED)-based receivers, can be implemented at lower cost for its lenient requirements on multipath channel information, but the ED-based receivers cannot distinguish interference and noise from the desired IR-UWB signals. Thus, the ED-based receivers are more vulnerable to noise and interferences than the coherent receivers [6]. Unfortunately, with high probability narrowband interference (NBI) signals present in the received IR-UWB signals, which seriously degrade the performance of the ED receivers. To mitigate this destructive effect, various algorithms have been developed, including the use of notch filters in the receiver end [7], digital interference cancellation [8], weighted energy detection [9], and the variance-detection (VD)-based receivers [10]. Among the above algorithms, the VD-based receivers have great potential to remove NBI, even in multipath environments, with low system complexity. In this paper, we focus our researches on comparing the performance of the ED- and the VD-based receivers for IR-UWB systems following the IEEE 802.15.6 standard in both additive white Gaussian noise (AWGN) channel and multipath channel with and without NBIs. Through computer simulations, the bit error rate (BER) and packet error rate (PER) for the ED- and the VD-based receivers with the binary pulse positioning modulation (BPPM) described in the PHY layer of the IEEE 802.15.6 standard [2] are thoroughly evaluated under various channel and NBI conditions.

This paper is organized as follows. In Sect. 2 the system model of the transceivers following the PHY layer of the IEEE 802.15.6 standard is introduced, and in Sect. 3, the BER and PER performance of the ED- and the VD-based receivers are evaluated through computer simulations. Finally, a summary about the advantages of the VD-based receivers over the ED-based receivers is given.

2 System Model

As the IEEE 802.15.6 [2], the UWB PHY frame format is formed by concatenating the synchronization header (SHR), the physical layer header (PHR), and the physical layer service data unit (PSDU), respectively, as show Fig. 1.

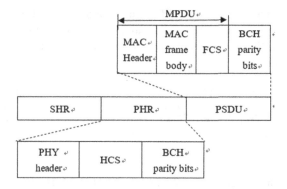

Fig. 1. UWB PHY frame structure

There are two modes of operation: default mode and high quality of service (Qos) mode. The default mode shall be used in medical and non-medical applications. The high QoS mode shall be used for high-priority medical applications. And this paper adopts the default mode to form the frame packet and implement the modulation work.

To form the physical layer protocol data unit (PPDU), the synchronization header (SHR) is transmitted first according to the transmitting order. The synchronization header (SHR) is composed of preamble and the start-of-frame delimiter (SFD). The first part is targeted for timing synchronization and the second part is for frame synchronization in the receiver. After SHR transmission, the PHY header formed by 24 bits which contains information about the data rate of the PSDU and length of MAC frame body is transmitted. To guarantee the correctness of the 24-bits PHY header, it is passed through the cyclic redundancy check (CRC) block and then through shortened BCH (40, 28) encoder.

In data transmission state, the MAC protocol data unit (MPDU) data coming from the MAC is stored in TX FIFO [11]. Before transmitting, these bits are passed through scrambler, BCH encoder, pad bits, and bit interleaving block to provide robustness against error propagation.

2.1 Transmit Pulse

In agreement [2], a pulse waveform $w'(t)$ of duration T_w shall be formed by either a single pulse or a concatenation of pulses and is given by Eq. (1):

$$w'(t) = \begin{cases} p(t) & T_w = T_p \\ \sum_{i=0}^{N_{cpb}-1} p(t - iT_p) & T_w = N_{cpb}T_p \end{cases} \tag{1}$$

Where N_{cpb} is an integer larger than one and T_p is the duration of $p(t)$. In order to reduce spectral lines due to long strings of pulses with the same polarity in the burst pulse option, spectral shaping through scrambling shall be used by either static scrambling or dynamic scrambling.

On the current stage, a few IR-UWB pulses such as the short pulse, chaotic pulse and chirp pulse can be taken into consideration and there is not a mandatory pulse shape. In this paper, the short pulse shape is chosen as the IR-UWB pulse. The pulse shall be given by Eq. (2):

$$r(t) = \begin{cases} 1 - \beta + 4\frac{\beta}{\pi} & t = 0 \\ \frac{\beta}{\sqrt{2}}\left[\left[1 + \frac{2}{\pi}\right]\sin\left(\frac{\pi}{4\beta}\right) + \left[1 - \frac{2}{\pi}\right]\cos\left(\frac{\pi}{4\beta}\right)\right] & t = \pm\frac{T}{4\beta} \\ \dfrac{\sin\left(\pi(1-\beta)\frac{t}{T} + 4\beta\frac{t}{T}\cos\pi(1+\beta)\frac{t}{T}\right)}{\pi\frac{t}{T}\left[1 - \left(4\beta\frac{t}{T}\right)^2\right]} & elsewhere \end{cases} \qquad (2)$$

The roll-off factor shall be set to $\beta = 0.5$ and $T = 1/499.2$ MHz. These parameters are specified by the agreement. Figure 2 shows the relative power spectral density (PSD) of the reference pulse centered at 3993.6 MHz satisfying the transmit spectral mask.

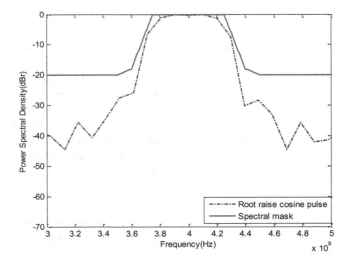

Fig. 2. PSD of the short pulse centered at 3993.6 MHz

2.2   Channel Model

In this paper, in order to investigate the performance of different receivers in the presence of narrowband interference, we adopt the CM4, IEEE 802.15.6 channel models [2]. The models discussed generally characterize the path loss of BAN devices taking into account possible shadowing due to the human body or obstacles near the human body and postures of human body.

Unlike traditional wireless communications, the path loss for body area network system is both distance and frequency dependent. The path loss model between the transmitting and the receiving node as a function of the distance is described by Eq. (3):

$$PL(d) = PL_0 + 10n \log_{10}\left(\frac{d}{d_0}\right) \qquad (3)$$

Where PL_0 is the path loss at a reference distance d_0, and n is path-loss exponent.

2.3   Receiver Model

As we know, various receiver structures for the IR-UWB systems have been proposed. In this paper, two different receivers are implemented. The ED-based receivers detect the presence of a signal by measuring its energy and comparing the energy with a reference threshold. The ED-based receiver structure is described as Fig. 3.

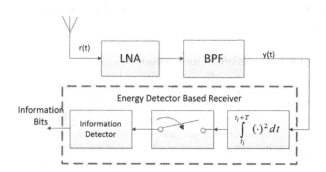

Fig. 3. The ED-based receiver structure

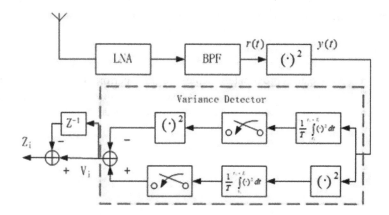

Fig. 4. The VD-based receiver structure

The VD-based receivers [10] recover information bits by measuring the variance of the squared received signal. In this structure, as shown in Fig. 4, the NBI component is shifted to the frequency band close to direct-current (DC) because of the square operation; and mitigated by a filter to improve the system performance.

3 Performance Evaluation

To study and evaluate the performance of IR-UWB system, the simulation work is developed. In this simulation, the transmitted IR-UWB pulses is short pulse waveform shown as Eq. (2). The bandwidth is set to 499.2 MHz and center frequency is set to 3993.6 MHz. The duration of a BPPM frame is 128 ns which strictly follows the standard, and the time shift to differentiate 1 from 0 is 64 ns. Correspondingly, the integration time is fixed at 64 ns in the receiver. In addition, the NBI bandwidth with 20 MHz and center frequency with 3.9 GHz is applied. In receiver end, demodulation work utilizing forward error correction code (FEC) decoding and hard decision is completed. What's more, the bit error rate (BER) and packet error rate (PER) are collected to analyze the statistical performance of the ED- and VD-based receivers in both AWGN and CM4 channels with and without NBI.

3.1 Additive White Gaussian Noise Channel

Figure 5(a) shows the BER results collected in AWGN channels. And these are obtained when the signal-to-interference ratio (SIR) is 0 dB, −3 dB and −6 dB. It is shown the ED-based receivers perform poorer than the VD-based receivers clearly. Accurately, both of the receivers can perform well without the presence of narrowband interference. But when the SIR is set to 0, the ED-based receivers almost collapse while VD-based receivers still perform well. In general, ED-based receivers are vulnerable to NBI and will corrupt once the NBI is present and the performance of the VD-based receivers degrade greatly only when strong NBI is present in the system.

Figure 5(b) shows that the packet error rate (PER) with ED-based receivers is unacceptable once the narrowband interference is present. While the VD-based receivers still perform well under the interference.

Figure 6 shows the results when the SIR is changed and Eb/N0 is fixed at 32 dB and 16 dB, respectively. Comparing with the ED-based receivers at BER of 10^{-3}, the VD-based receivers can approximately achieve a NBI performance improvement of 5 dB in AWGN. In other words, the ED-based receiver is vulnerable to NBI, while the VD-based receiver has an inherent ability to mitigate the destructive effects caused by NBI.

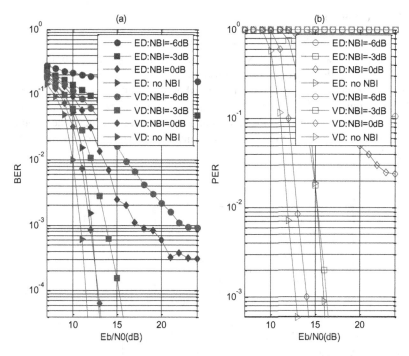

Fig. 5. (a) BER and (b) PER performance of the ED-based and VD-based receivers in AWGN channel

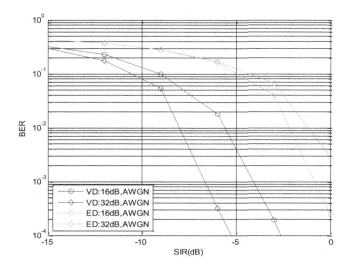

Fig. 6. NBI mitigation performances of the VD-based and ED-based receivers in AWGN channel

3.2   CM4 Channel

Figure 7 shows the BER and PER performance both in AWGN and CM4 channel model. Comparing with the AWGN channel as shown in Figs. 5 and 6, the multipath effects do degrade the demodulation performance of the VD-based receivers. This is because the strong inter-symbol interference when transmitting very short duration of the IR-UWB pulses and which results in a large number of resolved multipath components in the receiver end [8]. Furthermore, as we can see in Fig. 8, the stronger the narrowband interference is, the poorer BER and PER performance of the VD-based receivers become.

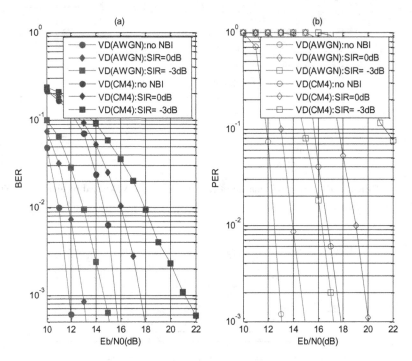

Fig. 7. (a) BER and (b) PER performance of the VD-based receivers in AWGN and multipath CM4 channels with different NBIs

The VD-based receivers perform better in both AWGN and multipath channels and have robustness on the existence of narrowband interference.

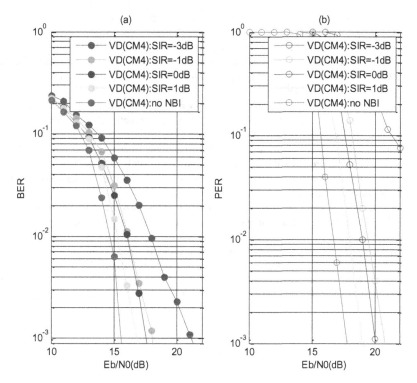

Fig. 8. (a) BER and (b) PER performance of the VD-based receivers in multipath channels with different NBIs

4 Conclusion

In this paper, we present the impulse radio ultra-wideband system based on the IEEE 802.15.6 standard with the energy-detection-based receivers and variance-detection-based receivers, respectively. And the performance of the system with and without the narrowband interference is evaluated respectively through the bit error rate and packet error rate. We find that compared with the conventional ED-based receiver, the VD-based receiver can achieve much better performance especially when NBI is present. However, the simulation results also show the multipath effects will degrade the VD-based receivers in the presence of strong NBIs and this still deserves further research.

References

1. Li, H.B., Kohno, R.: Body area network and its standardization at IEEE 802.15.BAN. In: Advances in Mobile and Wireless Communications, pp. 223–238 (2008)
2. IEEE BE: IEEE Standard for Local and metropolitan area networks - Part 15.6: Wireless Body Area Networks, pp. 1–271. IEEE STD. IEEE (2012)
3. Cao, H.S., Leung, V., Chow, C., Chan, H.: Enabling technologies for wireless body area networks: a survey and outlook. Commun. Mag. IEEE **47**(12), 84–93 (2009)

4. Hazra, R., Tyagi, A.: A survey on various coherent and non-coherent IR-UWB receivers. Wirel. Personal Commun. **79**(3), 2339–2369 (2014)

5. Weisenhorn, M., Hirt, W.: Robust noncoherent receiver exploiting UWB channel properties. In: International Workshop on Ultra Wideband Systems, Joint with Conference on Ultrawideband Systems and Technologies, Joint Uwbst & Iwuwbs, pp. 156–160. IEEE (2004)

6. Rabbachin, A., Quek, T.Q.S., Pinto, P.C., Oppermann, I.: UWB energy detection in the presence of multiple narrowband interferers In: IEEE International Conference on Ultra-Wideband, pp. 857–862. IEEE (2007)

7. Shaman, H., Hong, J.S.: Ultra-wideband (UWB) bandpass filter with embedded band notch structures. IEEE Microwave Wirel. Compon. Lett. **17**(3), 193–195 (2007)

8. Milstein, L.B.: Interference rejection techniques in spread spectrum communications. Proc. IEEE **76**(6), 657–671 (1988)

9. Steiner, C., Wittneben, A.: On the interference robustness of ultra-wideband energy detection receivers. In: IEEE International Conference on Ultra-Wideband, pp. 721–726. IEEE Xplore (2007)

10. Yang, A., Xu, Z., Nie, H., Chen, Z.: On the variance-based detection for impulse radio UWB systems. IEEE Trans. Wirel. Commun. **15**(12), 8249–8259 (2016)

11. Manchi, P.K., Paily, R., Gogoi, A.K.: Low power digital baseband transceiver design for UWB physical layer of IEEE 802.15.6 standard. IEEE Trans. Ind. Inform. (2017)

An Electric Charge Model Based on the Energy Harvesting WSN

Yang Zhang[1,2(✉)], Hong Gao[1], Yaping Li[3], Dailiang Jin[3], and JianZhong Li[1]

[1] School of Computer Science and Technology,
Harbin Institute of Technology, Harbin, China
[2] Key Laboratory of Mechatronics, Heilongjiang University, Harbin, China
zhang_yang@hlju.edu.cn
[3] Network and Information Center, Harbin Institute of Technology, Harbin, China

Abstract. The improvement of energy utilization efficiency has been an important research subject of EH-WSN. The existing studies usually use the energy model to analyze the network. As the harvesting and consumption of energy is affected by the real-time voltage, the energy model is not suitable for the EH-WSN that varies greatly with voltage. Notably, most of the present energy harvesting platforms adopt the linear regulator. As the charge quantity in and out of linear regulator is the same, we use the charge quantity to calculate the energy, avoiding the influence from the variation of voltage. Accordingly, this paper firstly proposes the electric charge conservation model based on the EH-WSN, avoiding the complicated computation of voltage and energy. The computation cost is greatly saved and the accuracy of the model is improved, moreover, an estimation method is presented for the charge quantity in this paper. Experiments show that the model is capable to operate practically in the IEA platform and accurately show the charge quantity variation of EH-WSN nodes.

Keywords: Energy harvesting WSN · Energy model ·
Electric charge model · Energy measurement · IEA platform

1 Introduction

There is continued effective researches devoted to the energy utilization efficiency of Wireless Sensor Networks (WSN). The progress of energy harvesting technology has presented a new chance for the development of WSN, while nodes are possible to harvest energy, such as solar energy, radio frequency energy, mechanical energy, heat energy, etc [1], and store the energy in the capacitor for sense, computing and communication. Thus the WSN gets rid of the battery limitation, achieves almost infinite network life and is called the Energy Harvesting WSN (EH-WSN). However, in most of environments, nodes could not harvest sufficient energy owing to the low density of energy, and the harvested energy has characteristics of vibration and imbalance. Therefore, nodes require much

© Springer Nature Singapore Pte Ltd. 2019
S. Shen et al. (Eds.): CWSN 2018, CCIS 984, pp. 157–165, 2019.
https://doi.org/10.1007/978-981-13-6834-9_14

lower power consumption, more accurate energy measurement and more efficient and dedicated energy management. The focus of research turns to the utilization efficiency of energy rather than the network lifetime.

To improve the energy utilization efficiency of the whole network, planning the energy of each node is necessary, therefore, the energy modeling for each node is needed. On the traditional WSN platform powered by batteries, the remaining energy and the consumed energy for each calculation and communication can be accurately measured and estimated as the power supply voltage is monotonically decreasing and the change is stable. However, in the EH-WSN, the node voltage will change greatly with the operation of the node, and the physical parameters of the node element will also have deviation (such as capacitance), thereby leading to a great change of the consumed energy by the same operation, so it is difficult to accurately estimate the energy. On one hand, it increases the extra computation and wastes the limited energy, on the other hand, it also reduces the accuracy of the energy model. Therefore, in the existing EH-WSN, most experiments were verified by simulation, which is far from the reality.

As the voltage of the EH-WSN node often exceeds the maximum operating voltage of the chip, most of the existing EH-WSN nodes use the linear regulator to regulate the voltage for power supply. The characteristic of linear regulator is that the input and output current is the same, but the output voltage is limited to the set value, which implies that as the voltage is stabilized by linear regulator, the charge quantity for each node to perform the same operation is the same. Therefore, we established the electric charge model based on the charge conservation that turned the complex energy calculation to a simple calculation of charge quantity, which greatly simplified the calculation of the node and improved the prediction accuracy of the energy model.

To achieve the electric charge model, the EN-WSN node is required to accurately measure the voltage and the charge quantity of the node. In previous research, we designed the IEA as the intermittent EH-WSN platform [2], which achieved the accurate electric quantity measurement with ultra-low power in the EN-WSN, and were capable to achieve more than 99.8% accuracy electric quantity measurement with the power about 157 uW. Depending on the IEA platform, the paper has made the following contributions:

1. The electric charge modeling based on the EN-WSN is presented for the first according to the characteristic of linear regulator that the traditional complex energy computation is transformed to the simple electric quantity calculation. It not only saves the computational energy cost of nodes, but also improves the accuracy of the model, so that the electric charge model can be truly applied to the practice.
2. This paper tests the operation effect of the electric charge model on the IEA platform in detail. Experiments show that the model reflects the true status of the charge quantity of node and is able to estimate the variation of the charge quantity.

The remainder of the paper is organized as follows. Section 2 provides the background and summarizes the related works. Section 3 describes the electric charge model. Section 4 presents the experiments. Finally, Sect. 5 summarizes the paper providing final remarks.

2 Related Works

The research of existing EH-WSN energy model usually adopts the equation $B_{t+1} = min\{B_t + W_h - W_c - e, C_v\}$, B_t refers to the energy at t time, W_h refers to the harvested energy, W_c refers to the consumed energy, e refers to the consumption energy of circuit, and C_v refers to the max energy that the capacitor is able to store. Where, e and C_v are known quantities, B_t can be calculated according to the voltage, the energy B_{t+1} of $t + 1$ time can be calculated by estimated W_h and W_c [3,4]. The existing studies usually need to suppose that the harvested energy is known or predictable and the energy consumed by an unit operation is regular, therefore, the total consumption can be calculated by accumulative calculation [5–9]. However, in the EH-WSN, the value of W_h and W_c is hardly to predict that it will be affected by the energy source voltage, the internal resistance, the operation of nodes and even the ambient temperature [10]. Therefore, the experiments of the above researches are all adopted simulation verification, which has not operated in the practice. The existing studies are working hard to improve the energy model, to the best of my knowledge, there is no research studied from the view of charge quantity.

3 Electric Charge Model

To calculate the energy with the equation of $E = \int U(t)I(t)dt$, learning the change of voltage and current with the time variation is necessary. For the battery powered WSN nodes, the change of battery voltage is slow, the voltage is relatively stable when the node performs a specific operation, therefore the current is also constant. The energy consumed by an operation is fixed, thereby calculating the total energy consumption becomes simple. Therefore, the battery powered WSN is suitable for the traditional energy model. Whereas, the EH-WSH node usually uses the capacitor with the capacity far smaller than that of the battery to store the electrical energy. When the node executes a specific operation, the voltage will reduce evidently and the energy for each operation is different, depending on the charging voltage, capacitance, and the characteristics of the components. When the node runs t time with a constant current I, the consumption energy will be $U_0 It - \frac{I^2 t^2}{2C}, U_0 - \frac{It}{C} \geq U_{min}$. When multiple operations are executed, it becomes complicate to compute the total consumed energy. Therefore, in the EH-WSN, the traditional energy model is not applicable any more.

Since the voltage of EH-WSN platform is often more than the maximum voltage of the node element, most of the existing EH-WSN platform has adopted the linear regulator stable voltage (mainly LDO) [11–13]. The linear regulator is capable to output the stable voltage, therefore, the current is also constant when the chip of the node performs a specific operation each time, that is, the consumed charge quantity is constant.

The characteristic of linear regulator lies in that the input and output current is the same, but the output voltage is limited in the set value, as shown in Fig. 1. This implies that the energy in and out of linear regulator is different, but the charge quantity is identical. For the node energy storage capacitors, although the energy consumed by each operation is not constant, the consumed charge quantity is fixed. When the node operates t time with a constant current I, the consumed charge quantity is It, which is far more simple than the energy calculation. As long as the voltage value of the capacitor does not exceed the threshold, its specific value need not be concerned. So we can circumvent the energy and simplify the calculation greatly. According to the conservation of charge, we can simplify the complex energy model into a charge model, as shown in Eq. 1:

$$\begin{cases} Q_{t+1} = CU_t + Q_h - \sum I_{Ci}t_{Ci} - I_q T \\ U_{min} \leq U_t \leq U_{max} \end{cases} \tag{1}$$

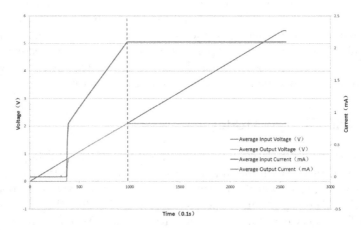

Fig. 1. Linear regulator with input voltage from 0 V to 5.5 V (type STLQ015M21R, 5K load)

In Eq. 1, U_t refers to the voltage of capacitor at t time, Q_h is the harvested charge quantity (measured by the IEA platform), $I_{Ci}t_{Ci}$ refers to the current and time for executing i task, I_q refers to the quiescent current of the node, U_{min} refers to the lowest voltage for the system work (usually the output voltage of linear regulator), and U_{max} refers to the maximum voltage for the system or capacitor, taking the lower value of the two. Only a small number of additions and multiplication can be used in the upper calculation, and there is no problem in the mixed execution of different operations. Compared with the traditional energy model, the charge model effectively reduces the computational burden of nodes, and is more suitable for the ultra-low power EH-WSN supplied by the linear regulator.

The EH-WSN nodes usually intend to predict the harvesting energy in the next period of time to plan the network strategy. However, the harvesting energy is not predictable as the energy harvesting is not stable in most environments. In a short time, we can assume that the energy environment will remain stable, then the value of Q_{t+1} can be calculated according to historical data. The voltage change of EH-WSN node is shown as Fig. 2. The node only works for a short time, and the voltage drops rapidly. Subsequently, the capacitor is recharged for most of the time, and the voltage increases slowly. In a short period of time, the energy harvesting device is equivalent to a voltage source with large internal resistance, and the equivalent circuit is shown as Fig. 3. Suppose the voltage of source is U_S, the internal resistance of source is R_p, the constant consumption current of node is $I_{Consume}$, the voltage of capacitor C_1 is U_{c1}, and the current of capacitor C_1 is I_{c1}, then:

$$\begin{cases} U_S = R_p(I_{c1} + I_{Consume}) + U_{c1} \\ I_{c1} = C\frac{dU_{c1}}{dt} \end{cases} \tag{2}$$

At t time, the voltage of capacitor C_1 is U_t, the initial voltage is U_0, then the following Eq. 3 is obtained with the substitution of current I_{c1}.

$$U_t = U_0 + (U_S - R_pI_{Consume} - U_0) \cdot \left(1 - e^{-\frac{t}{R_pC_1}}\right) \tag{3}$$

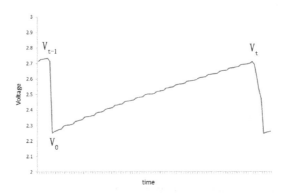

Fig. 2. Voltage variation at running time

According to Eq. 3, the node is possible to approximately estimate the harvesting energy in the next period of time. Firstly, we have to know the true value of U_0, C_1, R_p, U_S, thereinto, the value of U_0 can be directly measured. As the IEA platform can directly measure the voltage value of capacitor and the quantity of electric charge in and out flow. According to $C_1 = \triangle Q_H - \triangle Q_C/\triangle U$, the capacitance is directly calculated. Then, according to the inflow current $I_H(t)$ and capacitance voltage $U_{C1}(t)$, the source voltage U_S and the internal resistance

R_p is capable to be calculated by $U_S = I_H(t) \cdot R_p + \frac{(U_{c1}(t) + U_{c1}(t-1))}{2}$ in practical circumstance, the calculated value of C_1, R_p, U_S from single measurement can not be accurate, the Exponentially Weighted Moving-Average (EWMA) algorithm is adopted to smooth the value. As the value of U_0, C_1, R_p, U_S is obtained, the voltage value, the charge quantity and the energy of capacitor in next period of time will be calculated according to Eq. 3.

4   Experiments

The EH-WSN platform for the experiment is IEA 2.31 versions supplied by the solar battery AM-8702CAR. The rated capacity of the node energy storage capacitor is 1000 uF, and the actual value is 1083 uF measured by LCR meter. The node is set to wake up once every second to measure the current voltage and the quantity of charge harvested in the last second. The quiescent current of node is 8.5 uA, and it will consume 2.003 uQ for waking up once and 254.71 uQ for communication once.

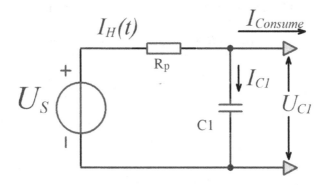

Fig. 3. Equivalent energy harvesting circuit

4.1   Accuracy of Electric Charge Model

To verify the accuracy of electric charge model of Eq. 1, we directly measure the capacitance and voltage per second with a high precision multimeter, at the same time, the node takes usage of electric charge model to calculate the electric charge quantity Q_{t+1} of next second according to the true value of U_t and Q_h per second. The comparison results are shown in Fig. 4.

In Fig. 4, the red line refers to the real change of the stored electric charge in the node capacitor, and the blue line refers to the calculated electric charge of capacitor in the next second according to the actual data and the model of this paper. The light source is LED, when the voltage is above 2.7 V, the node receives 50 ms data and sends 10 byte data packet. The node works continuously

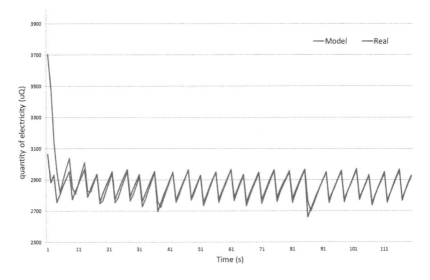

Fig. 4. Accuracy of electric charge model. (Color figure online)

for 120 s, owing to the lack of data, the initial measurement error of the model is relatively large. With the accumulation of measuring data, the computation error of model decreases rapidly and is less than 2% from the 10th second with an average error of -0.25%. The electric charge model can accurately express the change of charge quantity of EH-WSN node considering the above measuring error. Besides, at the 120 s moment, the capacitance from calculation is 1082.96, which is only less than 0.04 per thousand different from the real value.

4.2   Accuracy of Electric Charge Estimation

As known, the electric charge $Q = CU$, thereinto U is the voltage and C is a constant value of capacitance, therefore the electric charge estimation is equivalent to the voltage estimation. To verify the accuracy of electric charge model estimation, the node firstly works 50 s to calculate the values of C_1, R_p, U_S, which is 1079.16 uF, 22.1 KΩ, 5.84 V respectively. Then estimate the variation of capacitor voltage in the following period of time. The node is set to communicate when the voltage is above 3.2 V. The voltage will fall to a low level after communication, which is set as U_0 to estimate the voltage variation until next communication. The estimated voltage is compared with that of the true value, and the results are shown in Fig. 5. The light source is indirect sunlight.

In Fig. 5, the red line refers to the real change of the voltage in the node capacitor, and the blue line refers to the estimated voltage in the following seconds according to the Eq. 3. As Fig. 5 shown, the estimation line is close to the real line, indicating that the node is capable to accurately estimate the variation of voltage, the electric charge and the energy before next communication of the node. Notably, if the current consumed by the node varies, the accuracy of estimation may be influnced.

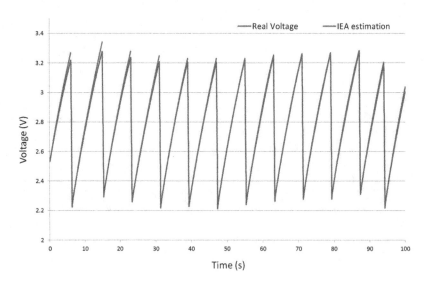

Fig. 5. Results of voltage estimation. (Color figure online)

5   Conclusions

In this paper, we proposed an electric charge model based on the working characteristic of linear regulator. Different to the traditional energy models, the electric charge model in the paper no longer takes into consideration of the complex variation of the voltage and energy when the node works, while calculates the charge quantity stored, harvested and consumed by a node. As the charge quantity variation is relatively stable, the method has greatly saved the computation cost and improved the precision of the model. Moreover, we proposed a new estimation method for the charge quantity. Experiments show that the average accuracy of the model is up to 99.75% at the IEA platform, which can better replace the original energy model and bring the EH-WSN more close to the practical applications.

Acknowledgement. This work is supported in part by the Key Program of National Natural Science Foundation of China under Grant Nos. 61632010, Project of heilongjiang university special funds of basic research foundations of universities in heilongjiang province, No. KJCX201825.

References

1. Park, C., Chou, P.H.: AmbiMax: autonomous energy harvesting platform for multi-supply wireless sensor nodes. In: Sensor, Mesh and Ad Hoc Communications and Networks, pp. 168–177 (2006)
2. Zhang, Y., Gao, H., Cheng, S., Cai, Z., Li, J.: IEA: an intermittent energy aware platform for ultra-low powered energy harvesting WSN. In: Ma, L., Khreishah, A., Zhang, Y., Yan, M. (eds.) WASA 2017. LNCS, vol. 10251, pp. 185–197. Springer, Cham (2017). https://doi.org/10.1007/978-3-319-60033-8_17

3. Ren, X., Liang, W.: Delay-tolerant data gathering in energy harvesting sensor networks with a mobile sink. In: Global Communications Conference, pp. 93–99 (2012)
4. Wang, X., Gong, J., Hu, C., et al.: Optimal power allocation on discrete energy harvesting model. EURASIP J. Wirel. Commun. Netw. **2015**(1), 48 (2015)
5. Vigorito, C.M., Ganesan, D., Barto, A.G., et al.: Adaptive control of duty cycling in energy-harvesting wireless sensor networks. In: Sensor Mesh and Ad Hoc Communications and Networks, pp. 21–30 (2007)
6. Nakayama, K., Dang, N., Bic, L., et al.: Distributed flow optimization control for energy-harvesting wireless sensor networks. In: International Conference on Communications, pp. 4083–4088 (2014)
7. Ren, X., Liang, W., Xu, W., et al.: Quality-aware target coverage in energy harvesting sensor networks. IEEE Trans. Emerg. Top. Comput. **3**(1), 8–21 (2015)
8. Wu, Y., Liu, W., Li, K.: Power allocation and relay selection for energy efficient cooperation in wireless sensor networks with energy harvesting. EURASIP J. Wirel. Commun. Netw. **2017**(1), 26 (2017)
9. Gelenbe, E.: Synchronising energy harvesting and data packets in a wireless sensor. Energies **8**(1), 356–369 (2015)
10. Hester, J.D., Scott, T., Sorber, J., et al.: Ekho: realistic and repeatable experimentation for tiny energy-harvesting sensors. In: International Conference on Embedded Networked Sensor Systems, pp. 1–15 (2014)
11. CYALKIT-E02 Solar-Powered BLE Sensor Beacon Reference Design Kit Guide. http://www.cypress.com/file/280601/download
12. Smith, J.R., Sample, A.P., Powledge, P.S., Roy, S., Mamishev, A.: A wirelessly-powered platform for sensing and computation. In: Dourish, P., Friday, A. (eds.) UbiComp 2006. LNCS, vol. 4206, pp. 495–506. Springer, Heidelberg (2006). https://doi.org/10.1007/11853565_29
13. Zhang, Y., Gao, H., Cheng, S., Li, J.: An efficient EH-WSN energy management mechanism. Tsinghua Sci. Technol. **23**, 406–418 (2018)

Privacy and Security

An Improved Privacy-Preserving and Security Hybrid Access Control Mechanism

Xiaohui Cheng, Fei Dai, Meng Hu, and Qiong Gui$^{(\boxtimes)}$

Guangxi Key Laboratory of Embedded Technology and Intelligent System,
College of Information Science and Engineering,
Guilin University of Technology, Jiangan Road No. 12, Guilin 541000, China
{cxiaohui,102016453}@glut.edu.cn, guilucky@163.com

Abstract. Based on the analysis of various access control mechanisms, a widely applicable privacy-preserving and security hybrid access control mechanism for systems is proposed. This mechanism, which is called attribute and role based hybrid access control mechanism of encryption and time (ET-ARBHAC), consists of two processes, namely the attribute-based access control (ABAC) process and role-based access control (RBAC) process. In ET-ARBHAC, ABAC procedure is designed to encrypt related attribute values and allocate roles and RBAC procedure is added a re-verified time mechanism to increase system security and save system resources. Theoretical methods and architecture of the mechanism were illustrated in this paper. This study provides precious theoretical contributions for researchers and theoretical references for system/website developers, system operators and system technology vendors.

Keywords: Access control · Resource saving · Security · Privacy-preserving

1 Introduction

With the urgent need for privacy and security, the industry and academia are constantly upgrading their security and have achieved many results. In terms of access control models, as research has continued to deepen, many access control models have emerged in past three decades, namely mandatory access control (MAC) [1], role-based access control (RBAC) [2], and Attribute access control (ABAC) model [3] etc. Among these access control models, RBAC and ABAC are most widely used and popular access control models. The research of RBAC was relatively mature and there were many related studies in RBAC [4, 5]. What is more, RBAC became an official standard as ANSI/INCITS [6] in 2004. However, it still has its drawbacks, such as role explosion, only receiving small-scale user access.

As for ABAC, the formalization and large-scale application of the research on the basic mode of ABAC is still in its infancy, and ABAC still has many unresolved issues such as authorization, management, auditability, scalability, hierarchical representation, etc. They have been largely ignored or left for future work [7] by some scholars.

Although hybrid ABAC models and frameworks are intended to solve these problems by extending proven traditional models, this is often done at the expense of flexibility or the elimination of the unknown nature of ABAC's identity. For the

© Springer Nature Singapore Pte Ltd. 2019
S. Shen et al. (Eds.): CWSN 2018, CCIS 984, pp. 169–180, 2019.
https://doi.org/10.1007/978-981-13-6834-9_15

increasing complexity of attributes, a policy-based access control model can be cited to control its flexibility and versatility, but each improvement often introduces new costs. Furthermore, most of previous hybrid mechanism did not pay much attention to the system privacy and security. As a consequence, the news of leaking users' privacy and system breakdown are increasing.

In order to tackle the problem of privacy, security and system resource saving, we propose a hybrid access control mechanism, called ET-ARBHAC. It contains two processes i.e., the ABAC and RBAC process. ABAC process is used to encrypt related attribute value and allocate the role, RBAC process is used to assign permissions. Besides, the re-verified time mechanism of RBAC process increase the security and save resources. Furthermore, we evaluate the feasibility of our mechanism by giving an example of experiment.

The contributions of this paper are as follows:

(1) Privacy, security and system resource conservation. In the ABAC process of ET-ARBHAC, all the attributes of the user were encrypted by the SHA256 algorithm and stored in SQL. As a result, the users' privacy could be protected. In the RBAC procedure of ET-ARBHAC, the time re-verification mechanism could guarantee the system's safety and save system resources because the users' role and its permissions will only valid during the preset period of time.

(2) Applicable for most systems. Our hybrid mechanism is designed for most of the systems and focus on the privacy and system resource saving. For most of the system or websites would require users to sign up and login. Then the user could attain the permissions and related resources. When designed systems or websites, the programmers could refer to our mechanism to achieve the system and get effect of privacy and security.

The remainder of this paper is divided into the following sections. Section 2 introduces recent research work of the improved ABAC models and hybrid access control mechanisms. Section 3 describes the related definitions and technologies of this ET-ARBHAC mechanism. Section 4 gives a detail description on design of hybrid access control mechanism. Section 5 analyses evaluation of the mechanism. Finally, Sect. 6 provides concluding remarks and gives our future works.

2   Related Research

The original study of the ABAC model was proposed by Wang et al. [8] They put forward the first "pure" and "universal" ABAC model in the form of a logic-based framework based on logical programming. Although Wang et al.'s framework introduces layered attributes, it focuses on attributes based on tactics and their evaluation are expressed, consistent and performance. Several key components are missing, including lack of object attributes (User attributes) and omit the formalization of ABAC aspects beyond policy and evaluation (only access control of services/operations is considered). Subsequently, Zhang et al. [9] proposed a unique ABAC model based on attribute-enhanced access matrices, called the "attribute-based access matrix" (ABAM) model. ABAM defines an access matrix in which each row is represented by a pair of an object and its attribute set (Si, ATTS(S$_i$)). Each column consists of a pair of objects and their attribute sets (Oi, ATTS(O$_i$)). Assuming certain strategies are met, each cell ([S$_i$,O$_i$]) corresponds to a set of access rights that the subject (S$_i$) may exercise over the object (O$_i$). The operation (or "command" in ABAM) can be performed on a given object by the given object only if the matching access required for the operation is found in the access matrix and the attributes of the principal and the object satisfy the following conditions. Rubio-Medrano et al. [10] introduced the concept of security token into ABAC's abstract model, which defines the relevant core components and attributes required for the minimum reference model.

With the deep research of ABAC technology, hybrid ABAC model that combines ABAC with other models began to appear in recent years. The purpose of the hybrid ABAC model is to combine attributes into existing access control models, or to extend the traditional access control model with unidentified or policy-based access control concepts. Shafiq et al. [11] provide a potential solution for their hybrid ABAC model, which includes a trust assessment and negotiation framework. Both frameworks provide confidence assessment of claims attributes and dynamically establish trust between collaborating organizations. Lee et al. [12] proposed that "attribute aggregation architecture" collects attributes from neighboring peers and evaluates them using a reputation-based trust plan, where "each peer decides its reputation against other peers based on its own experience. And assess the credibility of the peers. Shafiq and Lee's other studies by in dynamic trust negotiations may be easily applied to the "pure" ABAC model; however, most of the work in this area assumes that attributes originate from trusted sources. Model based on "attribute-centric" strategies, Kuhn et al. [13] have the peculiar of including attributes in the RBAC model role, which is just another attribute of the user, not necessarily a separate access control entity that assigns the rights. Jin et al. [16] character-centric attribute-based access control (RABAC) extends the NIST RBAC model created the first attempt to establish a formal role-centered RBAC-ABAC hybrid model. Cheng et al. tried to combine relational access control (ReBAC) with ABAC in their UURACA model [14] extends the user-to-user relationship access control (UURAC) model [15].

3   Related Definition

3.1   Access Control Model Definition

Attribute-Based Access Control Model
This solution is extended on the traditional ABAC models to encrypt related attribute value. The ABAC framework model has three major modules: rule execution point (abbreviated as PEP), rule decision point (abbreviated as PDP) and rule administration Points (abbreviated as PAP).

Rule Execution Point: After the subject issues an access application and the PEP receives the access application, the PEP immediately collects information based on different access requests from different subjects. The information includes a variety of resources, visitor attributes, etc. and serves as a set of formal information. Then the information were forwarded from the PEP to the PDP, PDP will make a corresponding decision to these information. The decision is the result of node's agreement or disagreement with this request.

Rule Decision Point: The main responsibility of the decision point is to determine the operation request from the PEP according to the access policies, and then return the result to the PEP.

Rule Administration Point: Guessing all the assumed plaintexts according to the method of exhaustion, and encrypting their attribute values with the SHA-256 encryption algorithm to obtain a mapping table. The mapping table is based on the unencrypted attribute values and the encrypted hash values. They are mapped one by one in the mapping table and used by the query.

Role-Based Access Control Model
With reference to the previous RBAC model, the following definition of the role-based assignment permissions in the role-based access control section for this article is made:

The user is represented by U, the role is represented by R, the permission is represented by P, and session is represented by S respectively;

PA: According to the user's different roles to give it different permissions, here used P $\times$ R representation;
UA: UA relies on the proposed attribute strategy to assign a role, represented by U $\times$ R;
User (s_i): Each session s_i refracts a user, denoted by S $\rightarrow$ U;
Role (s_i): Each session s_i reflects a role, denoted by S $\rightarrow$ R.

3.2 SHA-256 Encryption

In order to make the access control strategy adapt to the low power consumption requirements of the Internet of Things node and improve the computational efficiency of the encryption algorithm, the SHA-256 encryption algorithm is used here to make it meet the requirements of the hidden access structure.

SHA-256 is a compression-based iterative cryptographic hash function, updating eight 32-bit state variables A, B, C, D, E, F, G, H based on 16 32-bit words M0,..., M15 messages. The compression function consists of 64 identical steps. The steps of the transformation using fMAJ and fIL two functions:

$$\sum 0(x) = ROTR2(x) \oplus ROTR13(x) \oplus ROTR22$$

$$\sum 1(x) = ROTR6(x) \oplus ROTR11(x) \oplus ROTR25$$

Step i uses the fixed constant K_i and the extended i-th word W_i information. First, fill in the input message and divide it into 512-bit message blocks. The ME which denotes the message extension function takes as input a vector M with 16 coordinates and outputs vector a (W, N). The coordinates of the expansion vector W_i are generated according to the initial message M according to the following formula:

$$W_i = \begin{cases} M_i\ 0 \leq i < 16 \\ \sigma_1(W_{i-2}) + W_{i-7} + \sigma_0(W_{i-15}) + W_{i-16}\ 16 \leq i < N \end{cases} \tag{1}$$

The value of N is different from a hash function of the variable that gradual decrease (or expansion). The functions $\sigma_0(x)$ and $\sigma_1(x)$ are defined as follows:

$$\delta0(x) = ROTR7(x) \oplus ROTR18(x) \oplus SHR3(x)$$

$$\delta1(x) = ROTR17(x) \oplus ROTR19(x) \oplus SHR10(x)$$

Its loop iteration operation is shown in Fig. 1:

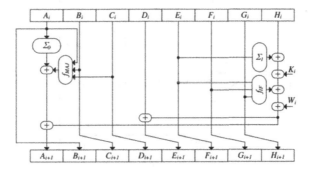

Fig. 1. A state-update transformation step for SHA-256

4   Design of the Hybrid Access Control Mechanism

In industrial and academic circles, many experts and professors are trying to help, as a result, some schemes are proposed. Under the basis of these study research, a security hybrid access control mechanism is put forward. In the following passage, the whole structure of the ET-ARBHAC is first illustrates, and then the ABAC and RBAC process of the ET-ARBHAC are described separately.

4.1   The ET-ARBHAC Mechanism Architecture

In this study, the ET-ARBHAC model is proposed, which is a synthesis of RBAC and ABAC models, with the advantages of RBAC and ABAC. The ET-ARBHAC mechanism consists of two procedures, ABAC allocating role process and RBAC allocating permission process.

When user starts to apply for access to the system, whether it is a user or a large number of user groups, visitor's attributes are extracted PEP and pass the attributes to the PDP. PDP will assign roles to the user based on the values of the attributes.

Then the PAP will encrypt the attribute by SHA-256 and store them into SQL. Above is the process of ABAC, and the user gets its role but cannot directly manipulate the system's resources. It also needs to be assigned different permissions based on the permissions of different roles on the RBAC procedure. Only through these two major processes can user operate system resources that need to be accessed to complete secure access.

The overall architecture model of ET-ARBHAC is shown in Fig. 2. We will describe the two processes of the ET-ARBHAC in the Sects. 4.2, 4.3, respectively.

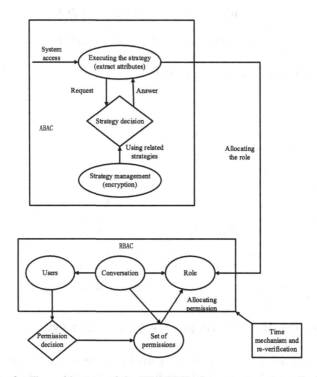

Fig. 2. The architecture of the ET-ARBHAC access control mechanism

4.2   ABAC Allocating Role Process

What is different from RBAC is that the method of attribute-based access control is based on the use of attributes to distinguish between privilege grants, and ABAC is relying on entities to achieve fine-grained access throughout the process. Since attributes are assigned based on attributes, attributes are quite important. Extracting a user's attributes can be its own status message, externally specific environment, or information that wants to access the system etc.

The basic components in the attribute-based access control strategy have the subject, resources, operations and conditions. The difference is that the above components are described through attributes. The attributes that are related to each other flexibly give different meanings according to different changes and requirements of the system. The definition of attributes integrates description of all the components in the strategy, and it breaks out the constraints that can only be based on identity. Now suppose that identity is treated as an attribute. In ABAC, no special function is given to it, and it has the same status as other attributes. In attribute-based access control model, the system uses the user's attributes to describe the user who made the access request. At the same time, the system uses the attributes of the resource to describe the applied resource.

Environmental attributes are often distinguished from subjects, resources and operations, which are non-static and can change in real time. It is similar to some externally-existing environmental information in the access process, the date that visitor submitted the application, the job that the visitor did, etc., which affects the system access of the visitors. The access control strategy decision process is updated in real-time with the real-time changes in the Internet of Things environment. In this case, the real-time permissions will also be different. Therefore, the environment attributes needs to be taken into account in access control process to ensure system security, and together with the attributes of the subject, resources, and operations as the constraint properties of access control process. The definition can be seen in the Sect. 3.1.

The initial access request and attribute-based access control request process are as follows:

The initial access control request (abbreviated as IACR): Collecting original information such as time, place, location and other attributes. Knowing about their relationship with the visitor, some of the original operations, for example, what kinds of operations and methods will be used when access resources.

The PEP first receives the initial access control request, which contains the required attribute values of the system. For example: Name = Xiao Ming, Age = 26, Place = Guilin, etc. The PEP does not need to know exactly who the visitor is, but knows the value of the attribute required by the policy. The model can adjust to large-scale user base because the attributes can be extracted at the same time and match the strategies. For instance, "user.type == student && user.type == teacher" OR "TIME > 8 AM AND TIME < 5 PM." This defines the user type and time that can access the system. The PEP uses the corresponding form to extract the visitor attribute value and send this value to the PDP. After that, the "visitor" of the "student and teacher" can freely access the campus within the specified time. Compared with the previous identity-based model, it was inflexible because it made decisions after discriminating whether the interviewer was Wang or Dai, Zhang or Li. Therefore, this model does not need to care about the visitor's specific identity as long as the visitor's attribute value satisfies the policy condition, the resource can be accessed.

When user first submits an access request to system, then it will enter the ABAC stage which contains several procedures. For details, see the following six steps:

(1) The Rule Execution Point (PEP) receives the initial access request from the user and extracts all the attributes of the use and send attribute value to the rule decision point (PDP).
(2) The PDP assigns roles to the subject according to attributes and policies.
(3) The PAP encrypts users' attribute values by SHA-256.

(4) PDP retrieves all the encrypted attribute values. By comparing the mapping table, if the hash value can be found in the mapping table corresponding to the attribute value, system allows user access, otherwise refuses.

(5) After the PDP gets decision results, PDP needs to forward the information to the PEP.

(6) The Rule Execution Point (PEP) is based on the decision result to execute. If the result is "YES", it means that the user is authorized to enter the RBAC process. If "No", accessing is denied.

In a nutshell, when the user needs to apply for access to the system, there are strategies to be executed and the attributes will be extracted and analyzed by the PEP. All the attributes will be judged by each strategy of the PDP one by one, and the strategies also have a scheme to manage in PAP. After above process, the user will be assigned role but without permissions to operate system if pass the PDP process. Otherwise, user's access request was denied. Then the system is under the process of role-base allocating permission process.

In addition, an analysis was made of the policy modification of the ABAC's rulemaking part under the ET-ARBHAC.

In the ABAC model:

$$R_1: policy_1, policy_2, ..., policy_k, ..., policy_n;$$
$$R_2: policy_1, ..., ..., policy_k, ..., policy_n;$$

$$R_i: policy_1, ..., ..., policy_k, ..., policy_n;$$
$$R_m: policy_1, ..., ..., policy_k, ..., policy_n.$$

Under this premise, if it is necessary to modify the specific permissions owned by $policy_k$, the n policy rules need to be searched again, until i policy rules to be found, which contains $policy_k$, then modify it. In general, the number of strategies is much larger than the number of roles. So the character needs to be traversed, which makes the modification easier. Even if the worst policy rules and roles are the same, the number of roles that need to be queried is at most as large as the policy rules.

4.3   RBAC Allocating Permission Process

According to Sect. 3.1 definition, such access control model mainly includes the following components: users, roles, permissions, and sessions. Once the subject's RBAC access request is approved, it establishes a session for the resource operation. Subject's role and its' permissions will be decided in the session, and the roles will cling to the permission set so that subject will get the permissions in the system. However, in reality, users can have different roles at the same time. Therefore, roles must be defined according to different requirements, and certain permissions must be assigned to the roles so that user gets the role to which the permissions are bound.

The role in this article can be compared using examples from everyday life. The "principals" and "teachers" that students often mention are all roles in daily life. Principals, teachers, etc., have different responsibilities in school. The process of performing duties is called "permissions".

The difference between the two is that in daily life, different people and even the same individual will have different roles in different circles. For example, XY is the president at school, but he also teaches in the class, so XY also have the role of teacher. As we all know, there are more than one teacher in the school. Therefore, the role of the teacher can be different people, and different teachers have various roles. Based on the analysis, the RBAC model is that different people can have different roles in this scenario and so as to obtain various permissions according to its roles.

Another specialty of the RBAC model is that the time re-validation mechanism is added, which allocate resources more rationally. With this mechanism, system resources could be saved. When a user obtains a certain role, he/she gets a series of relevant permissions immediately. However, the user cannot occupy a certain role forever. For example, the president in the university may exercise authority in accordance with the regulations and law to manage the school. After the president retired, his/her role was changed and someone will take his/her position. And the former president's permission will be delivery to the new president and he/she only gets his/her roles permissions. In this time mechanism, the role is based on the period of time and so the permissions are. The time reconfirmation mechanism can be see the example 1.

Example 1. Time reconfirmation mechanism:
for role in {…}

> if time >=T
> Permission {…} in role {…} is invalid
> if user.name == role.name AND user.id == role.id
> Permission {…} in role {…} is valid

In view of the above requirements, introducing time constraints into the model can more effectively use resources and increase the security of the system. This model introduces a time interval T where roles are assigned permissions only within the interval. In the RBAC model, the role gets permissions to manipulate system within a validity period. At the end of the time, the role is revoked and the permissions of the corresponding role are removed. The advantages of this mechanism are to avoid the user permanently occupying the role, reducing the possibility of illegal permissions. After a period of time, the character needs to be verified by the system again to obtain its permission. Therefore, the security of the system is greatly improved and resources can be allocated reasonably.

It should be pointed out that in this study, role-priority mechanisms are used to deal with the problem of role permissions conflicts. That is to say, in the RBAC role assignment process, priorities are set in advance for different roles. It is assumed that the permissions of a person's different roles are conflict, the role's permission with the highest priority will be guaranteed and invalidate the conflict permissions of his/her low priority role. In the future, we will add the role permission conflict detection mechanism, which prejudges the conflicts between different roles, and then preprocesses them in advance.

4.4   Merits of the ET-ARBHAC Model

Here are merits of the ET-ARBHAC model:

1. In the ET-ARBHAC, the SHA-256 encryption algorithm is used to encrypt subjects' information of ABAC process which ensures system's privacy.
2. Re-confirmed time mechanism in RBAC process ensures that the same role has different identities and rights that correspond to its identities within a certain period of time. As a result, it prevents users from occupying resources for a long time and cause waste of resources. For privilege conflicts of different roles owned by subjects, role-priority mechanisms are used.
3. ET-ARBHAC model can achieve large-scale user's visit as well as satisfy the user's dynamic change.

5   Evaluation

In order to test whether our mechanism is functional or not, a school management prototype system was made to test access control mechanism. What needs to be mentioned is that the system was designed with the ET-ARBHAC mechanism.

Now we give an example to illustrate the feasibility of our mechanism. When user David signs up in the system, its privacy information such as ID number, birthday, phone number etc. will be hashed by the SHA256 and store in the SQL. This is a counterpart of ABAC process (Table 1).

Table 1. User David's attributes hashed table

Attributes	User values	Hashed value (by SHA256)
Name	David	a6b54c20a7b96eeac1a911e6da3124a560fe6dc042ebf270e3676e7095b95652
Age	35	9f14025af0065b30e47e23ebb3b491d39ae8ed17d33739e5ff3827ffb3634953
ID number	360822198004127026	7d4375dbd188eccb8aadf9bc42516ba24c6f029b7fe5a0c615a5be36b3ac8593
Phone number	15236485475	22dc932fd90cb5d12c4fbeabdad575d972decdd07564fd92dc861d5fa1469ca7
Identity	Teacher/dean of the department	7b3aac14cdb269863d0a375d45a6ae41a0fc6759db59dae7c4f9ee4727087783
…	…	…

Also, we did performance experiment for the prototype system. Here are the experimental results of encrypted attributes.

From the Fig. 3, we could see when the subjects' attributes increase, the execution time of encrypted attributes also increase. But overall the execution time is bearable for users.

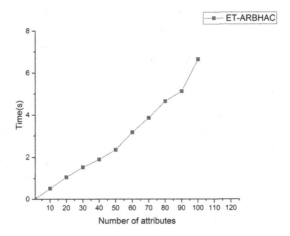

Fig. 3. The execution time of encrypted attributes in ABAC process

6   Conclusions

This article has analyzed and summarized the proposed ET-ARBHAC mechanism, which contains two processes i.e., the ABAC and RBAC process. The attributes are encrypted in ABAC and the permissions of roles will be assigned in the RBAC. This scheme can apply to various systems and have practical application value. In order to test whether our mechanism is functional and reliable or not, systems were made to test the mechanism. In the future, we will use more methods to optimize our mechanism and add optimized conflict detection in this scheme. The IOT devices will also be used in the system to test the mechanism.

Acknowledgments. As the research of the thesis is sponsored by National Natural Science Foundation of China (No: 61662017, No: 61262075), Key R & D projects of Guangxi Science and Technology Program (AB17195042), Guangxi Natural Science Foundation (No: 2017GXN SFAA198223), Guilin Science and Technology Project Fund (No: 2016010408), Guangxi Key Laboratory Fund of Embedded Technology and Intelligent System, we would like to extend our sincere gratitude to them.

References

1. Jiang, Y., Lin, C., Yin, H., et al.: Security analysis of mandatory access control model. In: IEEE International Conference on Systems (2004)
2. Bellettini, C., Bertino, E., Ferrari, E.: Role based access control models. Inf. Secur. Techn. Rep. **6**(2), 21–29 (2001)
3. Jha, S., Sural, S., Atluri, V., et al.: Specification and verification of separation of duty constraints in attribute-based access control. IEEE Trans. Inf. Forensics Secur. **13**(4), 897–911 (2018)
4. Sandhu, R.S.: Role-based access control model. IEEE Comput. **29**, 38–47 (1996)

5. Gouglidis, A., Mavridis, I.: domRBAC: an access control model for modern collaborative systems. Comput. Secur. **31**(4), 540–556 (2012)
6. ANSI-INCITS359-2004: Information Technology—Role-Based Access Control. American Nat'l Standards Inst./Int'l Committee for Information Technology Standards (2004)
7. Servos, D., Osborn, S.L.: Current research and open problems in attribute-based access control. ACM Comput. Surv. **49**(4), 1–45 (2017)
8. Wang, L., Wijesekera, D., Jajodia, S.: A logic-based framework for attribute based access control. In: ACM Workshop on Formal Methods in Security Engineering (2004)
9. Zhang, X., Li, Y., Nalla, D.: An attribute-based access matrix model. In: Proceedings of the 2005 ACM Symposium on Applied Computing, p. 359 (2005)
10. Rubio-Medrano, C.E., D'Souza, C., Ahn, G.J.: Supporting secure collaborations with attribute-based access control. In: International Conference on Collaborative Computing: Networking. IEEE (2015)
11. Shafiq, B., Bertino, E., Ghafoor, A.: Access control management in a distributed environment supporting dynamic collaboration. In: Workshop on Digital Identity Management, pp. 104–112. ACM (2005)
12. Lee, A.J.: Open problems for usable and secure open systems. In: Proceedings of the Workshop on Usability Research Challenges for Cyber Infrastructure and Tools (2006)
13. Kuhn, D.R., Coyne, E.J., Weil, T.R.: Adding attributes to role-based access control. Computer **43**(6), 79–81 (2010)
14. Cheng, Y., Park, J., Sandhu, R.: Attribute-aware relationship-based access control for online social networks. In: Atluri, V., Pernul, G. (eds.) DBSec 2014. LNCS, vol. 8566, pp. 292–306. Springer, Heidelberg (2014). https://doi.org/10.1007/978-3-662-43936-4_19
15. Cheng, Y., Park, J., Sandhu, R.: A user-to-user relationship-based access control model for online social networks. In: Cuppens-Boulahia, N., Cuppens, F., Garcia-Alfaro, J. (eds.) DBSec 2012. LNCS, vol. 7371, pp. 8–24. Springer, Heidelberg (2012). https://doi.org/10.1007/978-3-642-31540-4_2
16. Jin, X., Sandhu, R., Krishnan, R.: RABAC: role-centric attribute-based access control. In: Kotenko, I., Skormin, V. (eds.) MMM-ACNS 2012. LNCS, vol. 7531, pp. 84–96. Springer, Heidelberg (2012). https://doi.org/10.1007/978-3-642-33704-8_8

Image Processing

Significant Regional Detection Based on Precise Edge Learning

Wei Feng$^{(\boxtimes)}$, Jiliang Zhang, and Li Peng

School of Internet of Things, Jiangnan University, Wuxi 214122, China
fengwei@jiangnan.edu.cn

Abstract. The traditional saliency detection obtains significant regions by using the region contrast of color information. In complex and multi target images, the method often performs poorly, and the significant region can not be detected completely. Therefore, a significant region detection method based on accurate edge learning is proposed in this paper. First, in order to achieve better image cutting effect, we use multiple WMF (weighted median filter) to process the source image and then use the method of graph cut to divide the image to get some regions with similar features, that is, the segmentation graph. At the same time, we use background prior method to get the preliminary salient map. The edge learning area is obtained by combining the initial saliency map and the bootstrap map. The area is the foreground and the other regions are the background, and the convolution neural network VGG16 model is used to complete the detection. The algorithm is verified on the open dataset ECSSD. The results show that the algorithm has better recall and precision.

Keywords: Graph-based · Boundary learning · Weighted median filtering · Neural network

Human visual system can quickly when dealing with image processing, this is mainly thanks to distinguish from the complicated background area and prioritize significantly. This mechanism in today's era of data explosion has caused the attention of more scholars. Significant testing as computer vision field important preprocessing step used to reduce the computational complexity, is becoming more and more popular, is widely used in image processing, such as image scaling [1], image compression [2], target recognition [3], image classification [4], etc.

The main contributions of this paper are as follows:

(1) We propose a detection method based on accurate edge learning, which can highlight significant areas effectively;
(2) the application of graph cutting method can guide edge learning accurately and improve the detection effect;
(3) by modifying the VGG16 model, it is more suitable for significance detection.

S. Shen et al. (Eds.): CWSN 2018, CCIS 984, pp. 183–193, 2019.
https://doi.org/10.1007/978-981-13-6834-9_16

1 Related Work

At present, significance detection is gradually becoming a research hotspot at home and abroad, mainly divided into two mechanisms: top-down and bottom-up. A top-down mechanism typically has a specific target, and a computer with a task to find it, usually requires prelearning. The bottom-up mechanism is mainly detected by color, texture, boundary and other underlying features. Itti et al. [5] obtained images of different scales through gaussian filtering, and compared images of different scales with features such as brightness, color and direction for significant region detection. This is the earliest significance detection model. Yang and Yang et al. [6] applied the Absorbing Markov Chain to the detection of the significance region, and calculated the significance with the boundary region as the absorption point. Liu et al. [7] put forward firstly to extract color and position features for each area, and then the characteristics of the border area is set to the dictionary, sparse representation of image and its reconstruction error was calculated based on significant value calculation, the final fusion of multiple scales is worth to the ultimate significance test results significantly. Rahtu and Heikkila et al. [8] and Yao et al. [9] are building the joint conditional random field (CRF) the significance of detection model, by comparison with the different scales of regional and global contrast to significant test, but the detection effect is not ideal. Yao et al. [10] proposed a dynamic transmission based on cellular automata machine significant testing model, the algorithm can detect the significant areas of outline, but for the center position of daub effect is still very serious. Aytekin et al. [11] proposed the extraction of multi-scale features from deep CNN to obtain significant images. Kouhestani et al. [12] trained two CNN at different depths to capture local information and global comparison, and integrated local estimation and global search to predict the significance map.

In this paper, a method of detection of significant region based on accurate edge learning is proposed. First, we use multiple WMF (weighted median filter) to process the source images, then using the method of graph segmentation to cut images to gain a number of areas which characteristics are similar, this is the segmentation image. At the same time, the article uses the method of background prior to get the main edge information. The edge learning area was obtained by deleting the main graph cutting hyperpixels, so as to learn the foreground, edge and background. The convolution neural network VGG16 model was used to complete the detection.

2 Weighted Median Filtering and Graph Cutting

In this section, we will focus on how to calculate the conditional probability. Where, Sect. 2.1 introduces how to carry out weighted median filtering [13]. Section 2.2 describes how to perform graph cutting [14].

2.1 Weighted Median Filtering

The information contained in the image is very rich, and there is also a lot of noise, which requires us to filter out the noise. The weighted median filter is adopted to process the original image, which can effectively reduce the noise and simplify the boundary information in the image. However, the important boundary is usually not affected by filtering because of the high frequency of information on both sides of the boundary.

Move the image by using a window with a side length of r. In this paper, the value of r is 3, the central pixel point of this window is p, and the sum of all pixels in the window is R(p). For any pixel, q ∈ R(p) have a weight ω_{pq}. This weight is used to adjust the degree of correlation between the pixel point and the feature of the center pixel point, thus affecting the filtering effect. Formula 1 is the method to get the weight:

$$\omega_{pq} = n(q) \cdot g(F(p), F(q)) \tag{1}$$

Where, F(p) and F(q) are the eigenvalues of pixel points. In this paper, we calculate according to the color signature. n(q) represents the number of feature values that are the same between pixel q and neighboring pixel points.

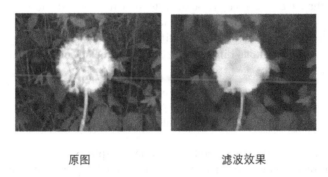

原图   滤波效果

Fig. 1. Filtering effect

The filtering effect can be improved by adding n(q). It also makes it easier to keep strong boundaries, g is the correlation function. In this paper, gaussian function is used, as shown in Eq. 2.

$$g = \exp(-\frac{|F(p) - F(q)|}{|F(p) + F(q)|}) \tag{2}$$

$$p = \underset{q \in R(p)}{median}\{F(q) \cdot \omega_{pq}\} \tag{3}$$

Finally, the main method of filtering is shown in formula 3, Fig. 1 is the comparison between the original image and the filtered image. According to the image. After filtering, the image is much less noisy, but the main boundary is enhanced, which provides better conditions for image cutting.

2.2   Graph-Cut

The method of image cutting can divide a picture into several areas, and there are similar features in the area. Compared with the current popular SLIC method, the area of image segmentation is larger. SLIC maybe causes image be overly segmented. At the same time, for the boundary, SLIC's boundary information is not complete enough.

First, think of the picture as an image set G with vertex set V and edge set E, then, the vertex set starts at every pixel, the edge set is the distance between the pixels. In this section, It is obtained by calculating the CIELab space distance of the pixel point. As shown in Eq. 4:

$$e(v_i, v_j) = \sqrt{(L_i - L_j)^2 + (a_i - a_j)^2 + (b_i - b_j)^2}, e(v_i, v_j) \in E, v_i, v_j \in V \qquad (4)$$

Edge sets also represent differences between vertices, which are the criteria for segmentation. In the same region, regional differences are used as criteria. Set the difference threshold in the region, if it is less than the threshold, it is the same region; if it is greater than the threshold, it belongs to two regions. At the same time set a standard of distinction between regions, which is based on whether the maximum edge set value of the edge pixel is less than the difference threshold value in the two regions, The threshold of interregional difference is $D(r_i, r_j)$,. The calculation method is shown in Eqs. 5 and 6:

$$d(r) = \max_{v_i \in r}(e_i) \qquad (5)$$

$$D(r_i, r_j) \leq \min(d(r_i), d(r_j)) \qquad (6)$$

Since the pixel point is a separate area when unsplit, you need to set an initial threshold for segmentation, otherwise you can't split it up, as the size of the segmentation area changes, the threshold needs to change constantly, therefore, formula 6 is adjusted as follows:

$$D(r_i, r_j) \leq \min(d(r_i) + r, diff(r_j) + z) \qquad (7)$$

$$r = \frac{k}{N_R} \qquad (8)$$

Where, z is the initial threshold value, which can be obtained by formula 8. K is the scale coefficient, which controls the size of r, indirectly controls how many regions the image is divided into, and NR is the number of pixel points in the region.

Fig. 2. Graph cut scale

As can be seen from Fig. 2, with the increase of k, the segmentation area keeps increasing, and the extraction effect of global information is also better.

3 Accurate Edge Learning

In this section, we discuss in detail how to use boundary information for accurate edge learning, where Sect. 3.1 describes how to get boundary information and Sect. 3.2 introduces the VGG16 model.

3.1 Boundary Information

Boundary information is not used in the usual significance detection algorithms, this is mainly because there is too much boundary information in a picture. The more complex the background, the more complex the boundary information, which is undoubtedly difficult to use for significance detection. With the deepening of significance detection, detection accuracy becomes higher and higher, and boundary information becomes a powerful means to improve detection precision.

In this paper, in order to obtain the main boundary information, i.e. the boundary of the foreground, weighted median filtering is applied to image processing in the second section, after processing, the main boundary information of the image is intact and most of the boundary in the background has been weakened. Then, according to the algorithm in literature [14], we can get the natural boundary in the picture which is the main boundary information. The processing effect is shown in Fig. 3:

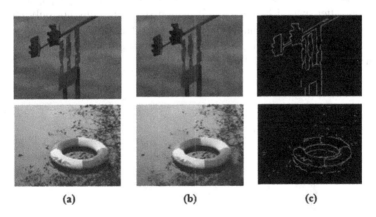

Fig. 3. (a) Source image (b) Filtering image (c) Boundary information

Therefore, we can get the boundary information content of the ith image cut hyperpixel:

$$B_i = \frac{1}{\left|\sum_{i \in K} b_i\right|} b_i \tag{9}$$

Where, Bi represents the boundary information content of the ith hyperpixel; Bi represents the total number of boundary points in the ith hyperpixel; K is the number of hyperpixels obtained by image segmentation.

Taken The information content obtained by formula 9 as the judgment standard, set a fixed threshold to delete and select the target graph to cut the hyperpixel area, to prepare for the next step of accurately learning the target image to cut the superpixel boundary.

3.2 Precise Edge Learning Under the Model VGG16

The VGG16 model [18] consists of 13 convolutional layers and 3 fully connected layers. Its convolution layer is divided into five stages. The maximum pooled layer with a connection kernel size of 2 and a step size of 2 after each phase. When you enter a size image into VGG16, the output scales of each stage are 1/1, 1/2, 1/4, 1/8, 1/16 of the input scales respectively, the useful information captured by each convolutional layer becomes coarse as its size increases. The specific structure is shown in Fig. 4:

In order to achieve the effect of accurate edge learning, new learning categories should be added in the study to achieve the precise purpose. In this paper, the outline of the main goal is extracted in Sect. 3.1, and the edge information is prepared to be used as the approach to accurate learning.

As indicated at the end of Sect. 3.1, the contour studied in this paper is a super-pixel contour after natural boundary information screening, this not only ensures the richness of the contour information, but also ensures that the traditional edge learning algorithm does not only learn the big contour information, and does not introduce too much complex noise contour information.

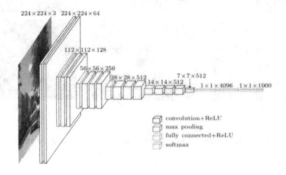

Fig. 4. VGG16 model

Therefore, the training of foreground, edge and background is carried out under the VGG16 model. A picture to be tested is divided into three areas for accurate learning.

Fig. 5. Exact learning (Color figure online)

The region marked red in Fig. 5 is the edge region of the exact study in this paper. In addition to the learning of the basic contour areas, the boundary features of the significant areas can still be learned [19]. Cooperate the foreground, the background study, and achieves the accurate study goal.

4 Experiment and Results

In this section, we used the algorithm proposed in this paper to test 1000 images in the open data set ECSSD. The experiment is based on the 64-bit Ubuntu16.04 operating system and NVIDIA GTX Genforce 1080 GPU. The software used is Matlab2014a and Python2.7. The applied deep learning framework is Caffe. This paper USES gradient descent (SGD) method to train the network. Set momentum to 0.9 and weight attenuation to 0.0001. Set the basic learning rate to 10–8. At the same time, when the training loss reaches one unit, the learning rate will be reduced by 10%. It took us 20 h to train, the convergence is achieved after 340k iterations.

4.1 Measurement Level

The measurement criteria of significance detection include precision, recall, mean absolute error and f-measure.

Usually, the PR curve is also drawn to comprehensively evaluate the advantages and disadvantages of the algorithm by calculating the area under the PR curve [20].

Among them, the precision ratio refers to the ratio of the correct significant area to the detection area. It reflects the accuracy of detection, as shown in formula 10:

$$precision = \frac{\sum g_z a_z}{\sum a_z} \tag{10}$$

The completion rate is the ratio of the correct detection significant area to the significant area, which reflects the comprehensive detection, as shown in Eq. 11:

$$recall = \frac{\sum g_z a_z}{\sum g_z} \tag{11}$$

F-measure value is used to integrate two evaluation criteria of indicators, so as to keep the balance between them, as shown in formula 12:

$$F - measure = \frac{(1 + \beta^2) \times precision \times recall}{\beta^2 \times precision \times recall} \tag{12}$$

The calculation method of mean absolute error MEA value is shown in formula 13:

$$MEA = \frac{1}{M \times N} \sum_{x=1}^{M} \sum_{y=1}^{N} |S(x, y) - GT(x, y)| \tag{13}$$

Where, gz represents the value of pixel point z in ground truth; Az represents the value of pixel point z in the significant graph of experimental results; M, N represents the length and width of the picture; S(x, y) represents the significance of the measured significance graph at (x, y); GT(x, y) represents the significant value of manually labeled ground truth at (x, y).

4.2 Experimental Results and Analysis

In this section, we compare the significant graph obtained by this algorithm with 6 mainstream algorithms, these 8 algorithms are respectively: IT [5], FT [13], FES [14], PCA [15], FB [16], QCUT [17]. The processing results of six images in the msra-1000 dataset are shown in Fig. 6. As can be seen from the figure, the detection result of the algorithm in this paper is better than other algorithms, with clearer boundary and prominent regions (Figs. 7 and 8).

As can be seen from the figure above, the algorithm in this paper is superior to the other eight algorithms in terms of recall rate. All three indicators are very stable. It can be seen that this algorithm is a very effective significant region detection algorithm.

In order to better evaluate the effect of the algorithm, we calculate AUC (area under curve), that is, area under PR curve, to evaluate the advantages and disadvantages of the algorithm and the other eight algorithms in this paper. The closer the AUC value is to 1, the better the algorithm effect will be. In order to compare the effects of each algorithm more directly, the MEA value, AUC value and f-measure value are listed in Table 1. It can be seen from the table that the algorithm in this paper is superior to other algorithms in every index.

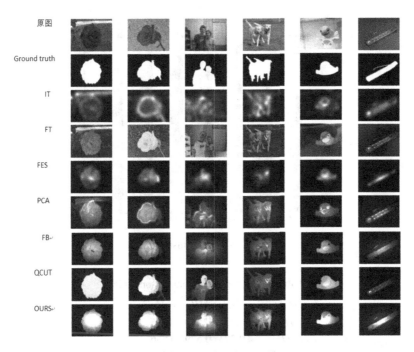

Fig. 6. Comparison results of the saliency map

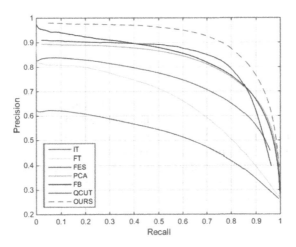

Fig. 7. PR curve

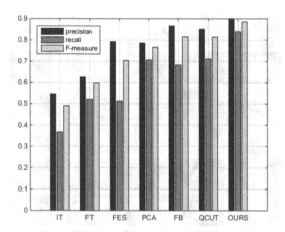

Fig. 8. F-measure histogram

Table 1. Performance comparison table

Athmetic	MEA	AUC	F-Measure
IT	0.324	0.489	0.485
FT	0.223	0.579	0.556
FES	0.219	0.725	0.778
PCA	0.142	0.795	0.798
FB	0.168	0.875	0.852
QCUT	0.114	0.882	0.884
OURS	0.122	0.954	0.911

5   Summary

In this paper, a method of detection of significant region based on accurate edge learning is proposed. This method can effectively enhance the significance of the boundary region of the significance graph. Reduce the smudge effect in traditional methods for complex background images, the method in this paper can also obtain the significant area accurately by learning the edge. The experimental results show that the proposed method based on accurate edge learning is superior to many existing methods in terms of accuracy and completeness.

References

1. Ren, Z.X., Gao, S.H., Chia, L.T.: Region-Based saliency detection and its application in object recognition. IEEE Trans. Circ. Syst. Video Technol. **24**(5), 769–779 (2014)
2. Li, S., Fang, L., Yin, H.: Multitemporal image change detection using a detail—enhancing approach. IEEE Geosci. Rem. Sens. Lett. Earth Interact. **9**(5), 836–840 (2012)

3. Ke, H.C., Sun, H.B., et al.: A video image compression method based on visually salient features. J. Digit. Inf. Manag. **12**(5), 333–343 (2014)
4. Wu, C., Du, B., Zhang, L.: A subspace-based change detection method for hyperspectral images. IEEE J. Sel. Top. Appl. Earth Observations Rem. Sens. **6**(2), 815–830 (2013)
5. Itti, L., Koch, C., Niebur, E.: A model of saliency-based visual attention for rapid scene analysis. IEEE Trans. Pattern Anal. Mach. Intell. **20**(11), 1254–1259 (1998)
6. Yang, J., Yang, M.H.: Top-down visual saliency via joint CRF and dictionary leaning. In: Proceedings of IEEE Conference on Computer Vision and Patten Recognition Providence, pp. 2296–2303. IEEE Press, RI (2012)
7. Liu, T., et al.: Learning to detect a salient object. IEEE Trans. Pattern Anal. Mach. Intell. **33** (2), 353–367 (2011)
8. Rahtu, E., Heikkila, J.: A simple and efficient saliency detector for background subtraction. In: Proceedings of the 12th IEEE International Conference on Computer Vision, pp. 1137–1144. IEEE Press, Washington D.C. (2009)
9. Yao, Q., Lu, H.C., Xu, Y.Q., et al.: Saliency detection via cellular automata. In: Proceedings of Conference on Computer Vision and Pattern Recognition, pp. 990–998. IEEE, Boston (2015)
10. Saliency detection via graph-based manifold ranking. In: IEEE Conference on Computer Vision and Pattern Recognition, pp. 756–764. IEEE, Portland (2013)
11. Aytekin, C., Kiranyaz, S., Gabbouj, M.: Automatic object segmentation by quantum cuts. In: International Conference on Pattern Recognition, pp. 112–117. IEEE, Stockholm (2014)
12. Kouhestani, M., Golfam, A., Aghagolzadeh, F., et al.: Subject salience in SOV and SVO word orders as a result of agent animacy. Xlinguae **9**(2), 37–46 (2016)
13. Brent, D.A., Gangadharan, L., Leroux, A., et al.: Putting one's money where one's mouth is: increasing saliency in the field. Monash Econ. Working Pap. (2014)
14. Zhang, Y.Y., Qin, Y., Lv, X.D., et al.: Saliency detection via PCA of image patches and ICA-R. Multimed. Tools Appl. **75**(8), 4527–4542 (2016)
15. Kim, J., Han, D., Tai, Y.W., et al.: Salient region detection via high-dimensional color transform. In: Computer Vision and Pattern Recognition, pp. 883–890. IEEE (2014)
16. Mehmood, I., Ran, B., Baik, S.W.: Automatic segmentation of region of interests in MR images using saliency information and active contours. Lect. Notes Electr. Eng. **215**, 537–544 (2013)
17. Gu, Z., Qin, B.: Nonrigid registration of brain tumor resection mr images based on joint saliency map and keypoint clustering. Sensors **9**(12), 10270–10290 (2009)
18. Qin, Y., Lu, H., Xu, Y., et al.: Saliency detection via cellular automata. In: Computer Vision and Pattern Recognition, pp. 110–119. IEEE (2015)
19. John, V., Yoneda, K., Qi, B., et al.: Traffic light recognition in varying illumination using deep learning and saliency map. In: IEEE International Conference on Intelligent Transportation Systems, pp. 2286–2291. IEEE (2014)
20. Honbolygó, F., Babik, A., Török, Á.: Location learning in virtual environments: the effect of saliency of landmarks and boundaries. In: Cognitive Infocommunications, pp. 595–598. IEEE (2015)

Author Index

Printed in the United States
By Bookmasters